ALCATRAZ GHOST STORY

ALCATRAZ GHOST STORY

ROY GARDNER'S AMAZING TRAIN ROBBERIES, ESCAPES, AND LIFELONG LOVE

BRIAN STANNARD

Skyhorse Publishing

Skyhorse Publishing books may be purchased in bulk at special discounts for sales promotion, corporate gifts, fund-raising, or educational purposes. Special editions can also be created to specifications. For details, contact the Special Sales Department, Skyhorse Publishing, 307 West 36th Street, 11th Floor, New York, NY 10018 or info@skyhorsepublishing.com.

Skyhorse® and Skyhorse Publishing® are registered trademarks of Skyhorse Publishing, Inc.®, a Delaware corporation.

Visit our website at www.skyhorsepublishing.com.
Please follow our publisher Tony Lyons on Instagram @tonylyonsisuncertain

Cover design by David Ter-Avanesyan
Cover photo by Brian Stannard

10 9 8 7 6 5 4 3 2 1

Library of Congress Cataloging-in-Publication Data is available on file.

Print ISBN: 978-1-5107-7824-5
Ebook ISBN: 978-1-5107-7825-2

Printed in the United States of America

Dedicated to all of those who have celebrated many birthdays in spite of their struggles.

Contents

Introduction

There are icebergs of humanity located within the ocean of single room occupancy hotels of San Francisco's Tenderloin. Stories are the current within this humanity, but these stories tend to remain submerged behind half-closed doors. Most outsiders rarely see or hear them. As a Project Open Hand driver delivering meals to the homebound and critically ill, I caught glimpses of this world, but I could only see and understand what emerged above the surface. There were bloodstains on the carpets, the stench of industrial disinfectant to cover the scent of sorrow, and whispers of "Five-Oh" as I maneuvered through the narrow SRO hallways. Faces appeared from the depths only to disappear again.

And then I was off the clock and free to set myself adrift in my own ocean of booze. I didn't possess the emotional infrastructure to navigate the memories of the workday, so I torpedoed them as best I could, causing 90 percent to sink beneath a beer and whiskey barrage. I emptied whiskey bottles to try to stuff the genies back inside. I would have been an alcoholic whether I was in Peoria or Paris, but working in San Francisco's Tenderloin haunted my mind and accelerated everything into a mental Doppler effect.

The origins for this story begin somewhere in the Tenderloin as I navigated the glass- and syringe-covered sidewalks in the early 2000s, but it just as well could start in a suburban garage where an empty vodka bottle thrown into the recycling bin transforms the isolation into sounds of a bowling alley. This is a story of train robberies, jail breaks, and big moments in history, but its heartbeat is addiction: the invisible yet grinding force that mates good intentions with bad ideas.

Contrary to conventional wisdom, many addicts don't exist in the spectrum of denial. A million damaged cells and an empty wallet are difficult to ignore. Instead an addict often ruminates on the possibility of their own dented goodness existing around the corner, if only they could extract themselves from the thorn bushes of active addiction.

If the puzzle pieces of fortune fall into place, the least of which include a well-knit safety net of forgiveness, the addict can over time move into an established landscape of sobriety. I am lucky to count myself as a citizen of this new landscape.

After Project Open Hand, I arrived at Alcatraz in my mid-forties, not as a convict but as a twenty-first-century tour guide. In an odd description for a former prison, Alcatraz presented itself to me as an opportunity, as it would be the first job I would begin as a sober person. Though currently sober, I carry residue of what I might deteriorate into if I resume drinking. It serves as a photo negative of the blurry light an active drunk feels they might possess if they could only pull it together; the anti-hero rubbing shoulders with the anti-villain while getting fingerprinted at the police station.

At the age of forty-five and a newly sober man working on Alcatraz, I first learned of Roy Gardner, a gambler who arrived at Alcatraz as a fifty-year-old convict. An addict is at heart a gambler, a person who feels uncomfortable with their present situation, so they take risks to either win big or dig a deeper hole. An addict rolls the dice as to whether another whiskey bottle or hit can rearrange the chemicals of their mind to improve everything. The possibility of disaster and epic loss is an appropriate risk.

While I never robbed a mail truck to try to make things right with my wife like Roy Gardner did, the shadow drunk that clings to my footsteps nonetheless identifies with Roy Gardner's decisions. Furthermore, he lived in the Tenderloin, the area that activated so much of my intrigue when I worked there. There were so many stories that I could only guess at, and here Roy Gardner was one of them. My introduction to Roy Gardner came through Michael Esslinger, the authority on all things Alcatraz, and Alcatraz park ranger Tom Ryan. But I had to know more.

The more I learned, the more unbelievable the story seemed, like the tall tales of a drunk guy at the end of the bar. There is a juvenile appeal to Roy Gardner's train robberies and jailbreaks, several of which were committed with a minimum amount of violence and a bumbling element of goofy friendliness toward his victims and the agents of the law. Roy Gardner was like an addict who operated on the teeter-totter of tenuous hope for tomorrow while becoming fluent in apologies to mitigate yesterday's damage. Gardner, like most addicts, including myself at my most scrambled moments, was consumed by a cocktail of one part grandiosity, two parts despair.

The previous version of myself was attracted to Gardner's wild escapes and robberies, many of which seemed launched out of a whiskey blackout. My forty-five-year-old, precariously sober mind, however, became drawn into his cinematic love story with his wife, Dollie. It was a love story fit for the big screen if only the third reel hadn't gone missing. By my mid-forties, I, too, was on the cusp of losing all that was important to me. We create ghosts for ourselves to serve as a fuzzy gold filling to heal the cavities in our minds that strain to navigate grief and mourning when it seems that a broken compass is the only tool available. Roy Gardner called this struggle "hellnighting." During its federal penitentiary era, Alcatraz confined over 1,500 inmates, all with their own unique and compelling stories, but I saw myself most in Roy Gardner and for this reason I kept gravitating back to him.

I try to explain the story of Roy Gardner to Alcatraz visitors, but I can never get it quite right. Perhaps I feel the gambler's mind of Gardner too often matches my own alcoholic instincts and I feel self-conscious about confessing sins to strangers who have just arrived to San Francisco from Australia, England, or St. Louis. Instead, I wrote down Roy Gardner's story here and will launch it into the void. This is a story of heartache, loss, and the upside-down journey an addict takes to preserve a garden that might need more sunlight and less water but is getting the opposite instead. It is a cautionary tale, directed at myself.

PROLOGUE

San Francisco

January 1940

The former boxer tilted his head in order to better read the paperwork presented to him. He was half blind, with a cataract threatening his good eye.

The blind eye wasn't a casualty of too many punches from an up-and-coming Jack Dempsey or some other external assault. Roy Gardner's eyes were losing their function because of absence. During long stretches of his life, his eyes had been starved of light. His pupils stretched themselves to their limits as they consumed more darkness upon more darkness until they could stretch no more and broke.

Inside the Halsted and Company Funeral Parlor on Sutter Street, there wasn't complete darkness, just the half-light of the undertaker's desk lamp. Roy wore a gray suit that squeezed a little tight across his broad shoulders, but it had to do. It was his only suit.

The undertaker respectfully looked away to allow Roy some time and space, the two elements that had never achieved good ratio for Roy in the past twenty years. He either had time, but no space. He had space, but no time.

Roy studied the paperwork and signed and dated most of the areas required of him. It was one day before his fifty-sixth birthday.

The undertaker pointed out one section of the paperwork that Roy hadn't completed.

"Who sir, is the deceased?"

"I am," said Roy Gardner.

* * *

As Roy Gardner planned for death, San Francisco was coming to life. He was departing as over one hundred thousand new residents would arrive within the city's boundaries by the end of World War Two. Many of the future residents would be the newly born, part of the upcoming Baby Boom.

In San Francisco's Outside Lands, new housing construction defied logistical wisdom and sprung up in the wind-whipped sand dunes of the city's Pacific edge, an area previously dismissed as a gray, fog-shrouded Hades hospitable only for ravens.

Returning soldiers from the Pacific Theater would also support San Francisco's upcoming population surge. The newly built Golden Gate Bridge, an engineering achievement celebrating humanity's potential, served as the receding vision for the young men sailing off to upend their own humanity in order to do battle and kill on the island cemeteries of Tarawa and Saipan. Returning to the Golden Gate Bridge represented a return to potential, a turning away from the bloodstained coral beaches, and many veterans decided to make San Francisco their new home.

Roy hadn't seen the Golden Gate Bridge in a while, and even then it was through his foggy, cataract-afflicted eyes as he cajoled tourists with tales of Alcatraz murder and desperation. He had worked on a tour boat that did rubbernecking laps around America's Devil's Island before making its return journey to the friendlier port on Treasure Island, the midpoint and terrestrial anchor for the Bay Bridge. The construction of Bay Bridge worked in tandem with the building of the Golden Gate as part of America's strategy to build its way out of the Great Depression. The Bay Bridge, linking San Francisco with Oakland, would become the gray workhorse to complement the show-pony Golden Gate. Roy's job on the tour boat ended, however, a victim of both the winter season and Hitler's Luftwaffe, which disrupted international travel and the 1939 carnival of San Francisco's Golden Gate International Exposition, which folded a month before scheduled. In the months since the Exposition's closure, Roy had been out of work.

After finalizing the bureaucracy of his own death at the mortuary, Roy walked onto Sutter Street and felt the odd warmth of January sunlight on his face. Rainstorms originating off the Pacific had battered San Francisco all week, but today offered a ceasefire. The rain clouds broke into scattered jigsaw puzzle pieces across the confident blue sky, as sunlight revealed itself like a man emerging out of a hangover.

Roy would figure out later how he would pay his remaining balance to the undertakers at Halsted and Associates, but for now he walked up a hill and then back down Hyde Street toward his downtown room. Along the way he would pass under the apartment window where Dashiell Hammett typed up *The Maltese Falcon*.

Roy walked toward his neighborhood which was still called downtown, but in later years would be known as the Tenderloin, an eventual epicenter of heroin, rotgut booze, street-level prostitution, and Vietnamese refugees struggling to gain a foothold in a neighborhood that was often terrifying and foreign for those born in America.

Now as then, the drain of the Tenderloin caught isolated men unmoored from family: the drunks, the paroled, and the otherwise brokenhearted. As Roy made his way to sea level, women became scarce, and the few that existed trended toward the B-Girl variety: smoky mirages who waited in tavern doorways looking for a sailor to roll. Roy descended the Hyde Street hill and approached the Hotel Governor on Turk Street, his home for the past year and a half.

There were no children in this neighborhood, save the newsboy who stood out front the Hotel Governor while hollering the summary of the day's events. The newsboy shouted loud as he was in competition with the street preacher. The preacher yelled about the Book of Revelations, while the newsboy answered, "'Finland Pushes Back Against Red Russian Invaders!' Give your donation to the Finnish Relief Fund! Help the Finns survive winter!"

The world was unraveling, but for now San Francisco was at peace, a temporary oasis while the rumblings of war grumbled across the curve of the earth, like a locomotive announcing itself in a person's bones, knees, and stomach before it could actually be seen.

Roy approached the newsboy, with whom he had a cordial relationship. With Roy's failing eyesight he received a verbal summary of the day's events from the kid rather than reading all about it. Count D'Or had good odds at Santa Anita and there was a debate about whether Seabiscuit could take it to the finish with a bum leg. Roy insisted that the newsboy call him Roy despite being an elder. Everyone called him Roy.

After his encounter with the newsboy, Roy entered the diner near the Hotel Governor and sat at the counter alongside the other men who would not be eating dinner with family that day. Later they would individually return to their empty hotel rooms that smelled of old rain and yesterday's booze.

* * *

A week later, when the newsboy assembled his January 11, 1940, papers, he would learn more about Roy in three front-page articles than he had in all the prior months the two made small talk together at the intersection of Turk and Jones. To the newsboy, Roy was a friendly face who dispensed nickels, gambling advice, and a few vague references to being a baseball player when they talked about the San Francisco Seals in the springtime.

On January 11, 1940, Roy did not stop by in person to visit, but he appeared on the front page of the boy's newspapers. The articles explained how Roy committed suicide in his room at the Hotel Governor on Turk and Jones, a catcher's throw to second base from the boy's newsstand. Per the articles, Roy packed his suitcases, left a tip for the staff, and put a warning note on his front door to prepare the maid. Roy had spent twenty years in various prisons, the newspapers explained, but he died in a cyanide gas chamber of his own creation.

Roy Gardner once held $120,000 in his hands and captured the attention of the American public with newspaper accounts of his train robberies and jail breaks. But at the time of his death, he struggled to pay the rent on his hotel room, and his social world became limited to the corner newsboy and the staff at the neighborhood diner.

PART ONE
1900–1920

"Roy was always a bad boy. No one ever understood him."
—*Mrs. O. K. Johnson, Roy Gardner's childhood neighbor in Colorado Springs*

CHAPTER ONE

Vallejo and the Bay Area

The First World War

The sound of Roy Gardner's laughter floated above the hammering and work whistles of the Mare Island Shipyard, making him heard before being seen by Florence Nelson. Roy saw Florence for the first time through the window of the candy store, her face a kaleidoscope amongst the jars of peppermint sticks. Newspaper reporters would later describe her as having the face of the Madonna. The sunlight illuminated the glass candy jars to create refractions and dancing prisms, but Roy might have only paid attention to the light in her hair. Her smile was an embrace. She stood in the candy store like a slender lighthouse, her presence a beacon.

With the shrieking of the work whistle, acetylene welders spilled out toward the pool halls and saloons that had yet to be shuttered by the Volstead Act, but Roy detoured away from the other men with their overalls and calloused hands and swaggered into the candy store that employed the sixteen-year-old Florence. He laughed at nothing in particular, and once he walked into the store, she noticed his gray-blue eyes that locked in with a focus reminiscent of a thoughtful owl. Then there was his smile. Roy wore his smile on his sleeve, which made him a well-liked employee, even if the same smile ruined his poker face and chances to win a few dollars from the boys in the after-work gambling sessions.

Florence Nelson worked at a candy store the day Roy met her, but for the majority of her life she would be a nurse. Her name was Florence, just like Florence Nightingale, but everyone called her Dollie.

"My name is Roy Gardner, but everyone just calls me Roy."

Dollie took notice of Roy's muscled frame and confident stride. He had the walk of a man accustomed to keeping his back straight to leverage heavy things. His boxing days were a few years behind him, but he maintained his build through manual labor. When Roy met Dollie Nelson for the first time, he was a strong man with a friendly face. His wavy brown hair was brushed back and covered a thick scar on the back of his head. Roy's powerful build served as a counterpoint to Dollie's petite stature, but she, too, was athletic and swam in the rivers and rode horses on the trails of the Gordon Valley near her home.

At the time Roy Gardner ambled into the Vallejo candy store, Dollie's father, Paulus Nelson, had recently passed away. Paulus, a Swedish immigrant, arrived in Napa in the 1870s to create an anchor for his next generation. Dollie's life had been restrained to a thirty-mile radius from Napa's Wild Horse Valley, the place of her birth, to the Mare Island Shipyard, the major hub of activity adjacent to the candy store. She was a student at Napa High School and had five sisters and a brother. Like Roy, Dollie's only brother was a welder, but in Robert Nelson's case he worked for the Southern Pacific Railroad.

The geography of Dollie's world was small, but she was surrounded by possibility. The waters of the Carquinez Strait flowed beyond Vallejo and into the San Francisco Bay. From there the estuaries continued west toward the open Pacific. Train tracks paralleled the waterways and bridges traversed the marshes to forge a path for the engines. Locomotives roared through the back end of nearby Port Costa. The massive trains and their ceaseless rumblings and *clack clacking* could potentially frighten a person into thoughts of dread, but the trains also projected power and promise. They moved like nothing else of this world, and they appeared to transport whole cities. At times it seemed their lines of cars would never end as they passed a person's path of vision. The trains grasped the contours of the earth and hitched along with the globe's spinning, creating their own cloud network of steam and coal dust.

In the Mare Island Shipyard, the metal cranes dominated the skyline. Long buildings with massive rows of windows merged the Industrial Revolution with the eternal need for humanity to put boats onto water.

The Great War would begin with naive earnestness later that summer, and the United States wouldn't enter the first of the World Wars until 1917, but the Mare Island Shipyard already served as a womb for newly constructed steel-hulled boats, warships, and dreadnoughts ready to disembark into the canals of the San Francisco Bay toward life on the open seas. Mare Island launched larger and larger ships birthed for industry and war with workdays defined by tonnage of ships created in the least amount of labor hours. It was here that Roy worked as an acetylene welder.

When Roy first met Dollie at the candy store, he regaled her with stories of the places he'd been; at the Oregon border he'd seen redwood trees so tall they looked like they could tickle the bottom of God's feet. He'd seen dynamite blast apart granite mountains in Colorado. He once posed as an Irishman and knocked out a Greek wrestler in an Oklahoma City boxing ring. Five years prior he visited a Mexican family in the Sonoran Desert. Had he been a less charming gringo the *campesinos* could have turned him over to Pancho Villa to be shot dead, but here he was now talking and flirting with Dollie. Roy said he even sailed to the Philippines where the air itself exhaled warm, steamy rain and he saw birds that matched all the colors of the sugar candy in the store.

Roy had traveled to all of these places, and yet he decided to linger in a candy store in Vallejo to be with Dollie. On the day Roy walked into the candy store in 1914, Dollie's life had been constrained by the eddies and estuaries of the Carquinez Strait and Napa Rivers. Now her life was set on course, pulled forward by the magnetism and north star of Roy Gardner. After their initial meeting, Roy would return on a regular basis to tell his stories while ordering ice cream sodas. He ordered sodas for her, too, and she accepted his invitations to go to local dances. Eventually they would swim at the beach or nearby lakes. Roy's body was built for the boxing ring, but he was also a graceful and powerful swimmer. It was as if the west edge of the United States with its lakes, locomotives, and dynamite gave birth to Roy Gardner. Despite Roy's past adventures and roving ways, he would always describe Dollie as the "one and only romance of my life."

The teenage Dollie said she was always fond of good times but had previously never gone with "steadies." Roy was "the one man to me." Boys her own age were awkward and unsure. Roy was big and bold, but with an easy smile that radiated a friendly casualness.

Roy Gardner and Florence Nelson, better known as Dollie, wed on June 1, 1916, a few weeks before her nineteenth birthday. He was thirty-two. Their wedding announcement in *The San Francisco Chronicle* described them both as "well known residents of Vallejo."

* * *

Soon after their marriage Roy quit the Mare Island Shipyard so he could start his own welding company in Oakland: the Auto Welding Works. He bought the business on an installment plan, but through hustle and saving, Roy consolidated with the Calox Welding Works at Third and Washington, a short distance to Jack London's favorite drinking spots on the Oakland waterfront that would later bear the author's name. The newlyweds relocated to a cottage in Oakland's Fruitvale hills. Their "nest," as Dollie called it.

While Roy worked long hours in the shop amongst Oakland's urban barns and block-sized warehouses, Dollie assisted with the bookkeeping. Roy toiled late into the night to finish orders and, to save money, he initially didn't hire a shop assistant, which enabled the purchase of more equipment.

To Dollie, Roy was one man, but he took up the space of two. "He is so big and daring and running over with life and affection. He always does everything in a broad, big way," she later explained to a reporter.

Roy developed a reputation as one of the best welders on the Pacific Coast, and his friendly demeanor drew in customers from far away who could have taken their business elsewhere. In time, enough work came in at such a steady rate that Roy hired additional help out of necessity.

Prosperity was in the grip of the newlyweds one year after purchasing the Calox Welding Works, despite a fire at an adjacent milling plant that damaged their own commercial property. Insurance covered the losses. For unclear reasons, Roy did not extend the fire insurance policy, and a second fire engulfed the block. Per the police report, a "miscreant" and "firebug" was to blame, and no one was ever held responsible. The second inferno consumed the entirety of the Calox Welding Works, and it burned down from top to bottom. One year's worth of labor and investment became smoldering ash. Nothing was salvageable. Roy and Dollie were down to a few dollars and outstanding debts.

Within this context, Dollie was due to give birth.

Dollie spent many nights plagued with insomnia. The memories of the building's immolation and the distinctive stench of piercing, charred rubble disrupted her sleep, but Roy provided a steady hand and reassurance that things would work out.

"We're young yet, and we have our health and the two of us have enough brains for a dozen families. We'll make a go of it again," he promised.

Jean was born in September 1917. Church bells from a nearby Catholic Church rang out when Baby Jean was first brought back to the Fruitvale cottage. Although not a religious man, Roy got down and said a prayer of thanks. He might not have been religious, but he possessed a gambler's respect for superstition. Jean's arrival brought new light into their home and provided a distraction after the devastating setback and bad omen of the Calox fire.

Roy sang "The Ballad of Casey Jones" to Jean as a lullaby. "'Come all you rounders if you want to hear, The story of a brave engineer.'" He lifted Jean through the air, up and down like she was the train chugging through Reno and over the Sierra Nevadas.

"'Casey said just before he died, There's two more roads I would like to ride, The firemen said which ones can they be? O the Northern line and the Santa Fe!'"

Roy and Dollie created a haven of laughter and new life despite their recent financial misfortune. The cottage in Fruitvale provided a glimpse of love while the rest of the world was bogged down in the unprecedented slaughter of men from Passchendaele in Belgium to Gallipoli in the Ottoman Empire. With the US now fully committed to the Great War, and German U-Boats sending Allied ships to the bottom of the Atlantic, the demand for more and more new ships continued. Roy had a solid reputation as a welder, and he soon obtained a job at the Shaw-Batcher Shipworks in South San Francisco, an area later known for the large "SOUTH SAN FRANCISCO THE INDUSTRIAL CITY" sign emblazoned into the San Bruno Mountains as a civic promotion to rival the HOLLYWOOD sign.

Roy put his entrepreneur dreams on hold for the moment. He needed work, especially with a new baby.

The family moved to San Francisco's Outside Lands, a foggy outpost near the Pacific edge. Much of this area was still wild and barren, a juxtaposition to the city's dense, urban core. The area's ruggedness appealed to Dollie's memories of rural Napa, where chickens, dogs, and horses outnumbered the people, and the live oaks provided a sanctuary for children playing hide-and-seek. The Outside Lands felt lonely and lost, however. The crashing waves of the Pacific created a sense of majestic wildness, but the land was bleak. Acres of sand dunes impeded trees from being able to take root. In the summertime when the rest of the Bay Area basked under dry heat, a battering ram of gray fog entrenched itself in the Outside Lands and pushed the warmth and sunshine east over the crest of San Francisco's Twin Peaks.

Despite the limitations of their new neighborhood, friends still came by on a regular basis to visit. Roy frequently invited coworkers over for dinner and the conversation flowed freely. It seemed that Roy had been everywhere, and he loved to read. He could talk about most topics, and his curiosity was endless.

If a man needed advice on whether to buy a used Dodge Roadster from a brother-in-law, Roy knew a good mechanic. Curious to learn about the nighttime constellations in the Southern Hemisphere? Roy had an old sailor story to tell.

"The men took to him at first meeting," Dollie explained.

Roy became a public speaker at the shipworks to help his welding department win the Liberty Bond and Red Cross promotional campaign set up to accommodate the patriotic fever gripping the country to compensate for its delayed arrival into World War One. Roy led the department, and it seemed he could have persuaded the Kaiser to shave off his own mustache.

As the head of the department, Roy maintained the thousands of dollars his fellow welders collected for the Liberty Bond Drives, and he often stored the funds overnight at home to be returned to work the next morning. Dollie expressed concern that Roy could get robbed by highwaymen in their foggy and isolated neighborhood.

"I'm a scrapper," he reassured her. Not a penny went missing.

If a coworker became injured on the job, Roy was there to assist. If a fellow welder died, Roy immediately organized a fund for the widow and surviving family. Only Mary Pickford, the silent film star, managed to eclipse Roy's popularity when she stopped by Shaw-Batcher as part of her own Liberty Bond Tour. Roy's solid work performance earned him pay increases and the family was saving money again. The financial loss of the Calox fire was an apparition in the past that they managed to outrun.

Roy was a beloved man at the shipyard and he was beloved at home with Dollie and Baby Jean. "Roy always loved us best," Dollie said. "He was a great home man. You should see him round the house, playing with the baby, teasing, joking, and laughing, always laughing."

Roy still had the itch to be his own boss and entrepreneur, however. The Calox fire nagged at him. He felt he accepted a challenge from the universe, lost, and he wanted a rematch. He put in his resignation at Shaw-Batcher.

The couple's two years of marriage already possessed a carnival ride's worth of whiplash extremes: long hours of hard work erased by one nocturnal fire to create immediate financial setback, a new baby providing joy, and more hard work leading to stability—just to leap into the unknown again. Roy's absolute confidence in himself, however, created an infectious enthusiasm. It was as if Roy could will things to happen through the sheer devotion of his abilities and intellect. He rarely entertained the possibility of things not working as planned. Roy had the ideas for his newest shop all drawn out and they would be able to cash in their own Liberty Bonds to pay for the new building and equipment.

Dollie would cite Christmas of 1918 as the high-water mark of their domestic life. The Armistice had occurred one month prior, and the end of the year presented "life and faith and pride in the present and hope and promise for the future," per Dollie's later account to a reporter.

Roy continued to sketch plans for what he envisioned to be his new welding shop, and he sent letters to various chambers of commerce throughout California to determine their next move.

His coworkers at Shaw-Batcher organized a farewell banquet in his honor at North Beach's Fior d'Italia Restaurant in the spring of 1919, about two months before the signing of the Treaty of Versailles. They presented him with a silver-mounted acetylene torch and a scroll engraved with the words, "You leave behind you many happy memories and take with you the loyal and heartfelt wishes of your friends." Over a hundred men signed the scroll.

One year after the farewell banquet at Fior d'Italia, Dollie received a telegram from Roy while she was visiting some relatives in Napa with two-year-old Jean.

Roy was in a San Diego jail.

Dollie would soon learn that while Roy's stories of defeating Greek wrestlers and sailing the open seas were all factually correct, he had omitted a few things from his autobiography when he first met her back in the Vallejo candy store back in 1914.

CHAPTER TWO

San Francisco and the Philippines

1900–1906

The Pacific Ocean pulled Roy Gardner west like a center of gravity. Roy's journey started close to the western banks of the Mississippi River in Trenton, Missouri, about fifteen years after Leland Stanford drove in the last spike of the transcontinental railroad. From the 1890s onward, trains provided the push and the Pacific Ocean provided the pull as Roy moved deeper and deeper toward the western edge of the United States. Roy's first westward stop was in Colorado Springs, where his family moved when he was eight.

His mother inherited money, but his father's risky investments in local mining operations bit at the heels of the family's financial security. The bad investments drained the inheritance, but his father achieved a counterbalance through a stable job as the operator of the Colorado Springs electric light plant, which provided a middle-class lifestyle for the family. Roy stayed in school until he was sixteen, but the Pacific Ocean beckoned him further west. The rest of his family moved to Oklahoma, not yet a US state, but a region awash in newfound oil wealth, creating overnight millionaires.

Roy decided to join the army, drawn by wanderlust and the opportunity to travel the world. In time he was stationed in San Francisco, a citadel safeguarding the country's western expansion at the beginning of the twentieth century. In an era when horses still provided transport for armies and the cavalry was immortalized in poetic epics such as the "Charge of the Light Brigade," Roy took up specialized training as a blacksmith, a skill in which he received high marks. One of Roy's sergeants further described him as an excellent pistol shot with a "pleasing personality." While Roy excelled at shooting inanimate targets, he became discouraged upon realizing this skill would need to be applied to shooting at real people in combat. Roy would describe his military experience as "two years wasted."

During drills and marches at Fort Scott in San Francisco's Presidio, Roy could see Alcatraz lurking in the Bay like a taunt. Alcatraz was still a military prison, a function it had served since the Civil War. While it would eventually lock down the likes of Al Capone and Machine Gun Kelly, Alcatraz in 1906 was a stockade that jailed uniformed drunks and deserters.

Roy studied the litter of ships pockmarking the San Francisco Bay, all the boats seeming to be escaping from somewhere or unmooring their chains to take a gamble in some other distant port. Beyond Alcatraz lay the much larger Angel Island. Alcatraz could swallow a man on the receiving end of a court martial, while the army base on Angel Island launched men like a cannon to the far reaches of the Pacific in support of America's war in the Philippines.

The US initially supported the Filipino independence movement against their colonial masters and mutual American enemy-of-the-month, Spain. Once Admiral Dewey blasted the Spanish fleet to the bottom of Manila Bay in 1898, however, American generals and politicians turned the Philippines into a schizophrenic kaleidoscope of changing intentions and lurching strategies.

Spain was defeated, and the US filled the occupier vacuum. The Filipino independence movement recalibrated its attention toward the latest foreign arrival. In the 1890s, the United States entered a war to support Filipinos against Spain, but less than a year into the twentieth century this war mutated into armed conflict against Philippine citizens themselves.

President McKinley, who once pled ignorance to the whereabouts of the Philippines, would eventually declare, "the islands were American property, that the army would proceed to take possession of them and that anyone resisting our authority would be repressed by force."

To create a softer approach to the conquest, educators and doctors shipped out to the Philippines along with soldiers and the marines. The US would put a different coat of paint on their land grab compared to the established European imperialists, but the results were mixed. One American general, Jacob "Hell Roaring Jake" Smith, gave orders to kill any Filipino over the age of ten and to turn the landscape into a "howling wilderness."

Anyone left standing, however, would be inoculated by a US doctor and taught to read by a US teacher. Anything not set on fire would be the foundation for new roads and train tracks as a US gift to the Philippines.

Four thousand US soldiers died in the conflict. Casualty reports included categories for suicide and deaths from tropical disease and heat exposure. Twenty thousand Philippine soldiers would perish, and the civilian death toll from bullets, famine, and fire went upward to two hundred thousand.

By 1902, the war in the Philippines officially ended with a muted whimper and the American public feeling like the past escapade was a heavy night of drinking that now had to be cleaned up.

Into this morass arrived the soldier, Roy Gardner, in 1904. He arrived in the Philippines from San Francisco on a ship named *Thomas*, a boat previously used to transport teachers and humanitarian workers in such large numbers that these benevolent faces of the US occupation became known as "Thomasites." The dual nature of the transport boat for both soldiers and aid workers encapsulated the bipolar nature of the US war in the Philippines.

The war was over by 1904, but occupation and infrastructure projects remained. Roy arrived on the island of Mindanao, the southernmost island of the vast Philippine archipelago. Pirates held as much sway over the swampy, tropical, and volcanic Mindanao as formal governments, and a Muslim autonomous region would continue to strive for independence from the Philippines long after the Philippines achieved its own independence from the US. One of the worst massacres of the occupation occurred in 1906 at Bud Dajo in the Mindanao island chain where roughly six hundred women, children, and poorly armed local soldiers were killed by offshore US naval guns and indiscriminate machine gun fire.

After his Philippines tour of duty, Roy shipped back to San Francisco's Presidio in the beginning days of 1906 with more time left to serve on his military obligations. He had a new tattoo and a tenuous line of credit. Daytime marches and drills in the Presidio persisted for Roy, while nighttime offered a perilous gauntlet down Pacific Street toward the booze mills, gambling dens, and bordellos of the Barbary Coast, San Francisco's "Devil's Acre." Roy had plenty of time to get killed by a bullet or the infected spit of a mosquito bite while in the Philippines, but he now risked getting his throat cut from within the dark walls of the Noggin of Ale, the Cobweb Palace, or other Barbary Coast haunts inhabited by men with nicknames like Hell Haggerty and Spanish Kitty, a female pool shark.

By 1906, most American citizens had forgotten about the Philippines, and Roy was hoping he, too, could be forgotten if he slipped off his soldier's uniform and ducked out of town. The brutality and grim conditions of the war may have soured him on finishing his military duties, but it is just as likely that he needed to go missing-in-action for the more mundane reason that he owed too many different people money due to his gambling debts.

Later in his life, Roy would say that spirits from beyond haunted his skull and guided his behavior. In the early days of 1906 Roy may have had a premonition that this would be the most advantageous moment to vanish from San Francisco's Presidio. Whether it was a spectral premonition, the fortuitous hand of God, or just dumb luck, Roy slipped out of San Francisco and deserted just before the worst natural disaster of the United States' 130-year history struck the San Francisco Bay Area.

On April 18, 1906, earthquake and fire destroyed just about everything in San Francisco, from prisoner records to the City Hall building itself. Ash and plaster dust trickled down from the sky like slowly falling snowflakes. Rubble covered everything at the ground level so that streets lost their names and functions.

Photos of the devastation offered a glimpse of what would befall the bombed-out cities of Europe and Japan in World War II. Thousands of San Francisco civilians became refugees, and hastily erected tent camps redefined the purpose of the Presidio. On April 17, 1906, Roy was a wanted man facing court-martial. By April 19, he was another person missing in action among the three thousand San Francisco residents who died in the previous day's calamity and apocalyptic fire. To his military superiors, Roy could have been one of the many unknown bodies crushed beneath the spontaneous tombs of crumbled brick or cremated in the inferno engulfing the city.

Roy's superiors may have thought he was among the dead of San Francisco, but at the time of the 1906 San Francisco earthquake and fire, Roy Gardner was already one month in Gallup, New Mexico.

CHAPTER THREE

Gallup, New Mexico, and Bisbee, Arizona

1906–1908

New Mexico was not yet a US state when Roy drifted in while fire burned down almost everything in San Francisco. Local jurisdictions operated as independent outposts. The FBI, the federal agency created to transcend the dislocation of small-town crime-fighting squads, was still just an idea. The science of fingerprinting was in its infancy.

Roy Gardner, the soldier based out of San Francisco's Presidio, was now a ghost. He shed his soldier uniform to become a miner.

Roy descended with the long line of humans that sank their fingers, pickaxes, and dynamite deep into the coat of Mother Earth to pick her pockets of copper. Within the depths of the mines, darkness had the capacity to become a demon lurking in all directions. A person's insides, always unseen, became turned outward to contribute to the void that paradoxically felt all encompassing. The darkness itself took shape in that it represented the complete absence of light.

As a boy in Colorado Springs, backroom speculators served as the cigar-smoking face of the Cripple Creek mines that hustled Roy's family out of their inheritance, and now Roy would take a chance that the mines wouldn't also rob him of his life. Fatal mining accidents occurred regularly during the time period. In just one example, 149 men, mainly Hungarian immigrants, were killed in a mine explosion at the CFI Mine in Primero, Colorado, in 1910.

In Gallup, Roy took his chance with such operations as the Snake and Opportunity Mine, but he eventually drifted down to the Copper Queen Mines in Bisbee, Arizona, a rough and tumble town within gazing distance of the Mexican border. On January 5, 1907, ten tons of dynamite went off by accident in Bisbee, creating a roar and shock wave felt thirty miles away. This could have been the opening salvo to greet Roy's arrival into town.

If the mines themselves didn't kill a man, the fistfights and gunshots back on earth between the Wobblies and the Pinkertons during labor strikes would.

Human animosity would finish the job Mother Nature failed to do. The mines provided money, but men were getting killed. Taking a job in the mine was a devil's bargain, and no one could agree on the wage for a potential deal with the devil. The word "strike" had many connotations in Bisbee: to strike a vein of mineral wealth, to strike it rich, to go on strike to protest work conditions, to be a scab or strike breaker, or to strike a man in the head who stood on the opposite side of the picket line.

In late March of 1908 Roy sank down into the Lowell Shaft when an avalanche of rock plummeted down into the darkness and crushed his head, an accident akin to a biblical stoning. He was knocked unconscious and near death, stuck at the bottom of a mine shaft that would be a convenient transition for a grave. His coworkers lifted him out of the mine, and a company doctor was called in to do surgery. A silver plate was put into Roy's skull to bridge the fracture, and Roy slipped in and out of consciousness for over a week. After a month's convalescence, Roy was on the mend. He had survived. Back in the land of the living, Roy submitted his quitting papers at the Copper Queen Mine. Roy arrived in Bisbee to pull copper rocks from the earth, and he would depart with a silver plate in his head. The silver plate would become a magnet for headaches for the rest of Roy's days.

CHAPTER FOUR

Northern Mexico

The Revolution, 1908–1909

Venustiano Carranza needed bullets and Roy Gardner needed a new gig.

After the Copper Queen Mines nearly killed him, Roy transitioned into running guns and ammunition for the Mexican Revolutionary Army for his next career development. The guns of the revolution wouldn't begin firing until 1910, but when Roy took the Southern Pacific train into Culiacán and Mazatlán after recuperating from his head injury, the revolution's significant players—Carranza, Victoriano Huerta, Emiliano Zapata, and Pascual Orozco—were assembling their chess pieces.

The fates and leaders of the Mexican Revolution shifted more dramatically than the tides on a full moon night, but Roy put his money on Carranza, a man as tall as Roy was strong, with a dour scowl to contrast Roy's mischievous smirk.

Roy roamed the Sonoran Desert on the Mexican side of the border, working odd jobs here and there and keeping his eyes and ears open for larger opportunities to avail themselves. A couple of Americans drew Roy into their scheme to transport guns and ammunition to the gathering army supporting Carranza. The plot to move guns was presented as a "cleanup," an opportunity in Roy's estimation for easy money, and he accepted. Roy was to make a drop-off in the town of Cananea.

Cananea lay on the Mexican side of the border about the same distance to the dividing line as Bisbee, Arizona, and the Copper Queen Mine were on the American side. Underground mineral wealth knows no boundaries, however, and copper riches spread under the rock of the earth in all directions. Cananea had its own copper mine, the Cananea Consolidated Copper Company, owned by an American, William Cornell Greene. In addition to Mexicans who received less pay than their American counterparts, the mine also employed a sizable number of Chinese immigrants.

In 1906, a labor strike broke out at the mine and the ensuing violence left a total of twenty-two people dead, including two who perished in a building fire. The Arizona Rangers arrived on scene to support the American management in quashing the labor unrest. The hesitation of Mexican dictator Porfirio Díaz to prevent the encroachment of armed Americans into a Mexican labor dispute created one more spark of resentment and anger within the populace, which further emboldened the revolutionaries a few years later. The murder of a Chinese immigrant during this tumult became the source material for the ballad "La Carcel de Cananea."

"La Carcel de Cananea," or "The Jail of Cananea," mourns lost love and the other tragedies and injustices of this life. Linda Ronstadt included her rendition of this *corrido* on her album honoring her Mexican heritage. The original lyricist of "La Carcel de Cananea" might have just missed Roy Gardner in passing, or Roy could have become the song's protagonist had they written a sequel. In early 1909, when the brief window of frost gave way to the dominating heat of the Sonoran Desert, Roy would find himself imprisoned within the adobe walls of the Cananea jail.

After finalizing the details of his latest gun-running assignment, Roy maneuvered his mule-drawn wagon across the border without any issue. His wagon contained boxes of ammunition interspersed with other items of legal commerce to create a camouflage. For approximately sixty miles he moved deeper into Mexican territory and avoided any conflict with bandits, *federales*, or any other number of armed men who could have found reason to shoot a gringo and take his cargo.

He approached Cananea, the town where he would complete his delivery and receive his payment. The journey had been long and not without its anxieties, but the mission unspooled with a consistent rhythm of open land that he passed through without incident. Roy and his mule-drawn cart traversed across the mesquite-covered plains, and he became comfortable in the familiarity and deepening monotony. As the mule shuffled into the small town, Roy was greeted by quiet and stillness which validated his thoughts that his assessment was correct: this would be easy money. Barefoot children chased goats and chickens across the dirt street, and there was little else. But then a dust cloud and cacophony of galloping hooves interrupted Roy's sense of relief.

Six men on horses surrounded Roy and his mule cart, and they did not present themselves as agents of the Cananea Chamber of Commerce welcoming him into town.

They were hardscrabble, hungry-looking men, and the dirt and dust of life outdoors obscured any sense of what kind of uniforms they might have worn. Some of the men didn't seem to have official uniforms at all, but they all had guns at their hip, if not in hand, and bandoliers slung across their shoulders. It may not have been immediately apparent to Roy that these men were a raiding party in support of Victoriano Huerta, a rival of Carranza, but this didn't matter as they made their opinion of Roy clear enough. He was dragged away from the wagon and separated from his cargo, which he would never see again.

There was little he could do. He was outnumbered by men on horseback, all of whom had guns at the ready, while he was a gringo in a strange land. By midnight he found himself thirsty and hungry and locked within the walls of the Cananea jail of song. No one would sing for Roy tonight, however, as he waited his fate inside the Mexican jail.

The next morning, a soldier dragged Roy out of the cell to face a judge and jury of sorts. The jury consisted of the men who captured Roy the previous day, and the judge was a new soldier, perhaps a superior officer. They discussed the situation in Spanish in front of Roy, whose only role was to accept whatever fate bestowed upon him. Roy was at least thankful that they gave him some leftover coffee and a plate of beans for breakfast. They returned him to his cell at the Cananea Jail, and the following morning he was dragged out again and corralled into a train packed with armed Huerta supporters.

Seven years later, there would be a national role reversal when Victoriano Huerta was held as a prisoner on a US train after he was caught flirting with German overtures to use Mexico as a safe harbor to launch U-boat attacks during the First World War. For today, however, Roy was the prisoner, packed into the hot and stuffy baggage car filled with Mexican soldiers. Roy received no ill treatment on this train ride despite the freckles on his sunburned skin, which betrayed him as a gringo with unclear motives in a hostile land. His guards shared some of their food with him.

The train continued south, deeper into Mexico, until it reached Hermosillo, the capital of Sonora, about 180 miles from Cananea. Here Roy was taken into another jail. The Mexicans succeeded at the task which would later befuddle American lawmen: transfer Roy Gardner from one jail to another jail via train without an incident.

Hermosillo would play a prominent role in the upcoming revolution. Its streets would see battles between Pancho Villa and General Manuel Dieguez, and Carranza would eventually use Hermosillo as a base of operations. But this would be of little comfort to Roy Gardner in 1909 once the prison door slammed.

Roy settled into the inky darkness and reflected that the inside of the stone prison was reminiscent of being stuck inside a mine. He evaporated into the silence where a person could begin to feel the noises of the inside of their own body, but his thoughts were interrupted by a man speaking in a thick Irish brogue from a nearby cell.

"Hello, Bill!" Roy said. Roy had no idea who the man was; he just called the man Bill because it sounded right. The man whom Roy christened Bill didn't correct him, just elaborated that his last name was Hughes.

Bill Hughes continued an Irish tradition going back to the San Patricios of the Mexican War, where the sons of Erin journeyed to Mexico only to get killed in front of a firing squad. Hughes explained that he wasn't too sure why he was sentenced to die, and Roy became convinced that a firing squad would be his own fate. The only uncertainty was when he would be executed.

Their conversation attracted the attention of two Americans named Dantzler and Chapman in adjacent cells. Dantzler and Chapman confided that they, too, were condemned to die, but no one knew their dates with their executioners.

Roy's guns and ammunition were confiscated upon his arrest, but he had managed to smuggle a knife with him into the cell. The men decided that once Roy received his sentence, they would figure out a plan of escape.

The three jail mates that arrived before Roy did not get executed, but they received no news about the possibility of being released either. Over the course of about ten days, Roy had ample time to reflect on whether one of the bullets he moved from Arizona into Mexico would eventually find its way into the rifle that would be shouldered by his own executioner. On the tenth day, the sentry took Roy out of the cell to receive his sentence. Roy didn't understand much of the Spanish legalese, but "three men will kill you soon" has a way of making itself clear in any language.

With the news of their imminent execution, Roy put his contraband knife to work. The doors of the cells were wood, about three inches thick. He and Hughes methodically cut through at night, making slow progress. When they needed to rest, they passed the knife to Dantzler and Chapman in the adjacent cell. The men whistled and sang to cover the sound of their sawing.

On about the fourth night of sawing, the men determined that their cell doors seemed compromised enough that they could be smashed open. Now they would just have to contend with the sentry guard. In their weeks of incarceration, the men had nothing but time to observe all the details and rhythms of the jail. When the night sentry arrived on duty, he made frequent passes by the men's doors and possessed the fresh steps of a man newly arrived to his shift. As the evening wore on, however, the prisoners observed that the guard's pace slowed and became lackadaisical and quiet.

The American and Irish prisoners decided that they would wait until about two in the morning to take advantage of the guard's drowsiness and bored complacency. For two hours they listened and waited as their faceless guard and soon-to-be victim walked by their cell door every so often. They used their ears to analyze any detail that could serve as a barometer of the guard's increase in apathy and decline in focus.

The guard shuffled by Roy's cell door and paused. This pause served as Roy's signal. From across his cell he charged at the door and burst through like a human battering ram. The crashing door knocked the guard off balance, and Roy's follow-up haymaker sealed the deal to knock out the guard. Hughes grabbed the rifle off the incapacitated soldier as they scurried along to determine the next course of action. Dantzler and Chapman smashed out of their cells as well and caught up.

In the frenzy, Hughes grabbed the guard's rifle, but lumbered on without taking the ammunition belt. Dantzler noticed this oversight and paused to grab the belt off the KOed guard before catching up with Roy and Hughes.

They encountered another sentry, but this guard was sleeping. The commotion of the running convicts awoke him with a start, but Hughes leveled the stolen gun at the guard before he could make a move. Dantzler grabbed the second sentry's gun and ammunition belt without much effort, and the American convicts scurried onward, leaving the second guard unharmed save for the wrath he would likely receive the next day from his commanding officers.

Under the cover of darkness, the convicts jogged in a crouch toward the walls of the prison, and Dantzler passed around the stolen ammunition belts so there would be a total of two guns with bullets divided among the four escaping convicts. The convicts had beaten their human captors, but now faced an even more daunting challenge: the Sonoran Desert, which twenty-first-century anthropologists would call the "the land of open graves" for its brutal, relentless capacity to kill undocumented immigrants from Mexico and Central and South America trying to make their way to the United States.

For the moment, the fugitives had the refuge of dawn, and the merciless sun would not be an issue for a few more hours. Roy and Hughes split off in one direction while Dantzler and Chapman went their own way. Four gringos with death sentences would draw too much attention if they all stayed together.

Roy and Hughes made as much distance as they could through the mesquite and desert lands, using the silhouettes of ridges and the lightening eastern sky as their navigation. The sun rose, and Hughes managed to shoot a rabbit, which provided some much-needed sustenance. He attempted to reload the gun in anticipation of more hunting opportunities or issues from humans, but a problem revealed itself: in the adrenaline-fueled rush of the escape, the fugitives overlooked that the stolen ammunition belts weren't compatible with both stolen guns.

In the haste to distribute the guns and ammunition, Dantzler had a fifty-fifty chance of getting things right, but he lost the coin toss. Roy and Hughes had a Springfield gun and the bullets for a Mauser. The Springfield bullets were with Chapman and Dantzler, wherever they might be.

A gun, even without bullets, might work as a poker player's bluff, should they find themselves cornered by angry humans, but as the sun rose to reveal the full landscape of the desert in front of them, Roy knew the gun would be a necessity for hunting. Without bullets it was useless. Frustrated, Hughes threw the Springfield gun into the scrub grass and tossed the ammunition belt in the other direction, making his own contribution to the Mexican Revolution should the items be recovered. Hughes decided to head in the direction of the Sea of Cortez, the body of water dividing the peninsula of Baja California from the Mexican mainland. Roy wanted to get back to the Arizona border.

The two fugitives shook hands and separated. They would never see each other again. Now Roy faced the vast agoraphobic expanses of the sun-blasted Sonoran Desert, completely alone.

Roy decided to move at night, remembering where the sun set so he could maintain his mental compass. Once the sun rose, he rested beneath skeletal scrub trees, or alongside crags of rock which provided shadow. There was no water or food.

He covered about twenty-five miles at night, bumping into the occasional cactus, and hearing the howls of nocturnal creatures who had somehow figured out a way to survive the landscape. The thirst was a hell, ironically a feeling like drowning, but with the common sensation of suffocation. A drowning person opens their mouth to gasp for air and gets water; a person cast out into the desert opens their mouth to somehow get hydration and only gets air. Under normal circumstances the parts of a human quietly do their job to keep the brain and body alive, but with desiccation approaching fatal levels, Roy could feel his body parts gradually failing and falling apart.

When he arrived in Mexico, he had the security of mules and provisions. The monotony of the landscape provided a comfort. Now the endless rock and plains appeared to mock him in its indifference. The land and sun would kill him. Then the sun would rise again, and the shadows would evaporate. The heat and insects would consume Roy's flesh, and the sun would rise again to bleach his bones. And that would be all.

While still clinging to mortality, Roy abandoned his shelter alongside the rock despite the afternoon sun and decided to keep moving. If the Huerta soldiers found him limping around and decided to shoot him, so be it. He no longer cared.

Rather than stumbling into sentinels of death, however, Roy approached a scene of green life in the middle of the desert. For about two acres he saw rows of trees alongside lines of berry bushes. The orchards bordered an adobe house. Roy may have thought this was a hunger- and thirst-induced hallucination, but the images became more focused and benevolent. A man and woman who appeared to be grandparents emerged from the house and beckoned to Roy. There were no angry men on horses. A boy of about twelve also entered the scene and they offered him water. Roy didn't necessarily understand Spanish, but they understood his suffering, and their generosity made Roy discover God, if only for a day.

They sat by the cool walls of the adobe; Roy shaking his head and laughing at his turn of luck, and the grandparents and their grandson chuckling in Spanish at the odd arrival of this wounded and weird gringo. In addition to water, Roy's hosts gave him tortillas and beans. As their sliver of the earth turned away from the sun to create long shadows on the adobe walls, the group sat in silence, not needing to say much to appreciate each other's company. Roy absorbed the kindness of strangers in a different country while the family might have tolerated Roy's presence at their home because they were kind and good and that was the only thing to figure. As the sun began to set, Roy determined that he better continue his northward march toward the border under the cloak of night.

The grandmother gave him a care package of berries, oranges, a canteen of water, and a chicken for his journey. As Roy left their adobe house with a revitalized spring in his step, the family conveyed to him in Spanish that he should stop by again if he was ever passing though. They were the good Samaritans making sure that the hungry and thirsty Roy Gardner didn't become another corpse for the buzzards in the land of open graves.

For eight more days Roy traveled on foot toward the Arizona border. He would have surely died had it not been for the hospitality of the family he encountered. By his eighth day of travel he was near death again, and now his shoes were falling apart. At last he made it to the border and onward to Naco, just outside Bisbee, Arizona.

Like a drunk seeking out a former lover at midnight, Roy returned to the Copper Queen Mining Company. Working in the mines was just a means to an end, however, to enable Roy to recuperate after losing his savings and practically his life in his Mexican Revolution debacle. By chance, Roy ran into Dantzler, who reported that Hughes and Chapman were captured and their eventual fates unclear.

While working in the mines, Roy reflected on what went right and what went wrong in his Mexican misadventure. Most everything went wrong. His experience with the elderly couple and their grandson was the act of divine providence or random luck that didn't reflect anything on his ingenuity or talents. The experience with the Mexican family was a pleasant thought, nonetheless, like an opium-inspired daydream that could conjure up a sense of home and warmth. The only moment from his involvement in the Mexican revolution that revealed gumption gone right, in Roy's estimation, was his haymaker punch that knocked out the first sentry in the Hermosillo jail. Roy bore no malice toward any human being, but the experience showed that he might be able to leverage fisticuffs as a better way to make money, compared to getting his head smashed to pieces by falling rock in a mine.

Roy quit the Copper Queen Mining Company for the second time, and "Young Fitzsimmons" was born.

CHAPTER FIVE

The West

1909–1910

Once back on the American side of the border, with his near-death experience with the Mexican revolution behind him, Roy committed to becoming a revolutionary of the boxing ring. He decided to associate himself with other Irish boxing luminaries of the time such as John L. Sullivan and Gentleman Jim Corbett, so he christened himself "Young Fitzsimmons." The new Gaelic persona had plausibility given Roy's reddish-brown hair and freckled shoulders, and he possessed strains of Irish ancestry anyway.

Roy, a.k.a. Young Fitzsimmons, made his way back to Colorado, the state of his boyhood. He hung around the boxing gyms of Trinidad, a turbulent coal mining town in the mountain shadows of the Spanish Peaks. A few years after his arrival, the Ludlow Massacre just outside the city would kill over twenty miners. Wives and children were part of the casualty list in what some historians described as the "deadliest strike in the United States."

In one of the neighborhood gyms, a man calling himself "Trinidad Gans" pummeled the leather bags, and the other boxers in training paused to have a look. Stale sweat lingered in the corners of the gym, but the boxers in training created a brisk and breezy sense of commotion. Trinidad Gans appeared to be the mayor of the place. The sweaty men and orchestrated cacophony of punches and grunts all seemed to pause and coalesce around one man, Trinidad Gans, skipping, jabbing, and punishing the training bags with knockout punches. One of these observers was Roy. Roy, who had no formal boxing training, emerged from the knot of men and challenged Trinidad Gans to a match. Roy was an unknown entity to the locals and most of the men told him to take a walk. Others oohed and aahed. Who was this new guy who just drifted into town? He was either crazy or stupid or both. The local promoter offered Roy fifty dollars if he could win and allowed for one week of training and promotion.

In July 1909, Roy appeared in a newspaper the first time. His story didn't appear under the name Roy Gardner, however, but as Young Fitzsimmons, the unknown boxer who KO-ed Trinidad Gans in two rounds.

This was the easiest money Roy had earned, and he decided he needed to move to a larger metropolis to up the ante. He chose Oklahoma City. Oklahoma was booming with money from newly discovered oil, and the overnight millionaires could be more amenable to investing in tawdry endeavors such as boxing when compared to their buttoned-down, old-money counterparts. Roy's family had also relocated to Oklahoma City, and it could be a homecoming given that Roy had been on his own since he joined the army as a teenager.

In later years, Roy's father would disavow Roy in the newspapers, but when the prodigal son showed up in Oklahoma City with rousing tales of escaping Mexican firing squads and KO-ing the top contender in Colorado, his father appeared to feel a certain masculine pride in his son. He became Roy's manager.

Another name change was unveiled, perhaps to avoid confusion with the heavyweight champion Bob Fitzsimmons. The man formerly known as Young Fitzsimmons now went by "Lawson" and Roy quickly tallied up five wins in the ring under this moniker, including a knockout against Tim Hurley, a boxer who also earned a paycheck as a Chicago policeman.

In a scene straight out of *Rocky III*, where Rocky Balboa accepts a challenge from Thunder Lips, played by professional wrestler Hulk Hogan, Roy a.k.a. Lawson accepted a challenge from Demetral, a Greek wrestler. Roy would earn fifty dollars if he could stay with Demetral for fifteen minutes without being launched off his feet. Roy made a significant number of new friends since he relocated to Oklahoma City, and the large contingent of Roy/Lawson supporters came down to the venue called the Casino to witness the spectacle.

When push came to literal shove, Roy experienced some rare doubts about accepting this match from the well-built Demetral, and the possible defeat in front of so many of his new friends increased Roy's unease. But Roy attacked Demetral's neck and hung on like a barnacle. For fifteen exhausting minutes Roy hung on, and the referee declared him the winner. The name Demetral, however, does not translate to "graceful loser" in Greek, and the wrestler pummeled Roy when Roy's back was turned after the match was already finished.

Roy regained his senses and the two began to wildly pound each other, which provided a more entertaining fight than the initial fifteen-minute challenge. The crowd went nuts, Roy saved face in front of his friends, and once the chaos faded into the cigar and cigarette smoke that created a haze within the overhead lights, he went home with fifty dollars.

Demetral demanded a rematch, but he upped the stakes for himself by requesting a boxing fight rather than a grappling contest. In his more familiar format, Roy won this match, too, in five rounds. Oklahoma City now started to feel like a small pond, so Roy set out on his own again. He broke ranks with his manager and father.

Like he would so often in his life, Roy moved west toward the Pacific Ocean. On his way west, he stopped in Pueblo, Colorado, where he experienced his first boxing defeat at the fists of Jim Flynn, a boxer who outweighed Roy by over twenty pounds.

Undeterred, Roy continued to California, which one politician described as the "Mecca for Pugilists." This description, appealing as it was for a scrapper like Roy, was increasingly seen as a pejorative by a growing and vocal contingent of pastors and ministers who wanted to rid California of this blood sport, which they felt attracted just as much violence outside the ring as in.

The outside spectators often mirrored the pugilists in the ring, as disgruntled gamblers slugged each other over losses, ethnic grievances were settled, and promoters restricted the sale of apples at prizefights, lest they get turned into objects with which to pelt the other fans or the referee. If the clergy didn't have enough to worry about with forbidden fruit becoming improvised missiles, then there was John Barleycorn and demon rum, not to mention the sight of bare-chested men sweating and fighting in front of swooning women, and perhaps a few swooning men, too. In 1910 there was an added threat to the established order in the form of the African American heavyweight champion, Jack Johnson, who had a habit of knocking out white men and having relations with white women.

Roy arrived in California in the summer of 1910, when Jack Johnson, the Galveston Giant, was due to defend his title against Jim Jeffries on the Fourth of July in San Francisco. Before the fight between these two heavyweights, however, came a fight between the governor of California, James Gillett, and San Francisco's mayor, P. H. McCarthy, sometimes known as Pinhead McCarthy.

Governor Gillett tacitly allowed the existence of boxing within the Golden State as long as the matches remained backwater and secluded donnybrooks. The Jack Johnson and Jim Jeffries fight, however, was billed as the "Fight of the Century" and was scheduled to be held in San Francisco, which was desperately trying to rebuild both its infrastructure and reputation after the 1906 earthquake and fire. A major sporting event could have been a civic booster, and indeed certain businesses and promoters were ready to turn a good profit, but the chorus of protesting clergymen grew louder and louder. Given the racial component of the scheduled prizefight where Jim Jeffries was labeled the "Great White Hope," riots were a possible outcome if either of the two pugilists won the fight. Bad press could knock down San Francisco's final approvals for the impending Panama-Pacific International Exposition, a world's fair that would transform and rebuild the San Francisco landscape. Gillett didn't want these plans dismantled by ruffians scaring away the more civilized gentry.

With carpenters working around the clock to complete the facilities for the Fourth of July event, and Johnson and Jeffries training at their respective camps in the Bay Area, Governor Gillett decried that boxing was a "public nuisance" which "corrupts public morals." It was less than a month before the clanging of the first-round bell. He also identified a sporadically enforced state law specifying that "sparring exhibitions" were within the bounds of legality, whereas "prize fights" were unlawful. Over $100,000 was set to be split between both boxers of the Jeffries-Johnson fight, which included payment for film rights. With the discovery of this legal fine print, the governor banned professional boxing from the state of California amid a wave of public adulation from religious leaders and fellow governors. San Francisco Mayor McCarthy had a dissenting opinion.

"Bunk! Bunk! Bunk! Cold feet for somebody! Just watch me. Will there be a fight? Bet your life," McCarthy said after the governor's ban. The promoters had already invested $30,000 in the San Francisco event, and McCarthy pulled off his gloves to defend this incursion on his local turf. Mayor McCarthy insisted the fight would go on, and Governor Gillett declared he would send state troops to stop it.

In the end, the governor won the round and the Jack Johnson and James Jeffries fight was hastily moved to Reno, Nevada, where Johnson won by a TKO in the fifteenth round.

California may have been a mecca for pugilists at one point, but Governor Gillett jabbed the prizefights back to remote clearings in the woods. Roy lived off his boxing earnings from Oklahoma and Colorado, and when that money ran out, he drifted down the coast from San Francisco to work as a dynamiter on the vertical cliffs that dropped into the ocean, the groundwork for what in time would be a roadway named Devil's Slide.

San Francisco drew Roy back, however. As the Christmas season approached, Roy found himself dining in San Francisco restaurants and taking in the night-life, savoring the amenities available to a man no longer condemned to die in a Mexican prison. San Francisco was on the rebound after the 1906 earthquake and fire, and Roy's desertion from his Presidio Army post was just one more item from the past that ended the fateful day of the Big Quake. Roy created a brand-new San Francisco problem for himself, however, as the last month of 1910 wound down to a close.

In 1910, Roy Gardner returned to California, the "Mecca for Pugilists," as his boxing career was peaking, hoping to cash in. But the "Fight of the Century" between Jack Johnson (pictured) and Jim Jeffries was hastily relocated from San Francisco to Reno, Nevada, after California Governor James Gillett enforced a previously ignored law that prohibited professional boxing.

CHAPTER SIX

San Francisco and San Quentin

1910–1913

Roy ambled around San Francisco's Market Street, not far from where he would die thirty years later. Shoppers maneuvered around rain puddles that reflected streetlights rebelling against the winter solstice darkness. People jostled each other and spoke in anticipation of the opera singer, Luisa Tetrazzini. Tetrazzini was due to sing a Christmas Eve performance on a specially constructed stage in front of the nearby Chronicle building as a promotional event to sell Red Cross seals. Newspapers reported a heightened police presence around the Chronicle building to manage the crowds, which were anticipated to be in the thousands.

Couples walked arm in arm while Roy strolled alone despite the Christmas season. He had reconnected with his family in Oklahoma City, but then drifted away. Roy hadn't worked since the summer. He downgraded to the low-rate hotels preferred by transient hobos and bedraggled inebriates. Roy walked through the crowds, most of whom were lost in their own sense of wonder at the Christmas decorations and the talk about the next night's Tetrazzini performance. The last dollar in Roy's pocket weighed down his thoughts.

A man could make money through honest work, but that just led to the need to do more work to make more money. The need for money was like a train's boiler, which constantly needed coal to be shoveled into its orange, glowing belly to make progress. On top of that, a man could get his skull bashed in while on the job. As an antidote to this struggle to push the boulder up the hill every day, Roy found comfort in gambling, but that, too, had its drawbacks: losing.

But winning a poker hand and a lot of money in just one moment always held a certain sway with Roy, in contrast to earning a finite wage over the course of a work week. The siren song of fast, easy money, even with its complementing threat of complete loss, prompted a buoyancy in Roy. It added an urgency to his blood flow and generated propulsion and a sense of purpose. Big bets created more upfront anxiety, but that just meant bigger relief once the chips were counted. Scientists of the mind would later identify these emotions as the byproduct of the brain chemical dopamine, a name linking it with dope fiends. The thrill of gambling would be identified as a similar brain response to the chase of drugs. Some people's minds were a deeper well for dopamine, and Roy's mind, guarded by a silver plate after his mining accident, was a vast reservoir.

Guided by these thoughts, Roy entered Glindemann's Jewelry Store at 818 Market Street. For a few moments he studied the trays of diamonds under the glass cabinets and contemplated his next move, as the proprietor, William Glindemann, and his assistants met with other customers. Roy's unease eventually attracted Glindemann's attention.

"I'm working up my courage," Roy said. "I might propose to my sweetheart."

Glindemann smiled and took on the persona of a wise uncle.

"The perfect gift for Christmas." Glindemann pulled out a tray of diamond rings and explained their various prices. "You're a handsome young man, I'm sure she'll say yes."

"I appreciate your vote of confidence," said Roy. "All of these rings look superb. I'll flip a coin to see which ring I should choose."

Glindemann chuckled and pivoted away to chat with other customers. He left the tray of rings out on the counter, mistaking Roy's sticky fingers for the sweaty palms of a young man in love.

Roy grabbed the tray of diamond rings and made for the exit. He initially didn't run to avoid drawing too much attention, and he figured he could disappear within the Christmas crowds.

Before Roy could make much distance, however, he heard Glindemann yell, "Stop thief!" from his store front. Roy could have launched a better head start had he made this grab and dash one night later, when Tetrazzini was due to sing across the street, with the predicted crowds and police focused elsewhere, but for tonight he would be the entertainment. All eyes were on him.

After Roy heard Glindemann shout, he ducked into an adjacent optometrist shop and ran out the back entrance onto Ellis Street in the direction of Union Square. He also ran right into Detective McLaughlin, who charged into the commotion. Seven years before the film debut of slapstick star Buster Keaton, there was Roy Gardner running up Ellis Street, with a tray full of stolen diamonds. Roy threw his hat onto McLaughlin's face and the misdirection worked—until Roy resumed his sprint, right into the overhand swing of Officer Fella's police club. Roy went down to the ground and experienced the second knock-out loss of his career. The diamonds ricocheted all over the street, and a few were never accounted for.

Detective McLaughlin handcuffed Roy in front of the bewildered crowd. Roy could accept that he lost this competition, but when the exasperated and out-of-breath Glindemann showed up, Roy felt shame for having caused so much trouble for the kind man who had earlier given him relationship advice.

Glindemann finalized the identification, and the police threw Roy into the back of the paddy wagon to be carted off to the city jail. The next day, Roy made another appearance in the newspapers under a new moniker: "Samuel Cox, The Daring Diamond Thief."

The article noted Samuel Cox's chattiness with his arresting captors and how he discussed horseshoes in addition to possessing a working knowledge of Bertillon fingerprinting, a new science of the time. Officer Fella was quoted as saying that he was close to shooting Roy had the clubbing not dropped him.

"I am usually able to overcome such contingencies," was Roy's response.

Roy spent Christmas in San Francisco's jail at the Ingleside station, too far away from downtown to hear the opera singer Tetrazzini. Instead, he heard the snores and farts of other men on Santa's naughty list.

Weeks passed until Roy went before the judge. His real identity had been untangled, though his 1906 desertion from the Presidio was never brought up. The hearing was a formality. Roy committed his crime on a busy street in front of hundreds of witnesses. The tray of diamonds was appraised at $3,000 and some never were recovered. The wet December streets reflected the streetlights to look like stars, but they could have been the diamonds flying in a thousand different directions all over Ellis Street. The judge sentenced Roy to five years. Roy's ruse during the theft had been to pose as a man getting an engagement ring for his girl-friend. Appropriately, Roy arrived at San Quentin Prison on Valentine's Day, 1911.

* * *

Upon arrival at San Quentin, Roy's head was shaved per the protocols of the period. The head shaving would prevent lice and mark him as a convict. He was now Inmate #24840. The prison authorities then photographed him, both for their own reference and to have photos available for wanted posters should there be an escape. In one photo, the authorities decked Roy out in a dapper fedora to antic-ipate what he might wear if he went on the lam. In this photo, Roy took on the rakish look of a matinee idol who decided to become a fugitive from the set of Keystone Studios.

San Quentin State Prison, like its Bay Area counterpart, Alcatraz, sits on what is now prime waterfront real estate, but at the time of its construction in the wan-ing days of the Gold Rush, it was considered an isolated outpost far from the urban center of San Francisco. Unlike Alcatraz, which would become a federal penitentiary, San Quentin was a state-run prison, and hosted executions. The first San Quentin hanging had occurred thirteen years prior to Roy's arrival, when an inmate met the end of a noose after being convicted of murdering two women in San Francisco.

For his Valentine's Day breakfast, Roy filed into the dining hall to have a meal of mush and black coffee with two thousand other convicts. Everyone moved like synchronized ants under the hawkish glare of armed guards stationed at regular intervals. The food was reminiscent of Roy's army days: mass-produced, watery sludge, with half-rotten meat cast away from the civilian world. The food was more successful in creating diarrhea than sustenance.

Per the custom for new arrivals, Roy was assigned to work in the jute mill, a pulmonary purgatory where convicts pulled and processed bundles of the stringy, fibrous jute plant to feed into roaring, insatiable machines to be made into twine. The machines belched out dust in angry storms and few convicts survived this assignment without developing a respiratory infection.

Problems of the lung continued for Roy when he was caught accepting a smuggled bag of tobacco from another convict, resulting in the punishment of extra work. Despite this setback, Roy was determined to toe the line so he could complete his sentence as soon as possible and leave prison while he still had his youth. Eventually he finished his hazing obligation in the jute mill and was transferred to the blacksmith shop, which enabled more critical-thinking opportunities in a trade he knew, in addition to providing the occasional chance for fresh air outside.

Prison offered the paradox of an endless boredom, where a convict had to shut off their mind in order to pass through the days, while simultaneously remaining on high alert to avoid trouble. Although Roy focused on doing his own good time, he couldn't back down if other inmates initiated an argument. Arguments in a prison setting led to a quick escalation of trading punches. After one such fracas Roy found himself reprimanded by the prison authorities and sent to the dungeon for three days while given half-rations. It was going to be a long, hard-won five years.

The days became mixed up in their monotony with the occasional change in work assignment to provide mental relief. Doing time meant just that, existing through calendar days to get to the next calendar day to inch just a little bit closer to a release date. Day by day, week by week, eventually bypassing a year. When Roy entered the dining hall for his 510th consecutive San Quentin lunch special, something seemed different. The lead guard yelled at the two thousand men to file in. They did. The guard yelled for them to stop at a specific mark. They did. The guard yelled at them to be seated. About 1,995 convicts sat, while five remained standing. The standing convicts now gave *their* orders to the other men.

Trays, plates, and even tables went flying throughout the dining hall. The riot was on. The general alarm went out throughout the prison grounds, and more guards came rushing into the chaos. The brick walls accentuated the noise of the rumble. The dining hall riot was a train without brakes hurtling down a mountain. After ten minutes of mayhem, shouting, echoes, and riotous seizure, the guards restored order.

All the men were marched back to their cells without food.

The following morning, the same two thousand inmates filed back to the dining hall for breakfast. This time there were more guards than usual, and the guards maintained the initial upper hand. The silence of two thousand convicts was perhaps more unsettling than the previous day's chaos. Two thousand sets of jaws chewing, and silverware clanking provided the only sound. No one spoke.

Until everything went crazy again. The previous day's mayhem may have just been an adolescent desire to blow off steam and have a food fight. For the second round of the riot, however, the convicts were bloodthirsty. Their target: the prison staff. Two thousand men with violence on their minds in a brick enclosure can't remain focused, however. A punch intended for a guard may have clipped another convict in the back of the head, and that convict took a retaliatory swing at the first convict.

Forks and knives dug into thighs, backs, and cheeks. Some men screamed in pain; others screamed in anger. Roy remained on his feet and noticed that one guard, Captain Randolph, was on the receiving end of a particularly severe beating administered by a group of convicts. An inmate wielding a fork squeezed past Roy and announced his intention to kill Randolph.

Under most circumstances, Roy maintained the convict code of interacting with the prison guards with a detached neutrality. A few individual guards may have distinguished themselves with their brutality, thus earning particular animosity from the convicts, but Roy never knew Randolph to be such a guard. Roy felt it unfair that Randolph should receive a spontaneous death sentence during a dining hall riot. As the inmate with the fork lunged toward the beaten Randolph, Roy grabbed the inmate's wrist and put him into a half-nelson.

For his efforts, Roy was stabbed in the back just above his kidney and received a nine-inch laceration. The riot ran out of steam as guards clubbed and whistled their way back into control. Roy was taken to the infirmary. During his recuperation, Caption Randolph visited to thank him for saving his life. In September 1913, Roy was eligible for his first parole hearing, and his parole was granted due to the strong recommendation provided by Captain Randolph. Roy left San Quentin approximately 930 days after his Valentine's Day arrival.

Roy returned to San Francisco upon his release, but he felt that he exuded the demeanor of an ex-convict. It was as if he trailed a scent of prison life that people could pick up on. Although San Francisco was founded by miners, sailors, harlots, and local politicians who shot each other in duels, Roy felt that he couldn't fit back into San Francisco with the brand of ex-con on his chest.

He moved up to the forests of Mount Shasta, close to the Oregon border, and began training as an acetylene welder at the Mammoth Copper Company. The perfume of the forest cleansed the dull stink of prison life. As a working free man, he had a schedule and a course of discipline, but he wouldn't get attacked by either a guard or another convict if he said the wrong words or didn't move fast enough. Lunch breaks with other working men provided the opportunity for jokes to create a sense of normalcy. Men outside prison could tell stories and enjoy their meals, whereas in prison a man could get stabbed in the back over breakfast. Work may have been drudgery before, but the experience of incarceration put things in a different light. At least he was working for a wage rather than just working to pass time in a prison environment. The forests of the region created a stillness and a grounding. Men here were a small part of something bigger, and their pasts didn't matter.

As a free man, Roy could make plans beyond getting through each individual day, and he developed a dream of saving and starting his own legitimate business, especially now that he was developing specialized welding skills. Robbing the Glindemann Jewelry Store was the biggest gamble Roy had taken, and he lost. San Quentin won. Roy was ready, however, to return to San Francisco for a rematch, but this time he had a new strategy. He was a committed working man.

When Roy was released from San Quentin in 1913, the wild days of San Francisco's Barbary Coast were fading into folklore. The Devil's Acre never found its footing after the 1906 earthquake, and the clamoring for national sobriety dropped a soggy towel on the bacchanalia.

In its place was the construction of the Panama-Pacific Exhibition, the showcase Governor Gillett fought to protect by banning prizefighting in California. The Exhibition would be temporary, yet it created a long-term legacy, including the Palace of Fine Arts, a neo-Greek temple gracefully reaching skyward, surrounded by swan-filled ponds. The monument would forever find its place on San Francisco postcards. In order to construct the fairgrounds for the Panama-Pacific Exhibition, San Francisco needed working men like Roy. Roy returned to San Francisco with confidence. No one asked about his past. They just saw him as a skilled laborer. Roy, always a garrulous storyteller, nonetheless kept his San Quentin experience a secret. No one needed to know. No one.

After finishing the job on the Panama-Pacific Exhibition, Roy heard of job opportunities across the Bay at the Mare Island Shipyard in Vallejo. He moved to Vallejo and became a welder who helped launch steel-hulled ships. One day, he passed a candy store where he saw Florence Nelson for the first time. He discovered that everyone called her Dollie.

"My name is Roy Gardner, but everyone just calls me Roy."

PART TWO
1920–1921

"You can't help but like the fellow—that's the worst part of it. He doesn't really deserve it."

—Arizona Republican newspaper article, dated November 17, 1921,
describing Roy Gardner

CHAPTER SEVEN

Tijuana and San Diego

Spring 1920

Like most people on the fifth day of a bender, Roy Gardner was alone despite being surrounded by a crowd. Mexico was a stormy mistress for Roy: first the date with the firing squad, then the slow burn in the desert, where he nearly died from dehydration and heat exposure. And now this. None of the ponies were doing what they were supposed to do. A long shot named Summer Sigh edged out the contender horse, Felicidad. *Felicidad* means happiness in Spanish, and Felicidad lost. That should have been a sign, but Roy kept digging.

Another round of drinks for him and his friends. Tijuana was pitched as a Monte Carlo south of the US border. There was no Prohibition. The Mexican Revolution continued to smolder, but the Tijuana boosters made sure that such unpleasantries didn't disrupt an American's need to quench their thirst before slinking back into their buttoned-down life on the north side of the dividing line. A guy next to Roy lost big and assumed the frustrated pose of a man in the crash position. Feeling bad for the guy, Roy bought the guy a drink out of commiseration, but Roy's own pockets were getting light.

If Roy's problems started while he was a little bit tipsy, maybe more inebriation would help untangle the knot. More drinks, more bets. The men earlier drinking and gambling with Roy were now gone. Who knows where they went. A new set of faces filled the stands, but Roy didn't cheer out of solidarity when these new people standing next to him won, and he didn't offer words of condolence when they lost. He had his own problems, and nobody was offering to buy him a drink anymore, anyway. The initial elation during the arrival in Tijuana and the rising mental tide created by the first few drinks bottomed out into an overcast, brooding fog. In a few short days, Roy Gardner lost it all.

The handicap of the gambler is that they can't see their future. It's not just that they lack the power to look a few seconds ahead to see what an opponent's cards will reveal, or which number the roulette ball will bounce on, but a gambler has no scientific way to know if their current moment is their apex. A gambler can't categorize with any accuracy whether their most recent breath coincides with the

Bangtails Line Up for Tijuana Classic

Tijuana, Mexico, promoted itself as a Monte Carlo south of the US border and a boozy alternative to its neighbors living under Prohibition. An ill-fated trip to the Tijuana racetrack activated the chain reaction of events that would land Roy Gardner at Alcatraz.

most advantageous time to walk away from the poker table, or if this is the time to stick around for a few more hands, that things are just about to get good.

Roy took a gamble when he decided to leave Shaw-Batcher Shipyards a year before his current descent into Tijuana. He had no way to know that the April 1919 farewell banquet at San Francisco's Fior d'Italia held in his honor by his fellow welders would be his apex for the year. He basked in the adulation and the friendship, but had he known how things were set to bounce, perhaps he would have paused for just a few more seconds to remember the smells of the food and record in his mind the exact timbre of the laughter of his coworkers and friends.

After Roy left Shaw-Batcher, he moved with Dollie and their toddler, Jean, deep into California's agricultural heartland in Fresno to open Standard Welding Works. The European and American powers signed the Treaty of Versailles in June 1919, thus ending the First World War while engendering its inevitable sequel. The global economy experienced an immediate contraction with the ending of the

Great War. Everyone's credit was ruined, international industry was destroyed, and former soldiers needed work. An international pandemic, the Spanish flu, compounded the overall misery that ironically coincided with the new peace. Things were slow to take off for Roy's new business.

Worse than that was the summertime heat of Fresno, located within the furnace of California's Central Valley, a basin that trapped heat between the walls of the Sierra Nevada on one side and the coastal ranges on the other. Prior to Fresno, Roy, Dollie, and Jean lived in the Outside Lands, the foggiest neighborhood in the foggy town of San Francisco. Their newlywed cottage in Oakland also experienced the cooling breezes of the Pacific Ocean to prevent summertime weather from ever going into triple digits.

Fresno in June, however, revealed to Roy that his old head injury from the mining accident and the silver plate in his skull couldn't tolerate heat. Roy became incapacitated with headaches. The heat made his skull feel like it was being crushed and tightened by a vise. By summer's end Fresno was unsustainable, both economically and from a standpoint of misery prevention.

Roy got a tip on a job lead in Los Angeles. Summers in Los Angeles can also tighten a man's head, but the height of the summer season seemed finished, and Roy needed money. Not viewing this relocation as permanent, Roy and the family moved into temporary quarters in the middle of Los Angeles. They had trouble finding lodging and took what they could find in the downtown section on Fremont Street. Dollie was unhappy living in the middle of urban chaos and congestion. Most of her life had been surrounded by the pastoral vineyards and creeks of Napa, and even their San Francisco residence was on the edge of town. In the middle of Los Angeles, everyone seemed to be on the make, and Dollie had difficulty finding friends.

Roy set out to prove this would all be justified in the end, however. He threw himself into completing his job contract, with a work ethic reminiscent of his days in charge at the Calox Welding Company back in Oakland.

Roy had a contract to make one thousand water heater tanks for the Union Tank and Pipe Co. Wanting to prove that the summer's incapacitation was a fluke, Roy worked around the clock. The sooner he finished this project and saved some money, the faster he could figure out his next move. In the meantime, Dollie was left on her own with a two-year-old in the middle of a new city that was not to her liking. Roy sensed Dollie's discontent, and his mind drifted and schemed of next plans while his body fulfilled its physical requirements to weld the tanks.

Roy finished the work obligation and received a lump payment of two thousand dollars. It was a lot of money to receive all at once, but it had been a lot of work. Roy vowed to pursue some leisure activities with Dollie and Jean to make up for his absence during the preceding months. He got a car to tour around. While the heat of a Los Angeles summer can be extreme, the mildness of its springs presented a tapestry to demonstrate why Los Angeles was quickly becoming the most populous city in California. Roy drove his family to Venice to see the sea moss blooming on the canals and then back around the lake at Echo Park so they could smell gardenias mixed with bougainvillea, climbing the walls of gardens like purple ropes.

In Los Angeles in the earliest days of spring, their car didn't even need a roof. They drove past a carnival, and on a whim, they stopped so Roy could win Jean a prize.

To maintain the momentum of this domestic pleasantry, Roy suggested that the family take a trip to nearby San Diego. Dollie was ambivalent. The past year had been hard and while a vacation sounded nice, maybe she'd prefer to relax in the familiar environment of home. But where was their home anymore? She still had plenty of relatives in Napa, which would always be her place of refuge. She knew Roy needed a break after his own challenges this past year. She suggested that Roy go to San Diego on his own to meet up with some of his friends, while she and Jean visited relatives in Napa. Roy consented to this plan.

As Roy took the Southern Pacific's two-hour journey to San Diego, he reflected on how he didn't want to repeat the past year. He wanted to go big so his family could be comfortable. He thought of ways in which he could surprise Dollie for their eventual reunion in Napa. He wanted to do something spectacular to make the new decade a home run. After arriving in San Diego on his own, Roy continued to Tijuana.

* * *

The whole justification for their past season of suffering was that there would be money in the end. But Roy just gambled it all away at the racetrack in Tijuana. How would he explain this Dollie?

He shuffled into the San Diego Post Office to see if there were any letters for him in general delivery. He wasn't sure what he was hoping to find. Maybe there would be a letter from Dollie saying that she loved him no matter what, and with that admission of infinite, unwavering love he would get a few drops of gasoline in his emotional tank so he could figure out what to do next.

Maybe there would be a job lead, and he could delay returning to Napa, but the state of the economy added to his headaches. No one was yet calling the Roaring Twenties by that nickname. In real time the decade's first year was feeling like the Rasping Twenties as the world put itself back together amid inflation and unemployment after the devastation of the Great War.

While Roy waited in line at the post office, something caught his attention. He listened to and observed the post office staff. In time he deduced that a large shipment of registered mail was heading for Los Angeles after midnight.

Once it was Roy's turn at the counter, he asked, "Can you check General Delivery? The name's Nelson, Robert Nelson."

Roy had a plan, a type of plan best served by an alias. The clerk looked unsuccessfully for Roy's imaginary letters, then Roy returned to his hotel room on San Diego's Front Street.

* * *

The next day, Roy woke up exhausted but shaky and excited. He felt like he'd been shot out of a cannon. He made his way to a restaurant close to his hotel. It was time to reclaim lost calories after his lost weekend in Tijuana. In addition to ordering a meal, Roy asked the waiter for the day's newspaper. The big story was a police raid on a "booze island" off Santa Barbara, and another article warned of radical sympathizers bent on overthrowing the government, but the top headline advertised a "Big Postal Robbery By Lone Bandit." Roy continued reading the article attributed to the Associated Press:

SAN DIEGO April 28—An unknown negro, shortly before 3 o'clock this morning, held up and robbed a United States mail truck about one block away from the post office, making away with one mail pouch filled with registered mail and securing loot believed to total more than $30,000.

The driver of the truck, Ray Stock, was on his way to the union depot to deliver mail for the Owl train for Los Angeles when according to his story to the police, a negro suddenly ran out from a sidewalk and presenting a revolver ordered the driver to stop and throw up his hands.

Forcing the driver to hold the mail pouches while he cut them open, the robber opened 31 sacks of mail, Stock said, but took nothing from these sacks. The thirty-second pouch was filled with registered matters and this the robber took with him after ordering the driver not to leave the place for 15 minutes.

The driver, however, as soon as the robber disappeared, hurried to the police station and officers were immediately detailed to run down the bandit. Thus far no clew to the identity of the negro has been secured.

Postmaster L.R. Barrow was notified and joined in the search. No
exact statement on the value of the mail matter secured by the bandit
is as yet available, but it is believed it will total about $32,000.

Roy was in the newspapers again, but for the moment he was the only one who
knew that the subject of the article was actually him. The jumble of inconclusive
and inaccurate information in the newspapers would help Roy gain time.

After his visit to the post office, Roy came up with his plan to recoup his
Tijuana gambling losses. He returned to his San Diego hotel room, waited, and
worked the angles. He had a pistol, which he may have procured for his trip to
Tijuana as a safety precaution, given his experience as a peripheral participant in
the Mexican Revolution. The pistol would be a prop for his San Diego robbery,
though Roy had no intention of actually shooting it. After retrieving his pistol
from his hotel room, Roy went back out into the streets of San Diego and waited
until well after midnight to act upon his plan.

Roy used shoe polish to darken his face, pulled his hat low, and lurked in the
nocturnal shadows close to where he expected the mail truck to make its exit onto
public streets. Although Roy was deliberate in not wanting to shoot the pistol to
hurt anyone, his decision to go in blackface could have gotten an innocent African
American man killed or falsely imprisoned.

Then it happened. Roy crossed a line he vowed he wouldn't cross after his
release from San Quentin. He was a robber again. That day, April 28, 1920, became
a dividing line in the life of Roy Gardner: before his mail robbery, and after.

During the robbery, Roy grabbed whatever pouches and envelopes he could
stuff into his coat pockets until he reached his main target: the sack with registered
mail that the clerk identified during the earlier visit to the post office. He growled
at the driver, Ray Stock, to be still and upon seeing the pistol and Roy's size advantage, Stock complied.

In the adrenaline-fueled rush of cutting thirty-two mail sacks while his other
hand held a pistol, Roy cut his leg and left a trail of blood on the street before he
could vanish back to his Front Street hotel room, a detail the newspaper article
also missed.

When Roy returned to his room, he locked the door and paused for a few
moments to make sure all was clear. It was four o'clock in the morning. Most people on the Pacific Coast were asleep. He reviewed in his mind the words of the post
office clerk: a sack of registered mail heading to Los Angeles. Roy needed $2,000
to cover his gambling losses so he could return to Napa and Dollie as a dutiful and
virtuous husband.

Roy rummaged through the first sack in his room, and his post-Tijuana
depression returned: most of the money in the sack was Canadian and useless as

a solution for his immediate predicament. But then he got to the Liberty Bonds and money orders. He counted out $5,000. The $5,000 grew into $20,000. With shaking fingers, he counted out non-negotiable paper totaling up to $65,000. The sum ballooned so high, Roy might not have been keeping an accurate count anymore, but what difference did the details make when the total net of his robbery exceeded $120,000? The stress in his stomach gave way to elation, like a tightly wound corset coming undone. For the first time in days, Roy collapsed in bed and slept, no longer encumbered by bad dreams and the anxiety of returning to his family with empty pockets.

Upon waking, he went to the restaurant to eat, read the newspaper's factually mixed-up account of the robbery, and plotted his next move. One hundred and twenty thousand dollars was too much money to hold, especially if the newspapers had more time to correct their details. Roy decided he would bury a chunk of the money outside town but remain in San Diego for a while. Once the news of robbery faded, he would return to collect his buried treasure. He could tell Dollie he found a temporary job, but he'd return to the Bay Area as soon as he could. He would assure her that with all of his hard work and saved up money he could take a break over the summer, and they'd buy an automobile to explore the redwoods or go horseback riding through the rolling hills of Napa.

Roy stuffed one of his suitcases with a significant portion of the money, and then filled his pockets with the balance. He'd stay checked in at his current San Diego hotel but spend the night somewhere else outside town after burying the treasure. If anyone asked, he could say he never left San Diego given his hotel receipt, but depending on the line of questioning, he'd have the option to say he was *not* in San Diego. In his haste to leave, he accidentally left one of the stolen mail sacks in the room. He also left one of his other suitcases, which had his name tag on it.

Roy hired an automobile to take him to the town of Del Mar, about twenty miles up the coast. Once in Del Mar, Roy approached the Stratford Hotel and hid the suitcase with a portion of the money under some bushes, the first phase in spreading around his wealth. After checking in under the name "M. E. Lawson," he left on foot to the main road, where he walked against traffic and cut through fields and orchards. He deliberately walked in circles to confuse people who might be observing him from afar. After locating a canyon that seemed a suitable hiding spot, Roy buried the treasure he carried in his pockets. Roy paused to take in the details of his location. He listened if the nearby waves hit the sandstone cliffs in a particular way to create their own unique echo and roar. Springtime wildflowers thrived in the fields of coastal grasses that edged toward the cliff drops. The grasses hid birds and the other creatures of the region, and now they would serve as sentinels keeping watch over Roy

Gardner's loot. Satisfied with the situation, Roy made his way back to the main road.

Roy walked in circles and loops to throw people off his trail, but the erratic behavior in and of itself was attracting attention, mainly from the staff at the Stratford Hotel. A clerk earlier noticed Roy hide the suitcase under some bushes. A conversation was had with the manager. The manager investigated the suitcase which had Roy's real name tagged on the side. The suitcase may have had blood smudged on the edges from Roy's leg wound during the robbery. Phone calls were made.

When Roy returned to the Stratford Hotel after burying the loot in the nearby canyon, he was met by Detective Sergeant Lopez and Deputy Sheriff Saxton.

"Are you Roy Gardner?"

"I am M. E. Lawson, member of the San Francisco Islam Shrine," Roy said, as he pointed to his Shriner's pin, indicating membership in the fraternal organization associated with the Freemasons that coopted fezzes and other Islamic imagery.

The detectives put the squeeze on him. His other suitcase with his name tag on it was found at his primary San Diego hotel, along with the mail pouch Roy overlooked. Roy acknowledged that while he was in possession of the stolen registered mail, he was being coerced by criminal elements to transport it to Los Angeles. Roy claimed that he did not rob the mail truck himself.

Roy could duck and jab, but the jig was up. Roy was in the newspapers again, but this time his photograph and real name supplemented the articles that appeared in the papers on May 1, 1920. Now the public would know him as Roy Gardner, the highwayman robber of the US Mails. He would share newspaper space with Venustiano Carranza, the Mexican revolutionary leader Roy once tried to supply with guns and ammunition. In May 1920, Carranza, like Roy, was also captured by enemy forces.

CHAPTER EIGHT

Napa and San Diego

April and May 1920

When Dollie and Jean returned to Napa during Roy's trip to San Diego, the winter rains finished their magic trick of transforming the hills that cradled the valley into a chlorophyll green. In late April the creeks flowed, and the rush of moving currents through channels could be heard before the creeks could be seen. In the bends of the creek where water pooled, water skippers and other insects found a seasonal home. By autumn the same creeks would be a graveyard of dry rock and fallen oak leaves. Spring, however, was a promise as the days grew longer and the wildflowers emerged as a benevolent yet consistent surprise.

Dollie told friends and family that the past year had its troubles, with the economic challenges in Fresno and the isolation of Los Angeles, but she felt that things were about to change for the better. Dollie was home. Napa would always be home. Napa was a familiar sweater that was well worn and well loved. While Roy seemed absent and lost in his labors these past few months, it had paid off, and they were well positioned for their next move.

She had received word from Roy that he was finishing one last work project for a friend, but that he'd be back to Napa soon with enough money saved where he wouldn't need to work during the summer, and they could all relax together and get their own place.

And then Dollie received a special delivery letter from an acquaintance in Los Angeles. The letter explained that Roy was being held on suspicion of committing a mail robbery in San Diego. The friend said that it was probably a big mistake but urged Dollie to get down to San Diego at once to help straighten things out.

Next came Roy's telegram. "I am arrested. Must stay in jail until tried. You will have to make the best of it until then. Don't believe newspaper accounts. Take care of papa's baby and yourself until I come back. I love you both, just the same as I always did."

Dollie's mind did somersaults. She could not digest this information in the abstract, so she focused on the concrete action of getting a train ticket. That was the only part she understood: *I am buying a train ticket for San Diego*. She took the first leg of her train journey from Napa to San Francisco, and from there she took the Owl Train to Los Angeles, reversing course from a few weeks prior. But her head was now filled with despair in contrast with the sense of hope she felt before. Two-year-old Jean remained with relatives.

Dollie didn't know what to think. She could see her hands but couldn't feel them. She assured herself that this would work out. As her friend said in her letter, this was a misunderstanding. But the thought of Roy in jail made Dollie weep. What was going on? Her sleep was broken and unsettled, which created more fatigue, yet she was on high alert. She looked at the other train passengers and wondered if they could understand her situation. She wondered if anyone else was going through a predicament like hers. But everyone seemed apathetic and quiet. Most slept on the train. They were going to a work obligation or to visit a friend, she assumed. She was going to jail.

The train arrived in the Los Angeles station, and Dollie got off to wait for the connecting train to San Diego. While waiting for the train to San Diego, Dollie tried to get something to eat at a cafe. She had no appetite, but she knew she would have to get sustenance to help keep it together. At the station newsstand, she saw a newspaper with Roy's photo and the headline: "San Francisco Man Turns Thug."

Dollie asked herself again, what was going on? An accidental arrest was one thing, but broadcasting his photo for everyone to see across the whole state?

Dollie bought the newspaper with shaking hands. *Do they know I'm this man's wife?* The article spoke of Roy's incarceration at San Quentin. *San Quentin? Is this real? They're saying Roy was in San Quentin for over a year after he robbed a jewelry store?* Dollie assumed that reporters sometimes mixed up a few details in their haste to make a deadline, but misrepresenting over a year of a man's life? If these dates were correct, then Roy would have just been released from prison when they met.

Dollie's train journey continued to San Diego. She did not want to know what she would discover here, but she had to know so she could resume breathing in a normal fashion. She hired a cab and asked the driver to take her to the San Diego jail. What did he think of her?

Upon arriving at the San Diego police station, Dollie was forced to wait in a lobby area with a gregarious police officer. He spoke of the mail truck robbery and referred to Roy as if he were already convicted of guilt. The officer weaved in the narrative of Roy's San Francisco jewelry heist and time at San Quentin.

Does this officer not realize I'm his wife? Dollie thought. *When can I actually see him?*

At last, she was brought back to Roy's cell. Dollie tried to take in the details. This was the worst day of her life thus far, and she would never forget a minute of it, but the cells of the jail were so bland she couldn't identify a color to describe them. The cellhouse was the color of nothing.

Everything echoed in the cellhouse. Roy heard Dollie's footsteps before he saw her, and the acoustics made her sound larger than her slender frame. Dollie's arrival represented hope and warmth for Roy, but it came with a coinciding crush of shame and despondency.

They clasped hands through the bars and kissed briefly and cautiously. Police officers stood nearby to chaperone the reunion.

"Is it true?" Dollie asked.

Roy inhaled. The police officers had pivoted away, but Roy knew they could hear everything. Roy prepared to perpetuate the lie he was telling about how he didn't actually rob the mail truck; he was at the mercy of other criminals who needed him to transport the money. Now he was about to lie to his own wife.

Before he could continue with the lie, however, Dollie continued. "Is it true? Did you rob a jewelry store in San Francisco and go to San Quentin before you met me?"

Roy exhaled. For the moment he could set aside the charade and calamity of San Diego and instead unburden himself of the big lie of omission he'd been perpetuating all these years. "Yes."

Dollie's fingers shook as she clasped Roy's hands through the bars. Tears streamed down her cheeks.

"What about the mail truck?" Roy was silent. "What about the mail truck, Roy? Please tell the truth so we can get this over with soon. Jean needs you. Get this over with quick. Please tell the truth." Roy remained silent.

"Did you rob the mail truck, Roy?"

"Yes."

"Why, Roy? Nothing makes sense right now."

"I lost all the money at the horse track. The story's as old as the mountains. I wanted to make things right."

"You have to confess. We have to end this as fast as possible."

"I will."

* * *

With Dollie's urging, Roy confessed, and the legal proceedings moved quickly. US District Judge Oscar Trippet sentenced Roy to twenty-five years at McNeil Island Penitentiary in Washington State. Roy explained to the authorities where the money was buried in Del Mar and they recovered all except 267 dollars. Whether raccoons or beachcombers found the loot is lost to the universe, but the financial obligation of paying it back to the state would fall on Dollie's shoulders. Roy had twenty-five years to work off the debt in prison industries, but 267 dollars would take a while earning a prisoner's pay.

The only surprise in the legal proceedings occurred when Roy stood up in the courtroom to address Raymond Stock, the driver of the San Diego mail truck. In a voice reminiscent of the tone he used to implore his fellow welders at Shaw-Batcher to buy Liberty Bonds, Roy said, "I want to apologize to you for the epithets I used. There was no malice in them. I was afraid you would resist, and I wanted to frighten you. I am very sorry. I hope that when we meet again it will be as friends."

Roy offered his hand, which Raymond Stock shook.

CHAPTER NINE

Los Angeles and Sacramento

June 1 to June 5, 1920

It was Roy and Dollie's fourth wedding anniversary. He was behind bars in Los Angeles, waiting to be escorted by Deputy Marshals Cavanaugh and Haig to McNeil Island Penitentiary. The claustrophobia of the cell, compounded by the arrival of Los Angeles summertime heat, most likely induced a headache in Roy. Dollie had returned to the Bay Area. Her plan was to get Jean so that Roy could see his daughter before being taken out of California.

After Judge Trippet brought down the twenty five-year sentence, Roy pleaded insanity, and volunteered his skull to be X-rayed. This tactic gained no traction. The judge passed the buck to the warden. The judge said the warden could respond to the insanity plea.

Deputy Marshal Cavanaugh introduced himself to Roy. He would be his escort on their thousand-mile train journey from Los Angeles to McNeil Island. First, they would stop in Fresno to pick up more prisoners. It would be like Roy's miserable past year in reverse. They would not pass through the Bay Area, however. They would only go so far west as Sacramento and then onward north to McNeil Island.

The deputies planned to communicate with Dollie when they were expected to arrive in Sacramento. Sacramento was within range of Napa, and she would take Jean there so Roy could see his two-year-old daughter in person one last time before beginning his sentence. As the prison train approached Sacramento, however, the marshal realized he forget to send word to Dollie. Roy would not see her.

He was allowed a phone call, however, at the Sacramento station under the watchful eye of the guard.

"Roy, go there and be a good boy until we are all reunited again, and you are free. It won't be as long as you expect, for if you behave yourself, you may be paroled in a little bit," Dollie said. Over the telephone her voice sounded even more distant than the sixty miles separating them.

She put Jean up to the phone.

"Good-bye, Daddy," the two-year-old said.

CHAPTER TEN

Oregon

June 7, 1920

After this phone call, Roy made his decision: McNeil Island Penitentiary would not contain the husband of Dollie Gardner.

The Short Line train continued on its northward journey out of Sacramento. Roy was ready to escape off the train as early as Marysville, just forty miles beyond the state capital. If the plan was to reunite with Dollie and Jean, why not do it while the train was still proximate to the Bay Area? But the marshals on the train were still fresh and cautious. Roy would need to wait until they started to get more comfortable. Maybe they'd get a little bit sleepy. Jumping off the train in Sacramento would have been Roy's first choice, but the train still had seven hundred miles on its journey until McNeil Island, and he would utilize this time and distance to figure out his plan for escape.

Earlier in the journey, the train stopped in Fresno where the marshals picked up another batch of prisoners for transport to McNeil Island. Roy struck up a conversation with one of the new prisoners. Tom Wing was originally from China but spoke fluent English. He was in lockup for a narcotics charge. The other prisoners, Roy learned, were in for auto theft.

The convicts en route to McNeil Island had their own train car, close to the chugging heart of the train's engine and separate from the civilian passengers. Roy made quiet mention of his plan to Tom Wing about escaping off the train. The way Roy explained it wasn't so much a plan, but a declaration of intent: *I am escaping off this train. Do you want off, too?*

Tom agreed that he was in. Roy asked Tom to translate and communicate to the other Chinese convicts if they wanted to take part in the escape as well. Tom reported that the others didn't have much time left on their sentences, and they didn't want to take a gamble on complicating their legal status.

The train continued northward toward the Oregon border. Rolling hills of evergreens that squeezed pockets of mist dominated the landscape. The country looked as if the gods were holding their breath. Six years earlier, this region inspired Roy to abandon his life of crime when he was just released from San

Quentin. Back then he fell into the rhythm of working outdoors with other men to finish a job. Eating at the same table and making jokes. They might not have had things in common before their work detail, but they were now united in completing a task that involved the interconnectedness of their minds and muscles. The jokes came easy at the chow table. Roy committed himself to this world of gainful employment, and the commitment had held for six years. He married and had a child. Roy appreciated the rhythm of the working man. But now he was bound to the rhythm of the locomotive ingesting tracks as it got closer and closer to Washington state and McNeil Island Penitentiary.

As the hours passed and the convicts kept to themselves without incident, the marshals eased into a casual looseness, just as Roy suspected. They talked of their plans for trout fishing on their days off. For the past several hours their human cargo had provided no problems. They had eaten in the dining car, moved back to their car, slept, and smoked cigarettes. Handcuffs aside, it would have been easy to mistake Roy for a man on the Portland Beavers baseball team, making his way back to a homestand. Per the protocol of the period, he was allowed to wear civilian clothes until his arrival at McNeil, where he'd be de-loused and issued a prison uniform.

Roy decided that it was time to act. For an hour they had seen nothing but forest. When he thought the forest might be ending, there was still more forest. Roy knew the next stop would be Portland. Endless forest on one side and a big city on the other seemed like a good split for Roy. The time to act was now. He could wait until the perfect moment, but if he waited too long, he'd be in prison.

As the train rounded a bend, Roy approached Marshal Haig.

"Look at that deer!" Roy exclaimed as he lifted his handcuffed wrists toward the train window. The plan was no more creative than a boy's misdirection, but it worked. One moment Marshal Haig was craning his head to look for a phantom deer in the Oregon wilderness, the next he was looking down the barrel of his own gun, which Roy had pulled from Haig's holster.

Roy alternated the gun between Haig and Marshal Cavanaugh. Roy ordered Cavanaugh's hands in the air, and Cavanaugh complied. Roy took the officer's keys, undid his own handcuffs, and handcuffed the officers together, the captive now the captor. Roy demanded money from the marshals, but they said that with their low pay they'd be robbing mail trucks soon, too.

Whether through force or persuasion, Roy received $200 from one of the Chinese prisoners. He waited for the train to decelerate into the Portland railyard. Marshal Cavanaugh asked for his pistol back, as it had been a gift. Roy opened the chamber of the gun and pocketed the bullets.

"This is a fine pistol," Roy said, as he pressed the revolver in Cavanaugh's free hand.

And then he and Tom Wing were gone. They jumped from the train and were absorbed into the Oregon wilderness like the phantom deer. The train rumbled northward toward Portland, but the McNeil Island train would reach its destination without some of its human cargo.

CHAPTER ELEVEN

Napa

June 1920

When Dollie returned to Napa in the first days of June 1920, she returned with an entirely different set of burdens. Six weeks earlier, she had a homecoming under the guise of a well-earned holiday, and her husband was due home with cash in pocket. Her circumstances were now upside down. Had a carnival soothsayer told Dollie about the change of events, she would have laughed and asked for her money back. But here she was. Her updated plan was to become a nurse and move to Tacoma, Washington, so she and Jean could be closer to Roy at McNeil Island Penitentiary.

One week after her wedding anniversary, and a few days after the Sacramento phone call, Dollie learned of Roy's escape from the train in a local newspaper. The article's brevity created more questions than answers. According to the article, Roy didn't so much escape as he became lost. Marshal Cavanaugh was a babysitter who failed at his task. The article about Roy's escape ended and transitioned into a separate article that reminded people about the final day to pay their income tax without penalty.

He was gone. That was it. Was he dead? She heard nothing else except for inquiries from the police asking her if she knew where Roy was. A few days later she read in the newspaper that Tom Wing, Roy's comrade in flight, was re-captured close to Portland, but still no word about Roy.

In time, she received a postcard from Vancouver, Canada. It had Roy's handwriting. She studied the postcard's handwriting again and again. She looked out the window to make sure no police were nearby. The postcard felt like an apparition of Roy, visiting her in Napa.

The postcard read:

> I am going to Australia, and if you don't come when I send for you, Dollie, it will ruin both of our lives. If any man ever harms you or little Jean, I'll come back and kill him, even if it is my own father. Good night, papa's two little girls—how I wish I could kiss you both but cheer up. It won't be long before we're all together again.

Dollie touched the postcard, knowing that Roy had touched this same card. This postcard would remain her secret. There was no other news from Roy. As the summer sun reached its late June solstice and Napa's famed vineyards struggled to find purpose beneath the restraints of Prohibition, the newspapers no longer provided any information, either. She read of bloodshed in Ireland. She read of politicians looking to restrict Japanese immigration. There was an earthquake in Los Angeles, but nothing about Roy.

The worst were the questions from Jean: "Where's Daddy?"

"He's on vacation."

Dollie suppressed tears as she reflected on the real answer to the toddler's question of "Where's Daddy?"

* * *

At night Dollie spoke to a tiny snapshot of Roy she kept by her bed.

"Where are you tonight, my poor boy? I wonder if you are hungry, or cold, or sick, and lonely for your two little girls."

Then she would say a prayer asking God to protect Roy and bring him back and allow the rest of their lives to be led in peace and happiness.

By the end of June, she decided to move to San Jose to work in a cafeteria connected to the seasonal fruit canneries. Jean would stay in Napa with Dollie's sister. Dollie needed a break from the police lurking around, but on a more practical level, she needed money. As the working representative of the Gardners, she still owed the authorities the $267 which they were never able to locate in the coastal canyons of Del Mar after Roy's San Diego robbery.

The authorities couldn't locate the buried $267, and now they couldn't locate Roy.

CHAPTER TWELVE

Parts Unknown

Summer and Autumn 1920

A person placing bets on the whereabouts of Roy Gardner in the early days of summer would be reasonable to consider Canada, Los Angeles, Europe, or Mexico. Dollie had an inside scoop on Australia, but she heard nothing else as the summertime heat of Napa's Gordon Valley dragged into an extended month of warmth in September. The earth stayed brown, and the rains wouldn't arrive for another month or two.

Was Roy experiencing the arrival of spring in Australia? Dollie could wonder, but she didn't know. His one postcard back in June was all she had heard.

The Los Angeles authorities placed their bet that Roy would be in the City of Angels, his last residence before his switch to desperado. Los Angeles in 1920 was on its way to doubling its size in just ten years. Most of its residents were originally from someplace different. It was a good place for a fugitive to get lost in the commotion of construction and daily new arrivals.

Other agents of the law, however, thought that Los Angeles was just a temporary stop as Roy made his way into Mexico, a country that already indulged his fluid relationship with polite society. A different line of betting called out Canada as the logical destination for a fugitive who started his getaway in northern Oregon. Dollie knew this hypothesis had its kernel of truth based on Roy's Vancouver postcard, but she wasn't talking.

Deputy US Marshal C. T. Walton, however, placed his bet on Europe and he had proof: an intercepted letter from Roy to a friend in Los Angeles. Europe, Roy wrote, was where he intended to go.

None of these bets would pay out. Roy ended up in Davenport, Iowa, a long shot that no one saw coming.

CHAPTER THIRTEEN

Davenport, Iowa

October 1920 to April 1921

When Johnny Cash performed at San Quentin Prison in 1969, he missed Roy Gardner by about fifty-eight years. The ghost of Roy Gardner, however, could have inspired "Wanted Man," a song written by Bob Dylan and received with howling enthusiasm from the San Quentin inmates when sung by Cash. The song provides an elementary school lesson in US geography as it chronicles all the cities where the narrator is wanted by the law. After Roy leapt off the train near Portland, he became the "Wanted Man" prototype. Cash could have added extra verses to describe Roy's activity during the last six months of 1920 and winter of 1921 as Roy moved from Portland, Oregon, north into Vancouver, then cut across the Canadian Rockies until making a reappearance on American soil in Minneapolis.

In Minneapolis, Roy transformed from a traveling fugitive to a traveling sales-man. Using the alias C. E. Patterson, Roy sold equipment for the United States Welding Company. His sales territory included North Dakota, Illinois, and Iowa. Agents of the law may have been keeping their eye out for Roy in California, but Roy managed to disappear in the Midwest.

The initial escape generated a brief newspaper article for just one day. His existence in 1920 illustrates how criminals initially had the upper hand in the Roaring Twenties: transportation outpaced communication. A bandit without any established notoriety could fade in and out of local police jurisdictions with rela-tive ease, if they kept their head down. Commercial radio would not find a place in family living rooms until the late 1920s. Individual police agencies remained disjointed and out of touch with each other, and only big-time criminals made the front pages of newspapers.

As the 1920s and Prohibition-related violence continued, law agencies would become better organized and the FBI would operate without the hindrance of state borders. But that eventuality had no impact on Roy in the early days of 1921.

By October, Roy was offered a teaching job in the welding department in Davenport's Automotive School. Roy would later claim that one of his students was Dean "Dion" O'Banion, the leader of Chicago's North Side Gang, who would experience a bullet-ridden demise by 1924.

For over six months, C. E. Patterson, a.k.a. Roy Gardner, fulfilled his role as a Socrates of welders without any interference from the law.

By the winter of 1921, authorities were still blind to the whereabouts of Roy Gardner. Their sleuthing bore no fruit, but they nonetheless had a tool not of their creation: a Midwest winter and two thousand miles of distance separating Roy from Dollie and Jean. Roy allowed himself one postcard to Dollie in the immediate aftermath of the Oregon escape. Aside from that he knew it was too risky. He assumed her mail was being watched. There's a good chance that Roy deliberately mailed his friend in Los Angeles the misleading letter saying he was en route to Europe to throw off the authorities. Perhaps he never had any intention of making it to Australia, either. He just wanted Dollie to know he was safe.

Six months had passed since Roy spoke to Dollie on the phone at the Sacramento train station. The sound of baby Jean's singsong voice filled his head. "Good-bye, Daddy!"

His June 1920 plan was to escape off the train and return to his family. He would have jumped off the train platform right then and there in Sacramento if circumstances allowed. Roy escaped, but he was spending Christmas alone. The flat expanse of the Midwest plains stretched to the horizon, just like the Pacific Ocean in California. It was a white Christmas, and it was a silent night, but that was the problem. There was no laughter with family.

The arrival of January brought a new year, but it also brought the coldest, loneliest part of the Iowa winter.

CHAPTER FOURTEEN

Napa

May 11, 1921

When her San Jose cannery job finished at summer's end, Dollie returned to Napa and found work as a housekeeper. It had been a little over a year since Roy robbed the mail truck in San Diego and about ten months since she received his Vancouver postcard. It had been ten months of silence, speculation, and sadness. Half of the financial obligations to the feds had been paid. She maintained her ambition to become a nurse when the opportunity availed itself. In the middle of a pleasant spring day in May, the phone rang in the kitchen while she was ironing. In the time period between World War I and World War II, telephones became increasingly common in American households, although long distance phone calls remained prohibitively expensive.

Dollie picked up the receiver.

"Does Dollie Nelson live here?" the operator asked.

This seemed like it could be the police, but why were they using her maiden name?

"Yes," she answered.

Then a man's voice came on, distant yet close.

"Is this Dollie?" he asked.

It was Roy. For almost a year she was looking for him: reading the newspapers, holding her breath, looking for an alias, studying photographs, studying obituaries, scanning faces in town, but now he found her.

"I want to see you and little Jean," he said. "I'm back in Sacramento."

Different parts of her brain thought different things simultaneously. She felt like she was wearing her right shoe on her left foot. She wanted to see Roy badly, but she was terrified, and she stuttered something to that effect.

"Now don't talk like that, dear," Roy said. "I'm all right and I must see you and the baby."

"Meet me at the O'Kell Ranch at my sister's house, for Jean is there," Dollie said.

Their phone conversation was brief, but she wanted to tell him everything. She wanted to hear everything. She felt like an adolescent in love all over again. The moment was fraught with danger and possibility and elation.

Sheriff Joseph Harris was also feeling a sense of danger and possibility and elation, but he was not experiencing sensations akin to teenage love. He was just a hunter who had found his fox. When Dollie hung up the phone receiver after her conversation with Roy, Sheriff Harris hung up, too. Dollie's phone was tapped.

* * *

Dollie hitched a ride with a laundry wagon driver, who took her beyond the Napa city limits to her sister's cottage at the O'Kell Ranch. Sheriff Harris passed them along the way, but Dollie didn't know his face. He was just a name and a nemesis in the abstract. The family that Dollie worked for mentioned that Sheriff Harris often stopped by to inquire about her and Roy.

The last time Dollie saw Roy had been about a year prior in a Los Angeles courtroom. Back then it felt like the floor had been pulled out from her, the air had been sucked out of her lungs, and vision had been pulled from her eyes.

But over the past year she became adjusted to the new reality of her life. As she rode in the laundry wagon to the O'Kell Ranch, she later explained to a reporter that she now felt like a battle-hardened soldier, stoic in the face of danger.

The driver dropped Dollie off at the cottage that preceded the larger ranch house. Dollie's sister rushed out to greet her.

"Roy is here! He arrived about an hour and a half ago. He was playing with Jean until the sheriff came. And he's down there now, hiding among the live oaks."

The sheriff's car was parked on the main road, perhaps thinking that Roy hadn't arrived yet and all they had to do was wait for the presence of Dollie to lure him in. With the police preoccupied with their roadblock, Dollie slipped down to the creek behind the cottage and saw Roy crawling through thick brush on the other side. The creek was half evaporated, leaving behind a bed of mud that sucked down Dollie's feet, but she clambered onward.

"Roy!" she called, but he scampered deeper into the brush. "Daddy!" she called again, using her nickname for him.

With this he turned back, splashed into the creek, and caught Dollie in an embrace, pulling her ankles out of the mud.

"My God, it's Dollie!" he said with a grin.

"Hurry! Get out of sight, the sheriff is here!" she warned.

Roy didn't move, however. He continued to embrace and kiss Dollie. Roy was back and in her arms. His clothes were smudged at the edges and his body exuded a warmth after being on the move beneath the midday May sun, but despite being a little grayer at the temples, Roy looked the same way he always did when he came home after a long day at the shipyard, warm and smelling of life.

"I'm so happy to be with you, Dollie, I don't care if they kill me now."

With Dollie's insistence they held hands and half-skipped over the tangle of rock and fallen branches to move away from the cottage. The canopy of yellowed live oaks created a zigzag network of shadows and camouflage on the ground below. Dollie's heart rate mimicked the excitement of a gambler who anticipated the gain of everything they ever wanted, coupled with the sensation of abject dread. She feared they could be shot at any moment. Roy waved this off with a cheerful smile.

"Don't worry, dear. They know I'm armed, and they won't come after me. I'm perfectly safe. Let's just think of the happiness of these few minutes. We've been separated for a whole year!" Roy explained that he earlier saw Jean making mud pies in front of the house. He had picked Jean up and she giggled, "Daddy!" Roy pointed out to Dollie that he still had the small, muddy fingerprints that Jean left on his collar after their hug.

"You'll always love me, won't you, Dollie, no matter what happens to me?" Roy asked. "God knows I don't deserve you or the baby, but I'm clinging to you both, as all that makes me want to live. I couldn't stand it another day. I had to come back. I want you to know one thing. I was ashamed to face you when I lost all our money in Tijuana. That's why I did that terrible thing, if I had any reason. But I can't figure it out myself. I don't know, I don't know."

Dollie implored him to not get caught up in the past, but she made him make a promise about the future. She made Roy promise before God and before his love for her and little Jean that he wouldn't shoot anyone even if he was under threat.

"I have never hurt anyone yet, have I, Dollie?"

With this agreement, they made the short-term plan that Roy would remain hidden in the brush until dark. If all seemed clear, he could make his way to the cottage, whistle twice, and then Dollie would go back out with him to the creek so they could be together again.

* * *

Dollie returned to the cottage and prepared a dinner for Roy with trembling hands. She had a difficult time concentrating. Any time a deer rustled over the dry, cracked live oak leaves that scattered the adjacent hillside, Dollie stared out the window to make sure Roy wasn't being pursued. She only had enough attention and focus to prepare rice, milk, and bread and butter.

With the onset of darkness, she heard Roy whistle twice from the vegetable garden. His signal. She met him outside with his dinner, and they returned to the creek. The crickets and bullfrogs made enough noise to camouflage their conversation, but it also made Dollie nervous that she also couldn't hear any approaching agents of the law. Roy assured her they were safe.

"Life is unbearable this way, Roy," Dollie said. "I never know if you are dead or alive, or what terrible thing is going to happen to you. I wish you could realize that it would be better for all of us for you to go to prison and serve your time and come out again in a few years a free man. I'll go up to Tacoma and take the baby with me, so that we can be near you. We can never know any happiness or peace of mind this way. You will be hunted down and sooner or later taken, and then it will be all harder for you."

Dollie persuaded Roy to surrender, but he gave one condition: he refused to surrender directly to Sheriff Harris, who he knew had stalked him to the ranch and was waiting up by the main road. Roy didn't want to give Sheriff Harris the satisfaction of winning.

"They will say that I was afraid, and that they had me corralled."

He requested that Dollie's brother-in-law drive him to Suisun City, a town surrounded by the tidal marshes of San Pablo Bay, just twenty miles from Napa. Roy would surrender to their sheriff, an uninvolved neutral entity in Roy's mind.

Their plan was for Dollie to return to the house while Roy remained hidden by the creek as the clock approached midnight. Once things seemed clear, Dollie would whistle twice, and then they would make their drive to Suisun City. If more deputies arrived, she would let out a warning whistle, and Roy was to remain hidden in the brush until further notice.

Dollie made her way back to the cottage with moments to spare before the arrival of more law enforcement, who decided to investigate closer to the cottage after their day-long stakeout on the main road bore no fruit. Dollie let out the warning whistle into the darkness, hoping that her signal didn't get lost amongst the croaking of the bullfrogs. The deputies searched the property. Dollie walked closer to the main road in the opposite direction of Roy and paced up and down as conspicuously as possible to create a misdirection and false impression to the authorities that she was still waiting for Roy to meet her.

By three o'clock in the morning, the sheriffs still couldn't find Roy. They declared a cease-fire and got back into their cars for their return to central Napa to get some sleep. Once their automobiles clambered away, Dollie waited a few minutes before scrambling down to the creek bed. She fumbled through the darkness to create a cacophony of snapped twigs and branches.

"Roy! Daddy!" she called out.

Crickets.

CHAPTER FIFTEEN

Roseville to Newcastle, California

May 20 to May 24, 1921

Following the 1848 discovery of gold in the western hills of the Sierra Nevada, thousands of prospectors journeyed to California looking to make their fortune. Roy Gardner crouched on a slope of these same hills seventy years later looking for his own version of gold.

He never surrendered to the Suisun City sheriff as he promised Dollie. He made it to Suisun City, but he just kept moving. After Suisun City he continued east into Sacramento and kept moving toward the mountains cradling Lake Tahoe. The flatlands and trapped heat of California's Central Valley gave way to hills and vertical rock formations. As a person traveled closer to the Sierras, the quality of the air changed. With the climb in elevation the air became both thinner and more conspicuous in a person's desire for it.

For several nights, Roy perched on a hillside to monitor the Pacific Overland *Train No. 20* as it made its way from the town of Roseville to Newcastle, with an eventual destination of Reno. His idea was to break into the train's mail car, in a close re-creation of his San Diego mail truck heist. A year earlier, his challenge was to break *out* of a train transporting him to prison, but now he struggled to figure out how he would break *into* a moving train. The train's mail car would be locked from the inside, Roy's current puzzle to solve. From the hillside perch, he noticed a large bend in the track where the train curved like the exposed ribs of a dog rolling around on its back. During this curve, the accordion shutter connecting the mail car expanded and presented a few moments of vulnerability. Roy's plan was to jump the train, and then work from the outside to exploit that moment of expansion to fit his hand into the clasps and enable his whole body to maneuver inside.

The plan was not without risk. If Roy couldn't work his whole body into the train's mail car by the time the train straightened and the accordion shutter squeezed shut, his arm would get crushed and most likely severed. For five nights,

Roy studied and replayed in his mind what he needed to do, and on May 20, he hid outside the Roseville train yard in the grass and weeds.

The train groaned and grumbled as it accelerated into the night. Roy sprinted alongside it for a few yards and then lunged up to grab a handhold before the train hit its top speed. He pulled himself up, and for a few miles Roy clung on, battered by the wind, until the *No. 20* approached the curve Roy had studied so carefully.

* * *

Railway mail clerk Ralph Decker was drifting off to sleep around 10:15 p.m. There wouldn't be much for him to do on the moving train until it reached Newcastle in about an hour. But rather than having a date with Mr. Sandman, Decker was jostled awake by Roy Gardner wearing a handkerchief around his face and brandishing a .45. Decker put his hands in the air as ordered, wondering how the man had gotten inside. The train roared toward the Sierras with everyone else onboard oblivious to the activity in the mail car.

Roy tied Decker's wrists. Then he began cutting open mail sacks one by one.

"Do you think there is anything in this?" Roy asked Decker. The initial shock of the intruder pointing the .45 gave way to a jumbled monotony. Roy went through fifty mail pouches while making conversation with Decker the entire time.

"Do you think this would be worth taking?" Roy said as he held up an envelope for Decker's inspection.

Roy spilled the contents all over the car like feathers in the aftermath of a pillow fight. Roy was a lone bandit, and he realized he needed some help. Decker was tied up, but he still had a mouth. Roy instructed Decker to bite down on an empty sack to keep it open so Roy could consolidate the registered letters he determined to be lucrative from all the other sacks he cut apart. Decker almost felt like an accomplice to the plundering. But robbery victim he was. Roy took Decker's watch and eleven dollars in addition to the looted mail.

Roy unlocked the mail car's door to prepare his lunge off the train and into the Sierra foothills. The landscape was black under the depths of night, but the rushing breeze of the opened door broadcast the predicament. This was going to be a hard fall. Roy would need his arms and shoulders available to break his tumble. The mail sack would need to be chucked out first.

If this were a heist movie where the director had the benefit of using the best take, Roy would pull the emergency brake signal, the train would slow, and he would throw the mail sack out the door just before Roy himself leapt off the train. The whole take would be one fluid shot.

Instead, Roy tossed the mail sack out, pulled the emergency brake cord, and nothing happened—except the laws of physics remaining in effect. The fast-moving train continued to create distance between the point where Roy threw the mail sack and his body as it remained on the mail car. Roy needed the train to slow down so he could jump off without being killed. He pulled the emergency brake cord again and again and nothing changed. Unbeknownst to Roy, he was using the wrong signal, so the train engineer ignored it. Finally, Roy slowed the train when he opened a stop valve.

Roy leapt off the train and landed hard on the ground. It was around 11 p.m. Dark. About seventy years prior, men scoured these hills looking for gold. Roy spent the rest of the night walking along the tracks looking in vain for the mail sack he threw off the train minutes before he had a chance to jump off.

Just as most of the prospectors never found gold, Roy never found the mail sack. But at least he knew what time it was courtesy of Ralph Decker's watch.

Roy made his way close to the main road but kept his distance to avoid detection. He saw a car accident and his instinct to help overcame his sense of caution. He rushed over to assist the driver, who lay bleeding on the pavement. Roy flagged down another driver and eventually the police arrived to help get the accident victim to the hospital. The police may have commended Roy as a Good Samaritan, unknowingly shaking the hand of the man who had just robbed the Pacific *No. 20*. With his good deed finished for the night, Roy made his way toward the town of Rocklin.

* * *

As the plundered Pacific *No. 20* decelerated into its destination of Newcastle shortly after 11 p.m., Ralph Decker reported the robbery immediately. Although Roy wore a handkerchief around his face during the robbery, Decker had ten minutes of mingling with him in the mail car to get a sense of who he was and what he looked like. The all-points bulletin went out.

When Roy evaded Sheriff Harris back in Napa, rumors spread throughout the region that Roy Gardner, the escaped bandit of the San Diego mail truck robbery, was back in northern California trying to connect with his wife and child. Local police departments might have been isolated when it came to fledgling criminals new on the scene, but newspapers were still hungry for a scoop. Roseville was twenty miles from Sacramento, which in turn was less than fifty miles from Suisun City, where Dollie directed police officials after Roy slipped away amongst the live oaks of Napa. Decker's description of Roy Gardner—a muscular man about five feet, ten inches, with reddish brown hair and a ruddy complexion—aligned with the description of the Roy Gardner everyone was familiar with. A robbed mail train established a crime pattern.

The next day's newspapers across the Pacific coast from Tacoma, Washington, to San Bernardino, California, described the robbery, with the accompanying hypothesis that Roy was the main suspect. Post Office Inspector W. I. Madeira announced from Oakland that there was a $5,000 reward for Roy "dead or alive." If Roy thought he could evaporate into the Midwest plains like before, he was out of luck. The Norfolk, Nebraska, *Daily News* spelled it out clearly enough in their front-page headline: "Authorities Believe Lone Man Who Looted Mail Car Is Roy Gardner."

Roy had graduated into a news sensation, and despite the limitations of the time period, he was now a known entity to police departments throughout the West. After looking all night for the ditched mail sack, Roy limped back to Roseville and a room at the Porter House Hotel, his headquarters since he evaded Sheriff Harris ten days prior in Napa. Roy went to the hotel restaurant for his usual breakfast and used the same meal ticket he had all week. Whether an indirect challenge or an ironic expression of naiveté, his regular waitress showed Roy a newspaper with his photo printed.

"This looks like someone I know," she said.

Roy also made sideways glances at another restaurant regular, Officer Kirby. Roy would later claim that he dined in the same restaurant at the same time as Officer Kirby every morning during his stay at the Porter House Hotel. The two cased each other like awkward teenagers, working up the nerve to ask the other to dance.

Staying in Roseville was a losing proposition. Roy may have decided to stay one more day so he could comb the train tracks for the chucked mail sack with the assistance of daylight, but that plan, too, fell apart. Postal Inspector George Austin explained to reporters that officials had already located the mail sack in the brush.

Roy finished his meal and left the restaurant. Officer Kirby took notice of it all from his own table.

Roy had a five-thousand-dollar bounty on his head and eleven dollars of Ralph Decker's money in his pocket. It was time to play poker.

* * *

The clinking and clanking of poker chips emanating from the Ridley Cigar Store was a siren song to Roy. Perhaps, he thought, he could make some quick winnings and *then* hightail it out of Roseville. Roy peeked in and asked if he could be dealt into the game. It was a robust, well-established game, but the other players consented. The only open seat had Roy's back to the door.

After a few hands, it was Roy's turn to deal. He spread the cards around the table in a rhythmic, clockwise motion. As Roy dealt out the last few cards, he noticed the men's faces change. They gazed at Roy with a grimness that made the poker game feel like a tarot card reading where the Card of Death was revealed.

The men in the room stopped inhaling their cigars, the jokes and guffaws stopped, and no one touched the cards Roy dealt out.

"Why so glum, everyone? We haven't started the hand," Roy said. No one said anything. One of the players nodded their head ever so slightly to cue Roy to have a look behind him. Roy twisted his head around to see Postal Inspector George Austin flanked by Southern Pacific Agents Dan O'Connell and Barney McShane, quietly standing guard with their pistols drawn. George Austin only stood five feet tall, but reporters described him as "five feet of nerve." The men of the room thought they were all on the brink of being robbed until George Austin clarified.

"Roy, we've got you. One false move and you're a dead man," Austin said.

Roy responded, "If you fire a gun into this crowded room you're just as likely to hit one of these men who have nothing to do with me. Let me finish this hand, and I'll come along quietly." The agents of the law agreed, and for the next few minutes the poker players finished their poker hand with three different pistols aimed across the room. With the round complete, Austin handcuffed Roy and led him out of the store.

He was put into a waiting automobile and taken to the Sacramento jail. Roy denied having any role in the robbery. Decker, the train mail clerk, was called in to identify Roy. A lineup of men, including Roy, were assembled. All the men had handkerchiefs around their faces to mimic the train robbery near Newcastle. Decker identified Roy without any hesitation.

"I have kept in mind that peculiar haircut," Decker explained.

This time Dollie would not miss Roy in Sacramento. She arrived at the local jail with a dessert of strawberry shortcake. She gave a statement to a reporter for the *Sacramento Bee*:

> He has done wrong and I suppose he must pay the penalty, but in God's sight he is more good than bad. A man who will walk into the shadow of a twenty-five-year prison sentence to see his wife and baby is a man, despite all else.
>
> His determination to see me and our baby, little Jean, is the reason he is in jail today. And if possible, I respect him and love him a thousand times more because he is in jail. He's my husband after all, and to me he's the finest man in the world.

Police officers declined Roy's request for a knife to help him cut his meals. Roy asked what difference did a knife make if he already had a smuggled razor blade anyway? The officers called Roy's bluff, and with a magician's flourish, Roy produced the blade which was sewn in his inner sleeve.

The officers beat Roy at poker, but he still had a few aces up his sleeve.

CHAPTER SIXTEEN

Sacramento

May 29, 1921

"I might as well tell the truth of the whole affair, it seems you will get it out of me anyway." After hours of grilling by police and postal inspectors, Roy admitted to his involvement in the Pacific Overland robbery.

With this unburdening, the authorities said that Roy went on to admit that he also had a hand in a September 1920 mail robbery in Centerville, Iowa. Fifty thousand dollars was stolen, but Roy said his accomplice "got away with the money."

Roy's interrogators also said he admitted to riding an Ogden to San Francisco train four times while casing it out. He went so far as to cut a panel to the mail car. Once talking, Ray couldn't stop. He admitted that a train in Colfax was also on his watch list. Despite the supposed confession, the Centerville train robbery was never formally pinned on Roy.

Roy would be taken to San Francisco to receive sentencing for his escape off the train taking him to McNeil Island Penitentiary, in addition to the Pacific Overland train robbery near Roseville. At the end of World War I, Roy left San Francisco to start his own business in central California, and he returned to San Francisco two years later having pursued that goal in his own peculiar way. On his return, Roy would not be attending a Masonic luncheon with a scheduled presentation on the art of making friends and influencing people, but instead was arraigned in court while handcuffed.

To the judge Roy said, "Mr. Austin has told your honor of a few robberies I committed. The Post Office authorities have accused me of every robbery west of the Mississippi River within the last year. He tells you everything against me, but nothing in my favor."

Roy could offer some extra gravy in his own personal sales pitch to the judge, but the objective facts remained: one robbed mail truck in San Diego. An escape off the prison train taking him to Washington. One robbed train making its way through the Sierra foothills to Reno.

CHAPTER SEVENTEEN

San Francisco

June 1, 1921

On June 1, Roy and Dollie Gardner's wedding anniversary, Roy was once again in a county jail awaiting federal sentencing. Two of their five anniversaries now involved Roy in lockup. Warden Hoyle predicted their marriage would be finished within three years, but Dollie told reporters she was ready to wait fifty years for Roy.

"This isn't a very good wedding anniversary, but there may be happier ones to come," she said.

San Francisco US District Judge Van Fleet sentenced Roy to twenty-five years at McNeil Island. The twenty-five years became a jangle of quarters in a person's pocket. Was this another twenty-five years on top of the twenty-five years Roy hadn't even started yet because he escaped before getting to McNeil Island back in 1920?

Judge Fleet used legal precedent and scholarship to guide his decision, but in the law school of Roy's mind, he had another opinion which he presented to the court.

"Although I am a bandit, at no time have I fired a revolver at any person, refraining even upon one occasion when I was knocked down while attempting robbery."

The judge responded that he "regretted to see so bright and intelligent a man in so serious a predicament." He added, however, that "I do not believe you are any different than any other man would be under such circumstances."

Judge Van Fleet announced his sentence: twenty-five years on top of twenty-five years. Dollie burst into tears at hearing the sentencing and turned to Roy.

"Take good care of yourself, Daddy, and I will be waiting for you," she said.

Roy turned to Marshal James Holohan in the federal court room and announced, "I give you warning, Mr. Marshal, that I'll not reach McNeil Island again. I'll get away again."

"I'd like to see that bird get away from me," said Tom Mulhall, former deputy sheriff of Santa Clara County and a seven-year veteran of the marshal's office. Mulhall would be Roy's escort for the second attempt at transporting him to McNeil Island.

CHAPTER EIGHTEEN

Sacramento

June 10, 1921

In June, gray fog descends upon San Francisco like a season-long siege. Baby sea gulls are born beneath this gray celestial blanket, and their squeaks interrupt the lapping and crashing rhythms of the waves.

The fog presses San Francisco with the precision of a surgeon's scalpel, for everywhere else in California there's a dry simmering heat with an accompanying fire threat. Roy marched amid a gaggle of law officers who sweated and huffed as they hobbled around a dried-up creek bed in Sacramento's Del Paso Park looking under rotten tree branches growing out of rocky embankments for $150,000 of stolen securities. The stolen loot was part of a separate train robbery in the Sacramento yards close to the time when Roy robbed the Pacific Overland *No. 20*.

Once Roy received his sentencing back in foggy San Francisco, he was taken by train under the escort of guards back to Sacramento in a repeat of the previous year's attempt to transport him to McNeil Island. Once in Sacramento, the journey would pivot north toward Oregon and Washington State. Before reaching California's capital, Roy told the guards that he knew where the $150,000 was hidden from the other train robbery. Roy insisted he didn't participate in this robbery, but thieves talk, and he'd been in lockup after his Roseville arrest sharing cigarettes with them.

The officers agreed to let Roy off the train to lead them to the loot as an opportunity for Roy to atone for his other transgressions. Roy marched the men through the fields of Del Paso Park as he looked for the exact tree. Roy went through the motions of craning his neck and picking up fallen tree branches, but in reality, he was looking for an escape. The surrounding officers would offer Roy no such opportunity, however. They had him surrounded with shotguns leveled.

Realizing the futility of escape under such circumstances, Roy announced to the officers that he must have been "double crossed" when the men told him of their hidden pot of gold. The police put Roy back into their automobile for the next phase of the prisoner transport to the train station at Davis, just outside Sacramento.

The agents of the law had their rematch with Roy Gardner after they lost him a year prior. For the June 1921 rematch, they took the extra precaution of fastening him with an Oregon boot: a heavy, doughnut-shaped iron that fit around a man's shin close to his knee with an extending component that locked into the heel of the shoe. This cousin of the ball-and-chain was invented by a man also named Gardner in the nineteenth century. With the Oregon boot locked on Roy's leg and handcuffs fastened on his wrists, Roy and Marshal Mulhall made their journey northward on the *Shasta Limited*. They were joined by David Rinckel, a Prohibition agent and former deputy marshal who had worked in Alaska.

The train journey had begun in an almost perfect re-creation of the previous year's train ride. Roy observed the same flocks of birds swarming for their own annual migration, as if the sky possessed invisible train tracks. In the prior year, Roy had gone on the lam, hid in Canada, lived in Iowa, robbed a train, and was recaptured. The trees and mountains outside the window of the train, however, stayed in their exact same spots as if they were waiting for his return. The roots of the trees gripped the earth in their own version of the Oregon boot.

During his previous escape, Roy had an able-bodied and motivated accomplice: Tom Wing. For the 1921 rematch, however, the only other prisoner on the train was a haggard counterfeiter in his fifties named Norris Pyron, who had only a few years left to serve and a nagging cough. They picked up Pyron in the town of Dunsmuir, a base camp community situated along the ascent to the Trinity Mountains. Roy concluded that Pyron wouldn't be of much benefit as an accomplice and continued to make his plans in solitude.

Similar to last year, Roy waited. He waited for the train to establish a drowsy rhythm. Everyone was on good behavior as the train headed north through California. The *click-clack* of the train traversing the track became a heartbeat. Shadows shifted across the landscape and the color of the sunlight took on different qualities. There were other passengers on the train, and these other passengers most likely caught glimpses of the shine of the handcuffs around the men's wrists as they were occasionally moved to the smoking and dining cars. Marshals Rinckel and Mulhall kept one of their own hands locked across the bend of each convict's elbow as added security and an advertisement to everyone that these men wouldn't be causing any trouble.

Roy was looking at a lot of prison time, but the unfolding spool of trees passing their window presented a calming effect. When the *Shasta Limited* made its first Oregon stop in Salem, additional Southern Pacific agents entered the train car transporting Roy to McNeil Island.

The lead agent announced, "Roy Gardner, you will not escape off this train in Oregon!"

Nighttime arrived along with the Northwest rains that assaulted the train windows like an artillery barrage. Roy estimated that they passed the spot where he escaped last year when they approached Portland, but it was just a hunch as he couldn't see much through the window with the darkness of the impending midnight hour.

Dan O'Connell, one of the Southern Pacific special agents, said that during the Oregon segment of the journey, Roy "behaved wonderfully. You couldn't have wanted a better prisoner."

The Southern Pacific agent barked that Roy was not to escape off the train in Oregon. So, Roy waited until the train crossed the Columbia River into Washington to reveal the smuggled pistol he'd been carrying since San Francisco.

CHAPTER NINETEEN

Washington State

June 11, 1921

For the third time in a year, Roy Gardner was about to leap off a moving train.

The midnight entrance into Washington was likely lost on the other the passengers, who took advantage of the late hour for sleeping rather than geographic analysis.

There was no sleep for Roy. He was anticipating. Once the extra agents disembarked back in Portland and the train sped headlong toward McNeil Island, he had to act. He roused Marshal Rinckel from his snooze. Roy said that he needed to go to the lavatory but added that he had difficulty completing this task on his previous attempts with the handcuffs on. Could he just this once take off the handcuffs so he could properly wash up a bit?

It had been a quiet eleven-hour journey with only two more hours to go. Marshal Rinckel may have declined this request at first, but Roy persisted. Roy was the top Liberty Bond salesman of his department during the Great War after all. Eventually Marshal Rinckel agreed to remove Roy's handcuffs, but Roy was still hobbled by the Oregon boot. Rinckel escorted a limping Roy to the train washroom. Marshal Rinckel undid Roy's handcuffs and stood sentry while Roy gimped in and closed the door.

Marshal Rinckel heard faucet knobs squeaking within the restroom and water splashing around. He may have heard Roy on the other side of the door coughing a few times to clear his throat. Then the most significant event of the train journey up until this point happened, and Marshal Rinckel would be unable to describe its sound. What is the sound of a pistol pointed at your own nose?

When Roy boasted to Marshal Holohan in San Francisco that he would escape off the prison train yet again, he was already in possession of the smuggled pistol. Roy's stomach had absorbed hundreds of punches during his boxing career and now it would absorb the presence of a smuggled gun hidden against tightened abdominal muscles. When the police officers frisked Roy before boarding the *Shasta Limited*, they ran their hands right across the pistol. His hard stomach camouflaged the steel of the gun.

Roy burst out of the bathroom quickly yet quietly, so as not to disrupt the nocturnal atmosphere of the train. He pointed the pistol at Marshal Rinckel and pressed his finger to his lips with his other free hand. The Oregon boot was a defanged instrument in the tight quarters of the train car when Roy had a gun, free hands, and the physique of a boxer. Roy pushed Marshal Rinckel along, causing him to backpedal. With a push, Rinckel toppled backward like a bowling pin on top of Marshal Mulhall, who was suddenly awoken from his own slumber. Mulhall initially refused to raise his hands, so Roy shoved the nose of the revolver into Mulhall's belly to force the situation. With the element of surprise, Roy managed to grab Mulhall's own pistol before Mulhall could put it to use, but no bullets were fired within the train cabin.

The rematch was going Roy's way. The only monkey wrench occurred when Pyron, the other convict, woke up, saw the commotion, and let out a holler that fell somewhere between enthusiasm and fear. Roy reclaimed control of the situation and ordered Pyron to be quiet and to help find keys. Pyron climbed out of his bunk and rummaged through the officer's belongings. He located the keys and an additional gun belonging to Rinckel.

Roy uncuffed Pyron and slapped the handcuffs onto Mulhall and Rinckel, with the added anchor of linking them around a steam pipe running through the train car. With the officers handcuffed, Roy ordered Pyron to hand over Rinckel's gun. Pyron was too skittish and frail to be of much use, and Roy wanted no gunshots. There were civilian passengers in the adjacent train cars, so the longer everyone stayed asleep, the better his chance for escape. Roy ordered Pyron to let Rinckel keep one of his rings that Pyron intended to take for himself.

"This is a jail break, not a burglary," Roy admonished.

Pyron reluctantly relented. Roy was the heavyweight in control of the situation, whereas Pyron was a tubercular man who was only moments before startled awake and dragged into the escapade.

Despite his earlier scolding of Pyron, Roy took about $160 total off Rinckel and Mulhall. This would count as robbery in the eyes of most legal scholars, but Roy viewed it as financial fuel for the escape. Marshal Rinckel asked Roy to at least let the officers keep a few of their dollars for breakfast and Roy agreed, peeling off a few bills and putting them back in the officer's pockets.

About three minutes into the rematch the statistics looked like this: two agents of the law were handcuffed to a steam pipe, Roy had three pistols and $160, but the Oregon boot still anchored his leg.

He frisked Rinckel and found a knife, which he used to jimmy the heavy doughnut off his shin, but he had trouble with the heel plate. He sized up Rinckel's feet and said that it was time to hand over his shoes. Rinckel pleaded with him to let him keep his own shoes. Roy considered the situation. He managed to disable the worst part of the Oregon boot, but the heel plate would still hobble him and leave distinctive footprints, which would aid his pursuers.

Marshals Rinckel and Mulhall would be admonished by their superior, Marshal Holohan, for letting Roy escape again on their watch. There would be a doubling down on Rinckel's humiliation if his shoes were taken.

Roy came up with a compromise: he would let Rinckel keep his shoes if the two marshals would solemnly swear that they would give Roy a twenty-minute head start before they sounded the alarm. The officers made their promise, and Roy made them promise again.

With this solemn agreement, Roy presented his smuggled gun to the hand-cuffed officers and announced, "Here's a souvenir, the gun you got stuck up with!"

He pocketed the bullets and tossed a .32 in their direction. He kept one of the officer's pistols for himself and allowed Pyron to keep the other officer's pistol, with the warning that Pyron was to not even think of firing until they were off the train.

The handcuffed marshals asked Roy what his next plan was.

"You'll hear from me pretty soon," Roy said. "I'll pull a big job that everyone will hear about."

Roy opened the train window. A belch of rain sprayed into the cabin and he made his exit. Pyron jumped out too, but once Pyron hit the earth, Roy was already gone. He became like the elusive Sasquatch, disappearing into the Willapa Hills.

The *Shasta Limited* rumbled northward toward Tacoma. Marshals Mulhall and Rinckel remained handcuffed to the steam pipe. They started to count.

CHAPTER TWENTY

Castle Rock, Washington

June 11, 1921

The sky looked like a battlefield wound. Its outer perimeter presented as a dark bruise shifting from an opaque purple to a vague gray while hemorrhaging rain. The depths of dawn obscured the Cowlitz River, a major route for steamboats transporting wares from regional farms, and the cascade of rain camouflaged the sounds of the river's moving currents. When Roy emerged out of the fortress of red cedar, which smelled of wet earth and medicine, he limped into the town of Castle Rock, Washington.

He looked like what he was: a man who had fallen out of a moving train in the middle of the night while getting drenched. He hadn't shaved in a few days, and, most significantly, he couldn't pinpoint the time of his last meal.

There's a good chance that Roy's wanted poster from the prior year was still hanging on the walls of the local post office. The speed of his escape after the Roseville capture and the geographic similarity would save authorities the trouble of printing and posting new notices.

More than anything else, hunger guided Roy's decisions as he drifted into town. He would eat and then evaporate into the forest to determine his next move. Roy took a gamble and hoped that the early morning hour would be the time when the local police would be making their shift change. During this transition, Roy would make a quick dash for food and then get out before word of the midnight escape saturated everything like the Northwest rain.

* * *

Cowlitz County Sheriff A. W. Hoggett had dispatched no fewer than five posses to search for Roy once the *Shasta Limited* made its first stop after losing its human cargo. The news of Roy's escape spread quickly by word of mouth, an opening salvo that preceded the onslaught of printed news that was soon to follow. Roy's last escape was confined to a vague, one-off news story. Now the stakes were higher. Roy had escaped again. He had taunted the authorities in court, and he still managed to get away. The authorities needed to alert the local communities of Oregon and Washington, but at what price? They'd be humiliated.

If Roy could escape from the authorities two times in a year in a near-identical manner, then his news story was about to appear throughout the country's newspapers via the Associated Press. In addition to the Associated Press, major cities had multiple competing daily newspapers, all trying to scoop each other and work their own angles, from the publishers down to the adolescent newsboys, who would scrap and fight with their rivals for the best street corners. San Francisco alone had six separate daily newspapers in the 1920s. Newspapers were the primary source of mass communication in 1921, and Roy Gardner just gave the editors their story of the summer.

If Sheriff Hoggett's gangs were looking for Roy, then Roy was also staring back at them from the front-page, above-the-fold photograph in Tacoma's evening edition of the *News Tribune*. Escaping from his captors one year prior generated a brief, factually to-the-point aside in newspapers, but Roy's encore performance created front-page accolades of "daring" and "sensational" and "spectacular" across the country.

Police officers in Sacramento provided day-after analysis as if they were sports commentators.

"Gardner is a crackerjack of a crook," Sacramento Inspector Sitton opined to a local reporter. "When I spoke to Gardner while he was here, I could tell by the glint in his eye that he had something up his sleeve. He was entirely too optimistic. Never once was he down in the mouth."

Several articles described him as a man of herculean strength who could bend nails with his teeth, a theoretical feat at odds with the adjacent articles advertising Roy's physical characteristics, which included six gold teeth and a front bridge.

Miss Sada Cowan, a screenwriter from Los Angeles, told the Associated Press that in a serendipitous play of events, she happened to be riding the *Shasta Limited* on the night of the escape. According to Cowan, the manacled Roy Gardner took a few moments to slip away from his escorts and he disclosed the full plan of his escape to her. He supposedly explained that she now had an idea for her next thriller, "straight from the main heavy."

Police officers scratched their heads and pointed fingers trying to figure out how Roy managed to smuggle a gun on the *Shasta Limited*. Jail officials in San Francisco repeatedly insisted they frisked Roy while he was in detention waiting for sentencing.

San Francisco Deputy Sheriff John Whalen said that a man had visited Roy and presented him with a clean set of clothes. When Roy changed into the suit, Whalen frisked him and during the process Roy joked, "If this suit could talk it could tell a lot of things, but if it could talk, I would not have brought it here."

Dollie's brother, Robert, also visited Roy while in San Francisco, but officials couldn't identify a solid lead as to the history of the smuggled gun.

Marshal Charles Austin, the man who captured Roy at the Roseville poker game, journeyed northward in an attempt to capture Roy again in his own version of a sequel.

During his previous year on the lam, Roy used boats, motorcycles, trains, and his own feet to shift himself from the forests of Oregon across the Canadian border and eventually to the plains of Iowa. After the most recent *Shasta Limited* escape, the authorities would add something to their own arsenal in their pursuit of Roy: airplanes. Military authorities from Camp Lewis, Washington, notified US Marshal Holohan that airplanes were dispatched over southern Washington in the hunt for Roy. The pilots had orders to drop phosphine gas bombs into the timber surrounding Castle Rock to help flush Roy out.

Sheriff Hoggett announced to the press that he expected a climactic gun battle once they had him cornered. The main flaw with this scenario, however, was that Roy no longer had a gun.

The loss of the gun was one of several problems Roy took stock of when he first limped into Castle Rock in the early morning of his escape. Motivating everything was hunger, a biological version of the Oregon boot that weighed down his thoughts and interrupted his ability to make decisions about any other topic. He found a cafe that opened early, serving morning travelers who very well might have disembarked the same train he fled earlier.

As he approached the cafe, he nodded a hello to a man walking toward him. *Nothing to see here, I'm just a man covered in mud and scratches and I haven't shaved in a while. I can also explain this limp.*

While the full weight of his escape wouldn't be printed and splayed across newspapers for a few more hours, Roy knew his reputation preceded him and he would need to eat quickly. He entered the cafe and pulled out some of Mulhall and Rinckel's stolen bills to advertise to the waitress that even if he looked like a vagrant, he had the means to pay for his breakfast. This was when Roy realized that although he still had the money, he had lost the officer's gun somewhere along the way.

The incessant rain made everything wet and heavy. Roy may have mistaken the weight of his waterlogged clothes as the weight of the pistol in his pocket. The loss of the gun was a setback, but it had already served its main purpose in allowing Roy to bluff his way off the train.

After Roy ordered his milk and mush, he noticed the same man he passed on his way into the cafe loitering outside while staring in through the window. The man's presence jangled Roy's nerves, so he made a quick exit before having a chance to eat. With daylight making its muted arrival through the knot of clouds,

Roy knew he had to get out of town. Church bells rang; Roy couldn't determine if the sound was an alarm or a reminder that it was the Sabbath. He headed toward Castle Rock, the twenty-five-acre geological outcropping and steppingstone to nearby Mount St. Helens that gave the town its name.

Roy wouldn't need to read the evening edition papers to learn that Sheriff Hoggett had five posses searching for him. He saw their feet and ankles marching past while he hid beneath the brush. The close proximity of the search parties at least meant Roy might avoid getting the phosphine gas dumped on him from the air.

The last time Roy felt this hungry was when he was stranded in the Sonoran Desert while escaping from Mexican prison. In that situation there was hunger, heat, and thirst. The Northwest rain forests lived up to their name and served up Roy's hunger with a side of saturation.

The rain only took brief pauses since he leapt off the train. A person would have been hard pressed to believe that the summer solstice was days away in the Northern Hemisphere. The hunger and rain created shaky shivers in Roy, but at least the rain muted the sounds of his movements within the forest. The posse moved forward and chased after the aural kaleidoscope of what sounded like thousands of ball bearings rattling within their skulls. They lurched left, then right, then back.

At this stage of the hunt, it was assumed Pyron was still with him. Sheriff Hoggett promised a shoot-out, and while some of the men of the posses licked their lips at this prospect, others feared they were stepping into an ambush.

Roy tracked the men tracking him, and with the arrival of a new evening's darkness he slipped back closer to town. In one version of the story, he found a barn with a cow that he milked. Getting his first sustenance in days, Roy felt a new sense of motivation and purpose. He had to get out of Castle Rock. Every law agent on the Pacific Coast was swarming in. Under the blanket of midnight, Roy made his way to the train tracks and started walking north. After about two miles, he came to a water tower adjacent to the tracks. He hid in the ditch running parallel to the tracks and waited. After about an hour, a train decelerated to a stop at the tower. The engineer got out to oil the engine, and the train's fireman started the task of taking on water from the tower.

While the men were preoccupied with their duties, Roy crept closer to size up a spot where he could hop aboard and steal a ride. As he approached, two police agents stepped off the train to anticipate this exact move. Roy crab-walked back into the enveloping darkness, but he remained close enough to eavesdrop on the police officers discussing his name and the previous night's escape. The officers walked along the idling train and looked in all the nooks and crannies and metal platforms as if they, too, were hatching their plan to train hop.

As the officers worked down the length of the train, Roy crept up to the front and hid against the train's cowcatcher as if he were a bandit figurehead. When he sensed the officers were sufficiently far enough away, he shimmied up to the horizontal cylinder of the train's boiler, a spot the officers had checked a minute prior. He pulled himself up and hugged the tube.

The officers returned to the front of the train and did a second pass. Roy would be found. He pressed his body into the steel curve of the boiler, and he held his breath. He slid his body as far away from the officers' line of vision as he could without sliding off the boiler. One of the officers stopped and concentrated, trying to decipher the significance of a crunch of rock from beneath the train. Eventually the officer kept walking, past still-hidden Roy.

The train whistle hollered its intention to resume its journey before *chug chugging* into the night and away from Castle Rock. Roy had leapt off one train the night before, and now he hitched a ride on another, hobo-style. Sheriff Hoggett's men returned to their local quarters to sleep and prepare themselves for their renewed manhunt with the arrival of dawn.

CHAPTER TWENTY-ONE

Centralia, Washington

June 13, 1921

The caption for the ad promoting Fatty Arbuckle's latest film, *The Traveling Salesman*, warned, "He missed the train and will be here all week."

Louis Sonney did not want to miss his train. Centralia, Washington, was a long way from Hollywood, but he knew if he took a job in a sawmill or in the coal mines like so many of the other men in his hometown of Bellingham, Washington, he might get stuck and never get out. So Louis Sonney became a police officer, but he dreamed of Hollywood and hitting it big. He did not want to miss his train.

Wherever Sonney landed, however, it seemed there was always coal. Centralia, named for its center location between Portland and Seattle, was a town of only 7,500 people but sixty trains went in and out of its Union Station each day, earning it the nickname Hub City. The trains needed coal to move, and the depths of the Washington mines helped provide the black-and-gray rocks that propelled the locomotives forward.

Sonney settled into police work to avoid working in the actual mines, but he still had to referee the violence between the mine industry's warring factions. The International Workers of the World union, also known as the Wobblies, had an office in Centralia. On the one-year anniversary of the day the guns went silent in World War I, shooting erupted during the town's Armistice Day parade when members of Centralia's US Legion broke off from the parade and confronted men at the local Wobbly headquarters, some of whom were also Great War veterans.

The identity of the initial shooter is lost in the fog of war, but six men would be shot dead in Centralia on November 11, 1919. The mutilated body of Wesley Everest, a union organizer and lumberjack, would be strung up at the Chehalis River Bridge, and left to dangle and decompose for at least a day. His corpse was taken down only to be displayed at the Centralia jail, as a warning to others to not cause trouble.

Sonney had no patience for this bloodshed and was ready to turn in his badge and go to Hollywood. In the promotional picture for *The Traveling Salesman*, Fatty Arbuckle's character chases after the train as it heads off to the horizon.

Louis Sonney was also a large man with a girth to match Arbuckle's, but he was fast, and he had a dream. He would not miss his train.

While daydreaming and walking his beat around Centralia's George Washington Park, Sonney first caught sight of the man whose head was bandaged like a mummy. Even his hands were bandaged, but his fingers manipulated a cigarette with a casual dexterity. The entirety of the man's head and face were bandaged, save for eye and mouth openings, all the better for smoking.

Whatever accident befell this man looked painful, but he nonetheless appeared calm and at peace as he sat on the bench basking beneath the June sunshine, which finally arrived to evacuate the previous week's rain. A nice, new-looking suit served as a contrast to the bandages.

There was nothing illegal about sitting on a bench while reading the newspaper and smoking a cigarette, but Police Officer Louis Sonney was curious and intrigued. As Sonney approached the Mummy Man, they could have started the conversation with the safe topic of the nice weather before moving to the sports page and how the Portland Beavers baseball team were on a losing streak. The Beavers were doing so badly that the man with bandaged hands could have gotten a job as their pitcher.

Inevitably the conversation would drift toward the reason of the man's bandages. The man explained that he was working as a mechanic in a garage in Tacoma when there was a gasoline explosion. The man's determined draw on the cigarette while bandaged from a gasoline explosion was a self-deprecating joke that told itself.

"My name's A. J. Wright," the man said and offered his bandaged hand to shake. Wright had stories about the dangers of working in copper mines in Arizona, an earlier occupation, but he never experienced anything as bad as this recent gasoline explosion.

Sonney reciprocated with his own familiarity with the dangers of mine work.

Wright said he was going to move along out of town after recuperating for a day or two. He looked like a mummy from a Hollywood movie. Sonney was wearing his police uniform, but his mind was on his own Hollywood aspirations.

Eventually the men would wish each other a good day, and Sonney ambled onward, leaving A. J. Wright with his newspaper. The sound of their conversation was replaced by the droning buzz of insects also enjoying the sunshine and the symphony of train whistles at nearby Union Station.

Roy Gardner, a.k.a. A. J. Wright, continued reading about the capture of Norris Pyron in Kelso, a town not far from Castle Rock. A teenaged boy saw a "skulking man" by a veneer factory, and then called in the local posse to assist with the follow up. The posse found Pyron hiding beneath some torn-up grass and when they leveled their rifles at him, he pleaded, "For God's sake don't shoot, I'm not Gardner!"

The article described Pyron as a "tired, old man who was pleased to get out of the hunted class." Roy and Pyron were described as "pals" in the newspaper story, but Pyron also said he feared Roy. According to Pyron, Roy's final words before they parted ways was that he'd "kill me if I didn't resist capture."

The manhunt action was still centered in Castle Rock from what Roy could gather. He was removed from the epicenter, thirty miles away in Centralia. The Southern Pacific put a $5,000 bounty on his head and the posses were searching behind every timber leading up to Mount St. Helens, while Roy sat on a park bench and discussed the pleasant weather with a police officer.

Although Roy managed to escape out of the crucible of Castle Rock, his story was making its way to the perimeter of the continent, restricting his options for living on the lam. A front-page article in Saskatoon, Canada, described Roy as a man who "laughs at locks and law officers."

Roy had a newspaper presence in Brattleboro, Vermont, and Tampa, Florida. On June 13, 1921 alone, Roy appeared in three different Iowa newspapers, the state where he had successfully hid out for several months in the previous year. Other newspapers speculated he was making his way to Mexico.

Emmett Dalton, a former outlaw and bank robber who served fourteen years in prison, wrote a letter addressed to Roy that appeared in many West Coast newspapers:

> Roy Gardner, you're a fool if you don't surrender right now. Now understand, I am writing this only to help you because I know what you're up against better than few men alive today do. You're an outlaw. Every hand is against you. Every door closed to you. The only way you can earn your living is crime. And what's going to happen? In some robbery you'll kill someone. That's murder and it means death for you. Another thing, you have a wife, a good, true wife. Surrender and I'll do my best to help you. Surrender, and you'll never regret it.

* * *

The last time Roy spoke to Dollie was on their fifth wedding anniversary when he was in lockup at San Francisco County Jail. She spoke to him through the newspapers, however.

"He is my husband and I am going to be true to him. I think it would have been better if he had gone to the island and served his time, but he makes the best of it. I wish him luck," Dollie was quoted in an Associated Press article.

"I lived with him for four years and I know him. He was straight and honest for four years. I don't know why he went wrong. I don't have the slightest idea where he is going or what he will do. But I hope to hear from him some day."

CHAPTER TWENTY-TWO

Centralia, Washington

June 15, 1921

A Seattle newspaper promotion announced that seven thousand pounds of free fish were being offered to the needy and deserving. Marian Howell, the proprietress of Centralia's Oxford Hotel, was convinced that one of her guests, the man calling himself A. J. Wright, might have accounted for 190 pounds of this fishiness. Howell first noticed the man bandaged like a mummy when he checked in at the Oxford.

He said he was a Tacoma mechanic and needed to recuperate from a gas explosion in an auto garage. He had a slight limp, but aside from the limp and bandages, Howell thought the man registering as A. J. Wright appeared a bit too robust and vital. His head was fully bandaged, except his mouth and eyes, but his eyes seemed to twinkle. Despite the bandages, she could still see Roy's eyebrows and they didn't look singed.

A. J. Wright went straight to his room and she assumed he slept for a while, but then he left to see the town. This didn't seem like the behavior of a man needing to recuperate per his story. She accompanied the hotel maid to his room. When A. J. Wright registered, he said he had arrived directly from a hospital after being discharged. In his room, they discovered a filthy, muddy suit folded across the chair. Charred working-man's overalls would have made sense, but the muddy suit looked like it belonged to a businessman who took a wrong turn and ended up at the battlefield of Passchendaele.

Howell resumed her post at the front desk and waited. Wright returned with a newspaper under this arm, and he said a jaunty hello. Howell barely mustered a fake smile as Roy/Wright trotted up the staircase to get to his room. She decided to phone the police to have them investigate.

"The restless, searching curiosity of women trapped me," Roy later said.

Officer Sonney arrived at the hotel lobby and Howell told him her suspicions. Officer Sonney explained he was familiar with the man, but he would be happy to go up and talk with him further.

CHAPTER TWENTY-THREE

Centralia, Washington

June 16, 1921

In the arrest photo, Roy Gardner and Officer Louis Sonney look like two actors palling around on a lunch break at Keystone Studios. They could be John Barrymore and W. C. Fields anticipating their first tumbler of gin for the day. Roy is handcuffed, but his mischievous smirk makes it all seem like a joke. His manacled wrists are in front of his body, allowing him to lunge at the neck of a nemesis had he chosen that route. The scene, however, looks loose and affable. It could be two guys playing dress-up for Halloween. With this photo Roy would earn the nickname "the Smiling Bandit," occasionally modified as "the Laughing Bandit."

Sonney beams like a ten-year-old who just won the first-place trophy. While the atmosphere of the photo looks like actors goofing around, the event actually happened: Louis Sonney captured Roy Gardner. The event was real but laced with theatrics. Sonney already had the title of the film in his head: *I Caught Roy Gardner*. Not the most creative title, but succinct.

The dramatic tension and thespian acrobatics started when Roy answered Officer Sonney's knock at the Oxford Hotel. Sonney had already told the story many times to reporters and fellow officers, and maybe he embellished the story with subsequent retellings. Maybe he added the detail of a gun, maybe there was a breeze that made the curtains dance like a premonition, but the basic architecture of the story follows: Officer Sonney arrived at Roy's room per Howell's request and after several knocks, Roy finally answered. His bandages still covered his head, but things were looking a little askew due to the unexpected arrival of a police officer.

Sonney was the good cop and bad cop all rolled into one. He reminded Roy of their earlier introduction at George Washington Park, a friendly meeting, but he added that Roy was now needed down at the police station for a few questions, that's all.

Sonney imagined that if this story were recreated into a movie, the next part would cue the theater organist to lay it on thick on the Wurlitzer. Roy refused Sonney's request. Their friendly rapport disintegrated. Roy insisted he was a sick man whose convalescence would not be disturbed. Just a few questions, that's all,

Sonney reiterated. Roy dug in and threatened legal action against this man of the law. Roy called for a doctor. Sonney grew angry.

Other residents of the hotel poked their heads out their doors to spy on the commotion in the hallway. We can make this easy, or we can make this hard, Sonney offered for the final time. Roy continued to protest. Sonney slapped one handcuff on Roy with its mate already on his own wrist and pulled Roy toward him like they were doing a tango.

"I am a sick man," Roy declared. "Without rhyme or reason, I'm handcuffed and marched as a criminal."

Sonney maintained his resolve, and the men stomped down the stairs and into the hotel lobby. Howell observed it all from her post behind the front desk. Roy continued to shout about the injustice of the situation as Sonney barreled forward like an ox pulling a plow.

Sonney dragged Roy along into the Centralia Police Station, where the bandaged Roy continued to plead his innocence with the repeated incantations that he was a wounded man who needed to rest.

This whole scene was in defiance of his doctor's orders, Roy protested, "I'm going to phone for a lawyer and I'm going to sue you for the amount of your bond. That's ten thousand dollars. What do you think of that?"

Police Chief Hughes assessed the situation. Newspapers chronicling Roy's escapes and his wanted poster decorated the station. Chief of Police Hughes did a quick perusal of Roy's wanted poster and the accompanying text of Roy's physical characteristics. He sized up the prey Sonney just dragged in.

"We don't need to take off the bandages," Chief of Police Hughes said to Roy. "Let's just roll up the right shirt sleeve and have a look at that forearm."

Roy did as instructed, and everyone had a clear look at the stars-and-stripes tattoo he had received at some forgotten port back during his soldier days. Roy never faced repercussions for deserting, but the inked legacy of that time would topple his chances of escaping from a different crime over a decade later.

The game was over. Roy ceased his hollering and eased into a relaxed sense of near triumph after a hard-won fight. The bandages came off and he shook the police officer's hands, a gentleman in defeat. Sonney was a little bit circle shaped, but he was absolutely fair and square in the mind of Roy.

The police officers cheered and slapped each other on the back. They had nabbed the most wanted man on the West Coast. The capture was supposed to require a fatalistic shoot-out, but it ended in a bloodless interrogation of a man dressed up like Lon Chaney.

Most importantly for Louis Sonney, he was in the center of it all. He pulled the levers. He had a starring role. In his mind he could see the credits rolling. He would not miss his train.

* * *

"This is a regular family reunion," the handcuffed Roy said as a who's who of law enforcement agents associated with Roy's past escapades descended upon Centralia.

"Hello, George," Roy said to San Francisco Postal Inspector George Lewis.

"Hello Marshal, it's been a good joke on you," Roy kidded with J. B. Holohan, the man who ordered planes to drop phosphine gas bombs on Roy.

"Why howdy, Coturri," Roy said to the special agent of the Southern Pacific Line. "I was within forty feet of you last Monday near Castle Rock. I looked you over, but you did not see me. I wanted to speak to you but didn't have time."

* * *

The reporters surrounded Roy like he was Babe Ruth breaking the home run record for another consecutive season. Roy's demeanor was described as "cheerful."

"The only thing I regret is that I haven't time to get a shave. I hate to appear at McNeil's Island with a beard," he explained.

"Were you in any of those dozen places where people reported they saw you?" one newspaperman asked.

"Lord no. I was right within a mile of Castle Rock all the time. I didn't even go to that funeral at Silver Lake where that kid said he saw me. I don't like funerals. Be sure and say in the story that all that stuff about me milking cows and stealing chickens is bunk. I never did anything like that. I didn't steal any bacon, either, be sure and say that."

Describing his three days on the lam in Centralia, Roy said, "I tried to bluff it through, but it didn't work. I had a good time and I will say that people who even might have known who I was treated me fairly well."

He added that the night before his capture he attended a home products educational exhibit.

Newspaper articles contained sub-headlines stating, "Bandit Well Liked" and his friendships were engendered, according to one prison official, by Roy's "hail fellow well met manner."

Roy described Marshals Mulhall and Rinckel, his escorts on the *Shasta Limited,* as "the two nerviest men I ever stuck up in my life. If I hadn't worked as fast as I did, I would never have gotten away with it."

When asked why he didn't shoot the marshals when they initially resisted, Roy responded, "I had never killed a man yet and didn't want to."

Law officers and reporters continued to ask how he received the gun that enabled the train escape, and Roy conceded that the prisoners in the San Francisco jail put up $1,000 to have two guns smuggled in, and Roy received one of them. He stressed that Dollie had nothing to do with it.

Dollie also met with reporters but remained in Napa. She painted a picture of the Gardner marriage as a haven of law-abiding domesticity prior to Roy's plot-twisting trip to Tijuana.

"I hope that he lands safely at McNeil's Island, as I intend to go there right away with our baby. And then if he is ever released, I know he will be willing to start life all over again with me for all his devilment has gained him nothing. He has never made a five cent piece out of his crimes except when took the deputies' money, and I intend saving my money until I have enough to pay it back."

When a reporter asked Roy what he planned to do next, Roy responded, "fifty years at McNeil's."

A thousand spectators packed Centralia's train platform to catch a glimpse of Roy with his captors. Roy held up his manacled hands and waved as best he could to the curious crowd. He "maintained his characteristic smile throughout."

CHAPTER TWENTY-FOUR

US Penitentiary, McNeil Island, Washington State

June 18, 1921

When Louis Sonney captured Roy Gardner in Centralia, they were already within sixty miles of McNeil Island Penitentiary. For the authorities' third attempt to deliver Roy to prison there would be no thirteen-hour train journey that would provide Roy with the accomplice of a darkened midnight. On the third train ride to McNeil, a woman approached Roy and offered him a piece of pie. He accepted, and despite his handcuffs he retrieved a chicken wishbone from his pocket and offered this to her as payment. Roy offered another wishbone to his captors.

"Here, Holohan, take one for luck, they hoodooed me." Roy produced four more wishbones from his pocket, remnants of the chickens he insisted he didn't steal.

"I believe in charms," Roy explained as he handed one each to M. L. Sticky, special agent of the Great Northern Railway, and Post Office Inspector George Austin. Roy also made sure the conductor of the train and a reporter each received one of the calcified charms as well, an odd gift when Roy concluded, "I saved these little wishbones, but all they brought me was trouble."

If Alcatraz was nicknamed "The Rock," McNeil would be "The Island." One of many islands filling the Puget Sound like broken pieces of a cookie, McNeil sprawled across six square miles of dairy farms and forests, roughly the same geographic size as San Francisco. The farms would provide much of the food for the convict population. Beyond the penitentiary and farms lay a tangle of ravines, springs, fallen trees, and impenetrable underbrush. Similar to Alcatraz, the fast-moving, icy currents enveloping the island would serve as a natural deterrent and moat to keep convicts in. The first cell house on McNeil was constructed in 1873, fifteen years before Washington became a state. The penitentiary would remain under federal jurisdiction for approximately one hundred years, closing for reasons similar to those that brought on the closure of Alcatraz, namely high costs of operation.

During its tenure, McNeil would imprison the likes of Charles Manson and Robert Stroud, later nicknamed the Birdman of Alcatraz. At the time of Roy's arrival at McNeil Island in 1921, the most recent escape had been sixteen years prior. Albert Bell, a mail thief like Roy, fled from his guard in March of 1905 and took shelter in a prison barn, where he remained undetected for three days, receiving food from an accomplice. Like Roy, Albert Bell also had a loyal wife.

During the transfer from the train to the prison boat, Roy made no attempt to exploit the transition to make a getaway. Roy was often compared to his contemporary Harry Houdini, but Roy didn't jump from the prison barge while handcuffed as Houdini might have.

McNeil prison officers explained to the press that Roy ate "an especially hearty breakfast" for his first meal and "slept well" on the night of his arrival. The prison physician said Roy was "the finest physical specimen he has ever seen."

Roy was registered, put into prison clothes, and entered the routine of the convict. Warden Thomas Maloney would soon be ordering Roy a work assignment. A McNeil inmate explained that when Roy arrived, he was handcuffed to two guards "and there were about eleven huskies following him. Roy walked in laughing. He seemed to think it was funny. Roy was always laughing. He was always raising the devil."

Roy was eventually assigned to an excavation crew that was putting up a new building.

"He's as strong as a bull. I've seen him with one hand lift four men, hanging to a pick handle," explained a fellow convict.

Once processed at McNeil, Roy would be a peer with old associates. Tom Wing, from the first train escape near Portland, was also at McNeil, as was Norris Pyron, the counterfeiter of the second train escape near Castle Rock. Ed Hagen, a Seattle police officer and former boxing opponent of Roy's, was doing time at McNeil Island for bootlegging. It's unclear if Roy ever socialized with these men, however.

Although imprisoned, Roy still had officers on the outside chasing their tails. He told them that fifty dollars of Marshals Rinckel and Mulhall's money was hidden underneath on old gas engine near a sandbar close to Castle Rock. Police officers followed up on this lead but ended up empty handed.

Despite his incarceration, the newspapers and outside world continued to talk about Roy. The Broadway Methodist Church in Chico, California, published their upcoming sermon topic for the following Sunday: "What Should Roy Gardner Do To Become A Christian? What Christian Work Could He Do During His Prison Life?"

A newspaper article of the day described Dollie, who was still in Napa, as a "true blue woman."

The article about Dollie contained a quote from Roy shortly after his capture: "Get word to my wife that I still love her."

"Tell him it's mutual," was Dollie's printed response.

CHAPTER TWENTY-FIVE

The West Coast

Summer 1921

Louis Sonney attempted to claim the $5,000 reward for capturing Roy, but the US Post Office pulled a bait and switch. They clarified that the reward only applied to the original capture of Roy, not the recapture.

They did offer Sonney a fifty-dollar token of appreciation, however. Sonney gave the fifty dollars to Dollie.

"Mrs. Gardner needs the money and I will turn it over to her," he explained to a reporter. Oxford Hotel proprietor Marian Howell was not considered for any reward money, although her suspicion and follow-up with the police set the snare that led to Roy's Centralia arrest.

Four different people squabbled over who was the initial captor of Roy Gardner, and thus the recipient of the $5,000: Barney McShane and Daniel O'Connell of the Southern Pacific, W. H. Locke of the Roseville railroad police, and Mrs. Verdie Pitsos, an employee of the Roseville restaurant Roy often dined at prior to his capture. Pitsos conversed with Roy while he ate at the restaurant. She noticed that the Roy Gardner photo in the newspaper looked like her restaurant regular and she pointed this out to him. He said that there was no way he could be Roy Gardner as Roy Gardner was most likely long gone after the Newcastle train robbery. Pitsos remained suspicious, however, and told the police, which she believed led to his capture at the cigar store poker game.

In another competing theory, San Francisco chief post office inspector Stephen Morse declared that the real hero of the Roy Gardner capture was the printing press. Morse explained that there would never have been a capture had it not been for the 17,000 circulars with Roy's description distributed throughout the West Coast.

Whether man, woman, or machine, the recipient of the $5,000 reward wouldn't be decided and announced until close to Christmas 1921. Uncle Sam would become Santa Claus.

* * *

During his first month at McNeil, Roy ironically received a work position distributing the mail to prisoners. He also sent a series of letters to the editors of *The San Francisco Bulletin* describing his life, with the hope that this would eventually be published as a book and the royalties could assist Dollie and Jean during his incarceration.

Dollie also met with a writer, Alma Reed, for a series of interviews that were published in serial form over the course of ten days in *The Los Angeles Evening Express*. The articles stressed Roy's law-abiding work history and their loving marriage until that fateful day when he went to the racetrack in Tijuana back in 1920.

CHAPTER TWENTY-SIX

McNeil Island Penitentiary

July 1921

"Get off the island!" a disgruntled fan yelled as Roy swung for a strike three.

One month into his confinement, Roy and his fellow convicts were doing their best impersonation of the New York Giants, penitentiary division. The prison baseball field was flanked by the prison's boiler house on one side and the Puget Sound on the other. At McNeil Island, officers played alongside convicts to ensure there were enough men to fill out the teams. The pool of eligible players was whittled down by segregation policies mimicking larger society: Black convicts had to play against other Black convicts, and Native American prisoners had their own separate teams as well.

Roy was a fast third baseman per a visiting reporter from *The Tacoma Daily Ledger*, who also wrote, "Although several of the men have high batting averages, they are said to be experiencing considerable difficulty in obtaining their release."

Despite Roy's occasional strikeout, another convict said that "in the ball games he would prance around and try to steal. The boys were for him, and they would yell and laugh when he got the other players excited with his antics on the bases."

* * *

Mother MacColl, a snowy-haired civilian prison reformer with past experience at New York's Sing Sing Prison, visited McNeil Island and invited the convicts to metaphorically "play ball with me. Let's have no fouls. My great Captain will umpire the game."

MacColl was elected by over 2,000 New York convicts to serve on the Mutual Welfare League, a prisoner rights organization whose membership was typically limited to convicts only. An exception was made for MacColl, who investigated reports of false imprisonment and took her information to courts, at times even pleading her case to then-President Woodrow Wilson. She arrived at McNeil Island to meet with convicts who were veterans of the first World War and those serving life sentences.

"I entered into a partnership with God when I was nine years old," she explained. "When I was a young girl I sang for drunkards and my life has been spent in such work. All my time and my money has been spent salvaging humanity."

Upon her arrival at McNeil she said, "I have never seen a place so calculated to bring men's minds back to God. Its spotlessness, its generous space, which does not confine, but only holds men in detention, its kind-hearted warden and miracle worker doctor, all are wonderful. As for flowers, I never saw them before until I reached the island. The discipline is strict, one hears not a loud word, there is no confusion and no apparent friction."

Roy's fifty-year sentence indirectly put him in the life sentence category, and when MacColl interviewed him, she described him as a "wonderful specimen of manhood." While there was no doubt that the body of Roy Gardner robbed both the mail truck in San Diego and mail train in Roseville, Roy explained to MacColl that his mind was not the pilot of his ship. Roy had first tested this strategy at his initial sentencing in Los Angeles, saying that his head injury from the Bisbee mine cave-in activated his own personal Mr. Hyde.

To Mother MacColl, Roy said, "I want to be operated on and lead the life God intended me to lead."

Two Greek convicts and two Japanese inmates all sentenced on circumstantial evidence became Mother MacColl's priority with the Department of Justice, but her meeting with Roy made the news in early July. MacColl's analysis appeared on the front page of *The Tacoma Daily Ledger*, next to news of the upcoming Jack Dempsey-Georges Carpentier fight.

MacColl summarized her take on Roy: "His tendency to crime is thought to be caused by a deflection of the cranium and it is possible that surgical care will eliminate it. He is to be X-rayed and the physicians at the prison will send to Los Angeles for X-ray plates which are said to show the seat of his trouble."

The now-discredited lobotomy treatment become a prescription for managing schizophrenia and depression in the 1930s, and Roy anticipated this medical development fourteen years ahead of the curve. Newspapers described Roy's proposed treatment as the "surgical cure for rogues," but it is unclear if McNeil Island medical staff entertained Roy's request to have any operation.

After news of Roy's request for a brain operation made the rounds, the editors of *The Stockton Daily Evening Record* asked the question, "Hasn't the world a right to think we are still a little wild and wooly here in the west, parading convicts after they are locked up? With all the romance that has been twined around the doings of Roy Gardner because of his daring, he is nonetheless a plain robber who according to his own story, has less excuse for being dishonest than most criminals. There is no excuse for Roy Gardner's being a bandit except a weak yellow streak and an ingrown ego. Surgeons can do nothing for that."

* * *

Louis Sonney, the officer who arrested Roy in Centralia, also visited Roy at McNeil that summer. After Sonney's visit, Roy mailed a letter to Centralia's chief of police, saying that Sonney should have full credit for his capture.

Although Dollie didn't visit Roy, she maintained her plans to move to Washington with Jean, and the family corresponded throughout the summer. Jean, now almost four years old, practiced her burgeoning writing skills. Dollie wrote two letters per week and Roy wrote "bright, cheerful letters" as often as the prison officials would allow. Roy's letters reiterated his hopes to reunite with Jean and Dollie once his sentence was completed.

In one of his letters, Roy wrote, "no matter where you go, your sweet character and goodness will win you friends."

CHAPTER TWENTY-SEVEN

McNeil Island Penitentiary

Labor Day, 1921

Federal troops arrived in Spruce Fork Ridge near West Virginia's Boone-Logan County Line during Labor Day weekend of 1921, as coal miners fought for the option to unionize. During the First World War, a twenty-four-year-old man had a better chance of reaching his twenty-fifth birthday if he enlisted in the American Expeditionary Forces rather than going to work in a West Virginia coal mine. In the first nine months of 1921, Gatling guns and howitzers were employed as coal miners, company owners, and local sheriffs held their ground in a conflict that rivaled the violence across the Atlantic in Ireland. Photos of the West Virginia conflict looked like a base camp at Antietam, as rifle upon rifle rested against the trees in anticipation for battle. By the time federal troops arrived on Labor Day weekend 1921, upwards of fifty men had been killed in the climactic Battle of Blair Mountain, the bloodiest labor conflict in US history.

In Detroit that same weekend, President Harding's labor secretary, James Davis, announced, "In the past Labor Day has been a holiday in honor of the man who toils. This year it is a day that millions would rather celebrate, not by taking a holiday, but by going back to work on a job."

Davis proposed public works projects to assist the estimated six million Americans looking for employment as the country and world struggled to recalibrate after the cataclysm of the Great War.

In the Pacific Northwest, rain made way for sunshine to enable a Labor Day swimming and diving championship at Tacoma's Garrison Beach. Over thirty medals were distributed, and a carnival ball with dancing followed.

The arrival of sunshine also invigorated the McNeil Island Penitentiary's Labor Day baseball game, as 250 convicts, including Roy, gathered to watch two prison teams compete. By the fifth inning, the score was tied with runners on base. The batter made a Babe Ruth swing for the fences that connected with a *CRACK!* Men on base made their sprint. This would be the RBI to end the stalemate, and the outfielder whipped the ball back toward shortstop, who then pivoted toward home plate. There was a commotion of activity as players ran, and spectators jumped up and down while hollering advice and obscenities. The players coalesced around home plate to either prevent or encourage the go-ahead runner chugging around the bases.

Roy sprinted in the opposite direction as if he were chasing after an invisible, deep fly ball in the farthest corner of left field. There was another *CRACK!* And another *CRACK!* Who was batting? The play wasn't finished yet.

Convict Everett Impyn ran a few yards behind Roy until he collapsed to the ground by the left field line, his cessation of motion a discordant note against the hullabaloo on the diamond. The correctional officer in guard tower 1 reloaded his rifle, aimed, and there was another *CRACK!* A third inmate named Lawardus Bogart toppled in mid-sprint, not far from the prone body of Impyn, whose blood turned the green grass a deathly, black red.

The yelling stopped as the players and spectators shifted their gaze to the events occurring just beyond the perimeter of the baseball field. A few players made tentative moves to assist the dying convicts, but guards shouted and whistled at everyone to step back and get into their prison lines.

Roy continued his sprint away from the baseball game and toward the farms and forests that ringed McNeil Island beyond the prison boundaries. As the convicts cleared the diamond, four more guards joined the shooting from four separate towers to create a crisscross of lead across the field, replacing the day's fastballs and double plays. Two bullets caught Roy in the back of his legs, and he collapsed, the grass of the earth appearing to suck him down as if he were already in his grave.

Like Lazarus, however, Roy pulled himself up and continued to run. He made his way to a group of cows grazing beyond the baseball field, and he pushed and slapped their haunches to create a stampede. The correctional officers in the guard towers lost sight of him.

* * *

The day had been a showcase for McNeil Warden Thomas Maloney. It was a showcase until Bogart, Impyn, and Roy used pliers pilfered from their work detail to cut through the prison fence and make their run for it. Warden Maloney and his guest for the day, Heber Votaw, the superintendent of federal prisons and President Harding's brother-in-law, sat beneath the temperamental Northwest sunshine to watch the cliffhanger baseball game between the convicts. Then everything went off script as they witnessed one convict getting shot to death, another being critically wounded, and Roy Gardner making a jail break.

Warden Maloney had a public relations disaster on his hands in front of the very man he wanted to impress, and he was about to make things worse. Once the shooting stopped, he and other prison staff rushed to the field to tend to the dying

Bogart. Impyn was already dead and beyond the scope of medical attention. With the prison doctor on scene, Maloney charged to the wooded area on the perimeter of the prison to search for Roy. Many witnesses saw Roy get shot, but no one could find a body.

Maloney gave the order: "Smoke him out."

Correctional officers set fire to the brush and forests and Maloney got enough smoke to camouflage a platoon of soldiers. Unless Roy was dead, he could utilize the smokescreen to disappear deeper into the acres of forest covering McNeil Island.

By nightfall Roy was officially unaccounted for.

Bogart remained teetering on the brink of death in the prison infirmary and told staff that Gardner "said the guards would shoot, but that they wouldn't shoot to kill or wound."

Prison doctor Charles Jento reported that Impyn's final words before dying from his bullet wounds on the field were, "Gardner told us those fellows couldn't hit the broad side of a barn."

Speculation grew that Roy deliberately selected Bogart and Impyn as his accomplices and decoys. Bogart and Impyn were processed at McNeil after Roy's arrival, and they had only been at the prison for a little over a month. They were convicted of raping a nurse at Fort Lewis. Due to the nature of their crime, they were unpopular with both the correctional officers and other convicts, one of whom described them as "degenerates." The same convict explained that Roy "picked the only two men in the prison that the guards wouldn't hesitate to kill."

Bogart explained that Roy led the breakout and snipped the wire of the fence as they watched the Labor Day baseball game. During a compelling part of the game with all eyes on the field, Roy climbed through the hole in the fence, started his sprint, and ordered Bogart and Impyn to follow, likely knowing that if he had a lead, their silhouettes would serve as human shields once the guards in the tower started firing.

Warden Maloney had no clue if Roy was still hiding on the island or if he somehow made it to the mainland. Residents of McNeil Island who weren't officially employed by the prison volunteered to assist with the manhunt, but other McNeil residents confided to reporters, "It's no crime to rob a railroad," creating suspicion that Roy would get ongoing civilian assistance in his getaway.

Two women residents reported to prison staff that during the Labor Day baseball game, they saw a motorboat make its way up Puget Sound and approach the bluff of the island. The women said they saw occupants of the boat wave and an inmate spectator, possibly Roy, wave back shortly before the time of the getaway. Warden Maloney wasn't sure if the story was a result of active imaginations or if the women were seduced by Roy's charms and deliberately misleading the manhunt. John Rodell, a McNeil prison guard, corroborated the women's story, however. Waving to civilian boats on Puget Sound was a prohibition of prison rules, but convicts often did it anyway, and Rodell may have initially mistaken the waving during the baseball game as a celebratory gesture rather than a signal to a seafaring accomplice.

But Warden Maloney still couldn't figure out how Roy could have evaded the immediate manhunt to get to the water's edge with two bullets in his legs. No one in the guard towers reported seeing boats making a getaway through the maze of Puget Sound once the escape unfolded.

Adding to the mystery was that no blood was found where Roy was presumed to have been shot, but a prisoner library card was found a mile north of the road marking the penitentiary boundary, in an area off limits to prisoners.

A San Francisco traveling salesman came forward to say he had picked up a hitchhiker in Tacoma that he was now convinced was Roy and dropped him off in Seattle.

"Every prisoner would like to see Roy make a clean getaway. He was the most popular man up here. I guess the public thinks he's a good sport. Well, he's a fine fellow," a McNeil convict said to a reporter.

As the first day after Roy's escape drew to a close, a reporter for *The San Francisco Chronicle* wrote, "Whether he has succeeded in reaching the mainland or whether he is still in hiding on the island is a question which Warden Thomas Maloney, director of the manhunt, frankly admits he is unable to answer."

CHAPTER TWENTY-EIGHT

San Francisco

September 7, 1921

For the third time in thirteen months, reporters confronted Dollie to get her opinion of her husband, who many now described as "the Human Eel" due to his slipperiness. Dollie said that she had received a letter from him the Wednesday before the escape that was "cheerful" and gave no hint of an imminent escape, though he would not have disclosed any of these plans due to prison censors. A teddy bear for Jean's fourth birthday accompanied the letter. Dollie was actively finalizing her plan to move to Washington at the time of Roy's escape. She had taken the ferry from Napa to Vallejo and then to San Francisco as part of her larger journey northward.

Commenting on his escape, Dollie said, "I can't help but say that his action was inconsiderate of me, for all this makes my burden all the more hard to bear." She shifted gears, adding with a smile, "Everyone tells me they hope he gets away. He is a daredevil swimmer. I have seen him swim far out into the sea at the beaches and return in three quarters of an hour not a bit tired and full of pep. I believe he escaped this time just to show the officers he could do it. You can never tell what Roy is going to do next. He may even wait a while and return to the prison and say, *Here I am warden.* But if he gets out of the country, I will certainly be willing to join him."

She added, "I was to leave Sunday for the north to be as close to him as possible. He wrote to me once a day and mailed the letters as often as the rules permitted. Often in his letters he referred to the time when he would finish his long term and when he and our little daughter would be reunited again. I guess he didn't write yesterday morning."

CHAPTER TWENTY-NINE

McNeil Island?

Mid-September 1921

Roy Gardner was everywhere and nowhere.

Posses of armed men, both McNeil Island Penitentiary correctional officers and volunteer residents of the island, trudged through the thick underbrush of the forests bordering the prison in their search for Roy. The hunters waited for Roy to make a mistake. They waited for him to reveal himself. People kept watch on the apple orchards covering the more cultivated parts of the island. If the prison staff could have given a gun and a badge to the dairy cows they would have. Forty-seven people scoured the island for Roy.

One posse heard twigs snapping beyond a fallen log, and the cadence of the ruptured wood suggested a grown man stepping down. They found him! The men leveled their shotguns and fanned out as if they were fingers of a hand preparing to become a closed fist to crush Roy within their grasp. After silently creeping forward they made a climactic lunge forward. The posse became confronted with their mirror image: another posse creeping through the forest, thinking that the first posse was Roy, too.

"All the farmers on the island come out with guns, pitch forks and clubs when the siren blows," a McNeil convict explained. "And the siren sure sets up a yell when a man gets away. All those farmers are out for the $50 reward. Can you figure 'em? They ought to slip a man $50 and tell him to be on his way and good luck. I hope Gardner makes it. He's a good guy."

The armed search parties pumped lead into the wooded void of McNeil Island as the various posses heard phantom noises and saw cryptic figures moving about.

A murder of crows taking to the dawn sky became mixed up with Roy.

A group of men stalking Roy heard gunshots, and they assumed the escaped bandit was taking pot shots at them. They dove for cover, cocked their pistols, and after a few beats they crept forward. The search party leader pushed aside branches and held his breath in anticipation of the climactic showdown. The source of the blast, however, was revealed to be the prison pumping engine backfiring.

This *Los Angeles Daily Times* cartoon appeared on September 8, 1921, shortly after Roy Gardner's prison escape from a McNeil Island Penitentiary baseball game, adjacent to the waters of the Puget Sound. The cartoon also acknowledges the US debt from World War I, which contributed to a recession in the early 1920s.

Women residents of the island reported prowlers in their cottages, and the prowlers could never be found. A teenage resident reported seeing a man clambering through blackberry bushes, only to disappear. A mysterious rowboat was spotted ashore and when officers approached to investigate, the same rowboat vanished. Footprints and bloody strips of clothing were found on Winters Point, a stretch of sand adjacent to Pitt Passage, the narrowest stretch of water separating McNeil Island from the myriad other islands that Roy could have used for hiding places. The area was heavily guarded and isolated by a sharp cliff and timber, but a camouflaging fog had descended upon Puget Sound since Roy's break from the Labor Day baseball game.

Prison boats circled the island and the seaside currents became a never-ending mirage of arms, legs, and tufts of hair poking through the water, but they revealed nothing but more shadow upon closer inspection. The mysterious rowboat was eventually identified as belonging to one of the island ranchers, and the boat was determined to be on its own property anyway.

Prior to his escape, Roy said with increasing frequency that he felt that his head injury from the Arizona mine accident was the source of his bad behaviors. Like a fisherman's tall tale, where the fish gets bigger with each retelling, Roy started to elaborate on his head injury by suggesting his mind was controlled by spirits from beyond. In September 1921, however, Roy was doing the haunting.

As before, both Southern Pacific and Northern Pacific railway officials joined the hunt. Their bruised egos from Roy's previous escapes and robbery motivated their desire for revenge.

P. J. McMurray, a Northern Pacific railway man, declared, "He is right on this island and can not get away. He will kill somebody this time. Gardner has everything to lose this time and he will certainly put up a fight."

Louis Sonney also joined the hunt, serving as the proverbial good cop. Sonney had established a friendship with Roy in the months since the Centralia arrest and was perhaps the only law enforcement official who had the rapport to coax Roy out of hiding with words rather than bullets.

Roy's long-term nemesis, US Marshal James Holohan, arrived from San Francisco and said, "I am of the belief that he is in hiding on the island. At the last election about 75 percent of the farm vote on the island was Socialist. This strengthens my belief that Gardner is being protected by persons living on the island."

Roy was a larger-than-life figure whose notoriety was increasingly based on his absence from prison.

"Gardner isn't a cruel man," a McNeil convict said. "He isn't a murderer in any sense of the word. He has never hurt anybody and he never will. He isn't that kind. He is just a daring man gone wrong."

Clare Davis of *The Stockton Evening Record* provided a dissenting opinion, however, in an editorial.

> I shall have to confess, though, that my admiration for his daring has gone cold. It is a dreadful thing to say, perhaps, but I believe the best thing that could happen to Roy Gardner, to his poor, little pathetic wife and baby and all concerned would be for him to lose his life in this escape. He will always be a criminal and a weakling. He is a weakling. He is not man enough to take his medicine and try to lead a straight life.
>
> Friends, the saddest thing in Roy Gardner's life is that he is running away, not from McNeil prison, but from himself. He is running away, skulking in the bushes, hiding from the man he might have been. That is his tragedy. He has thrown away his birthright for a mess of pottage.

Fatty Arbuckle's bootleg liquor party in San Francisco knocked Roy off the front page. An aspiring actress named Virginia Rappe was found dead in the Fairmount Hotel, the scene of Arbuckle's bacchanalia, and investigators believed she was sexually assaulted prior to her death. After three manslaughter trials, Arbuckle would be acquitted in the court of law, but the public would never forgive him.

CHAPTER THIRTY

McNeil Island

September 20, 1921

Prison doctor Charles Jento stated for the record that it was his belief that Roy was shot twice during the Labor Day baseball game escape, and that he stumbled into the tangle of forest and bled to death from his wounds. This was no longer a manhunt, in his opinion, but a search for a body.

With the arrival of autumn, and no sign of Roy two weeks after the escape, Warden Maloney declared that Roy had either left the island or was dead. Maloney restored all prisoner privileges, and life at the penitentiary resumed its normal routine.

Like a thrice-spurned lover, the authorities of McNeil Island Penitentiary decided that the relationship with Roy Gardner wasn't working out. If he were to be found alive, plans were set in motion to transfer him to Leavenworth Penitentiary in Kansas.

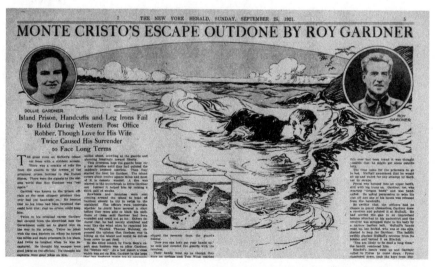

Although Roy Gardner remained unaccounted for after his Labor Day escape from McNeil Island Penitentiary, his story spread to the East Coast, and he gained comparisons to magician and escape artist Harry Houdini. He also picked up a nickname, the Human Eel, due to his slipperiness.

CHAPTER THIRTY-ONE

The West

Autumn 1921

If Roy Gardner was no longer on McNeil Island, he was reportedly seen all along the western states and provinces of North America, appearing and disappearing like the Flying Dutchman, per one newspaper description.

"Has Roy Gardner Turned Attention to Circus Trucks?" a writer for an Olympia, Washington, newspaper asked, after three men robbed $30,000 from a Sells-Floto Circus truck making a stop in Vancouver, Canada. An eyewitness claimed that one of the robbers looked like Roy.

A cook at a Bellingham, Washington, restaurant reported to police that a man resembling Roy Gardner ate dinner at his place the previous evening.

Back in Canada, a Vancouver man was mugged of $80 and the assailant was described as an unkempt man who looked like he had been living in the woods. Perhaps this was Roy Gardner, the mugging victim surmised.

Roy was supposedly seen at a roadhouse in Butte, Montana.

Newlyweds in Nevada en route to their Florida honeymoon claimed that Roy Gardner approached their lunch table and asked for directions to Marysville, California.

In the visitor registration book at the California State Fair's Mendocino County exhibit, a jokester wrote, "Roy Gardner and family, McNeil Island." The Secretary of the Mendocino Chamber of Commerce commented that Roy probably took a liking to the exhibit as it displayed tall trees.

In the coastal lumber town of Raymond, Washington, a group of men in a neighborhood barber shop gossiped about how they, too, had seen what appeared to be Roy Gardner hanging around a nearby pool hall, while others saw him eating at a diner.

"Funny you should mention Roy Gardner," interjected George Wilbur. Wilbur had opened a restaurant in Raymond about a year earlier after his arrival in the town of four thousand, but his ledger books failed to move out of the red, perhaps due to his habit of allowing friends to dine for free.

Wilbur boasted to the men in the barber shop that he used to ride the rails with Roy back in California, and it just so happened that George needed a loan so he could get back to the Golden State to get access to Roy's buried loot, the location of which George had an inside track on.

"Loan me a grubstake," Wilbur said, "and I'll pay you back with huge interest once I get to Roy's hidden cache that not even Uncle Sam could find."

The men in the barber shop either dismissed Wilbur's boast outright, or complained that they, too, had their own financial problems in the country's current predicament of inflation and unemployment. The town of Raymond was in a steady population decline that wouldn't rebound until the next world war. Wilbur left the barber shop and within a day or two he disappeared from Raymond altogether. Wilbur's disappearance coincided with a local citizen, George Peoples, reporting his car stolen to Raymond chief of police William Shumway.

As Roy's escape from McNeil Island inched toward the one-month anniversary mark, *The Los Angeles Evening Express* announced their contest inviting readers to submit their theory on Roy's whereabouts with the winner to receive fifteen dollars. One reader familiar with the Puget Sound suggested that Roy grabbed hold of one of the many logs found in its waters to use as a flotation device. Others thought he was still hiding on the island but would eventually get bored and reveal himself through a spectacular robbery.

CHAPTER THIRTY-TWO

The San Francisco Bulletin

September 26, 1921

The best theory on Roy's whereabouts would come from the man himself. Roy went straight to the top and wrote a letter to President Harding which he mailed to the assistant editor of the *San Francisco Bulletin* with the added request that the editors serve as his power of attorney in his hope that they could grease the wheels and get President Harding's attention. The editors analyzed the handwriting and compared it to previous letters Roy sent the newspaper earlier in the summer. The handwriting matched. The envelope bore no postmark. The September letter read:

Dear Sir—This appeal to you is from a penitent criminal fugitive seeking just one more chance to prove to the world that I can be a man among men. I am now a fugitive convict with two twenty-five-year sentences awaiting me. It is true, Mr. Harding, I have committed a number of crimes for which I am truly sorry.

I have spent many sleepless nights in and out of prison trying to figure a way to atone for and undo the things I have done. I have broken the heart of the dearest little woman that ever lived, my wife, and my little baby, Jean, is growing up with the stigma of her father's shame upon her. Mr. Harding, I am going to ask you to grant me one more chance by suspending the sentences now awaiting me.

I am not asking for, nor am I entitled to a pardon. In fact, I am not entitled to any consideration from you whatever, but I am hoping and praying that you will grant me my one and only chance to prove to the world that a criminal can reform and be an asset to society and a good husband and father.

Mr. Harding, if you will grant my appeal I promise before my God that you will never regret it. Let me be a protege of yours, to point to in years to come as a man to whom you extended a helping hand and pulled from the mire when everything seemed lost.

If necessary I will work my fingers to the very bone to repay those whom I have wronged. The man doesn't live who is more sorry than I am for the crimes he has committed.

As I understand it, the object of sending a man to prison is not to punish him, but to reform him and try to return him to civil life a useful member of society. If you will return me to society and my wife and baby, Mr. Harding, I solemnly promise that I will devote the remainder of my life to honesty and integrity.

By looking up my record you will find that I have committed a number of so called desperate robberies. That is a mistake because I am not a desperate man. I have what the police call a 'clean' record. In my entire criminal career I have never killed or injured any person. Please bear that in mind, Mr. Harding, when you decide this appeal.

I am now confined to my bed suffering from two bullet wounds that I received in my recent escape from the federal prison at McNeil Island. Mr. Harding, if it takes mental and physical suffering to reform a man, then I have been reformed a hundred times over, because I don't believe the man who lives who has suffered both mentally and physically as I have.

In closing, let me ask you to please grant me just one more chance to make good, If I fail in any sense of the word, then I am ready and willing to go back and serve every day of my time.

Yours in all sincerity, (Signed) Roy G. Gardner

* * *

In addition to his appeal to President Harding, Roy provided a detailed description of the escape to the editors of *The San Francisco Bulletin*. He wrote that he was indeed shot twice; the first bullet hit him in the fleshy part of his thigh and caused him to stumble, but he managed to continue moving. At this point, Inmate Bogart passed him, but Bogart only made it about twenty yards further before spinning around after getting struck in the back and collapsing. As Roy passed the prone Bogart, Roy said he felt "awfully lonesome about that time. Seven rifles spitting at me and badly wounded with 75 yards to go."

The second bullet caught Roy in the shin, and he fell but managed to get himself up and climb over a second fence, where he then hid beneath the brush beyond the perimeter.

In Roy's account, Warden Maloney and Dr. Jento moved within ten feet of him and when the order went up to set the brush on fire, Roy "figured that was no place for Dollie Gardner's husband" and he crawled back to the fence. He remained hidden against the fence and around dusk he heard reporters asking Warden Maloney questions, including an inquiry of the name of the guard who fatally shot Impyn. Warden Maloney responded that he didn't know and wouldn't tell him even if he did know.

Roy wrote, "I could tell him who shot me all right."

Roy remained hidden and at midnight, he coughed to create a diversion from the guard patrolling the fields. When the guard approached to investigate, Roy moved in the opposite direction to take shelter in a nearby prison barn, where he was able to get water "that revived me like a good shot of hop." He collapsed in the loft of the barn and passed out for about two hours due to loss of blood. He remained hidden in the barn in the daytime and at night he milked the cows for sustenance: "That milk sure was a life saver."

Roy said that he remained hidden in the barn for two days and two nights, and then made his way to the north part of the island under the cover of fog and darkness. On Saturday and Sunday, he observed the boat traffic and then early Monday morning he made his swim to Fox Island. "If I had not had the tide with me I never would have made it because it was the coldest swim I ever expect to take. It probably felt colder on account of my having lost so much blood, but at that I believe a polar bear would freeze in that water. I thought I was a powerful swimmer, but I don't think so now. That swim sure got my goat."

Once on Fox Island, Roy explained, he lived off the land, eating berries and dairy milk from cows. Roy concluded by saying, "I can't tell you where I went after I left Fox Island because you would have a line on my present whereabouts if I told you that. I can say this much, though: I am with a friend who is a real friend and here I will stay until my leg is entirely healed, if it takes six months. Please tell my little wife not to worry. I am sure everything will be o.k. soon. I wish you would tell the whole world for me that I am through as a criminal."

Roy's final request to the editors of the *San Francisco Bulletin* was that they publish President Harding's response to his appeal.

* * *

"Ridiculous," was Warden Maloney's reaction to Roy's appeal to President Harding and his description of the escape. "It's all a fake; it would be impossible for any man to swim to Fox Island as this letter states. No man of intelligence would attempt it. It's the farthest point of land from McNeil Island, with the exception of only the mainland at Stellacom. It's better than two miles across there and I'll agree with whoever wrote that bunk that a polar bear would freeze to death in the water."

* * *

When the news of Roy's appeal and his accounts of the escape began its eastward migration from San Francisco to the other big city newspapers of the country, Dollie added her own appeal to Roy. With Roy's fate unknown, Dollie canceled her plans to move to Tacoma. She remained in Napa and stressed that she knew nothing of his whereabouts.

Using reporters as her surrogate voice she pleaded to Roy, "In your letter to President Harding you said you had ended your criminal career. To show you really mean this, go back to McNeil Island. You can not be a hunted man and lead an honorable life. Show President Harding and everyone you are the man I have always said you were. Most anyone can be taken back, but it takes a Roy Gardner and a real thoroughbred to go back of his own accord and take his chances with the rest. Roy, do this one thing for my sake and little Jean's."

* * *

It is unclear if President Harding ever considered Roy's appeal, but a wealthy citrus grower in Monrovia, California, named Hal Siemens added his own two cents to the discussion—or in this case, 200,000 cents—when he wired President Harding a proposal where he would employ Roy at two thousand dollars a year and give him a "clean start again" if Roy's appeal were granted. Nothing ever came of this proposal.

CHAPTER THIRTY-THREE

Raymond, Washington

September 30, 1921

About sixty miles off the ragged Pacific coast of Washington lies the town of Chehalis, a convenient pivot point for those looking to make a straight-ahead journey south toward Portland and further still to California. In their own version of the expression, *Why buy the cow if the milk is free?* a motorist stole some gasoline from a Chehalis garage to put into their stolen car. While the thief wasn't caught, witnesses took down the license number of the car as it sped off, and it was determined that the car belonged to George Peoples of Raymond, Washington, who had reported his car stolen to Raymond chief of police Shumway.

Shumway was already following up on a lead from the cook at the restaurant owned by George Wilbur. The cook said he saw a man who looked like Roy Gardner at the restaurant and that Wilbur instructed his staff that this man got to eat for free. Shumway wanted to talk to Wilbur about this, but Wilbur had abruptly left town along with the rest of his immediate family, who left separately a day before he did. He left behind a pile of unpaid bills, and a group of neighborhood men chuckling at his earlier tall tale that he knew the whereabouts of Roy Gardner's California loot.

Chief Shumway also got a tip that a man who looked like Roy Gardner was seen at a rooming house upstairs from a local pool hall. Upon investigation, Shumway learned that one of the rooms had been recently vacated and the previous occupant left behind bandages and other medical supplies. In addition, a writing tablet was found in the room. At first glance the tablet appeared blank, but the indentation of the handwriting from the torn-off pages could be seen. The indentations could be read in places, and the words matched the sentences that appeared in Roy's letters to the editors of *The San Francisco Bulletin*.

It all added up: Roy Gardner had been hiding in Raymond, sheltered by George Wilbur. Shumway made this announcement, and an arrest warrant was put out for Wilbur.

The car belonging to George Peoples was found abandoned at a Vancouver, Washington, auto camp. At the time of its discovery, it was surmised it had been ditched several days prior.

George Wilbur mailed a letter to Shumway from San Francisco, saying he hadn't been aware that there was an arrest warrant for him until he read about it in the newspapers. Wilbur wrote that he would return to Raymond to settle things. San Francisco Marshal James Holohan and a group of his officers surrounded the San Francisco address where Wilbur mailed his letter, but Wilbur never made an appearance. It soon became apparent that Wilbur would do his part to contribute to the population decline of Raymond, Washington, as he never returned there, either.

CHAPTER THIRTY-FOUR

California

October 1921

Nighttime inched toward the domination of each individual day and crisp breezes punctuated the diminishing sunlight as the West Coast settled into autumn. Once authorities pieced together that Roy had stayed in Raymond for approximately four days, they made a credible assumption that he was back in the San Francisco Bay Area. The dragnet was already tight, especially around Dollie in Napa, where the authorities guessed Roy might try to return.

But then a group of teenagers from central California came forward to tell the police that a man calling himself Roy Gardner had taken them on a harrowing hell ride. The escapade started in Bakersfield, where the teenagers accepted a stranger's offer to give them a ride to Los Angeles, a spontaneous idea the teenagers came up with in a fit of juvenile wanderlust. The ride would be an adventure, they thought, and they had an uncle in Los Angeles to give their impulsive plan a semblance of direction.

After the teenagers accepted the ride from the stranger, the driver hit the accelerator, stop signals be damned. The driver recklessly sped through washouts, and he flashed a pearl-handled pistol after declaring he was Roy Gardner. Despite the presence of the pistol, the man gave no indication he intended to shoot anyone. His driving style would be the weapon if they didn't survive the trip.

The man mocked physics while taking curves too fast, and when darkness fell, he often turned off the headlights as other cars approached. The car was stolen, the man said. They stopped at a diner for food, and the teenagers noticed that the man had a pronounced limp, which he said was a result of getting shot in the legs during his McNeil escape.

Once within Los Angeles city limits, the man took a circuitous route, saying he was looking for a new car to steal before making his final sprint to Tijuana. Eventually, he dropped the boys off at Seventh and Spring Streets, in the heart of the business district, at 11:00 p.m.

The teens immediately went to the Los Angeles police and described their tale. The police showed the teenagers photos of Roy Gardner, and the boys said they matched the man who picked them up. The all-points bulletin went out, and authorities scrambled to create roadblocks at the border.

A day later, a man approached the police and confessed that he was the one who picked up the teenagers and claimed to be Roy Gardner as a joke. Despite Prohibition, the whole thing sounded like a bad idea hatched while drunk rather than a sober man's idea of a prank.

Once again, the authorities had no idea where the real Roy Gardner was.

* * *

Mailing a letter wasn't as severe a crime as robbing a mail train, but the act would get a doctor accused of aiding and abetting a fugitive. A doctor in Newport, Washington, a sparsely populated area near the Canadian border, wrote a letter to a colleague in Los Angeles reporting that a wounded and bedraggled Roy Gardner had approached his back door in the middle of the night. The doctor treated Roy's wounds and gave him a sandwich, and Roy disappeared as quickly as he arrived. The recipient of this letter presented it to the authorities. Despite his adherence to the Hippocratic Oath, the doctor who wrote the letter had some explaining to do.

As it turns out, the Roy Gardner in question was a mentally ill local man also named Roy Gardner, who was affiliated with an Iowa insane asylum close to where the doctor lived about a dozen years prior. Although Roy Gardner the bandit spent some time in Iowa and was increasingly leaning on the story that his brain injury had caused his outburst of criminality, the whole thing was a coincidence of names where the timeline didn't match up.

One month after Roy's escape from McNeil, a writer for the *Stockton Daily Evening Record* wrote, "Seeing Roy Gardner is going to be popular from now on. We may as well be prepared to be told that he was seen at four points of the compass many miles apart on the same day."

CHAPTER THIRTY-FIVE

Moose Jaw, Canada

October 1921

By mid-October, Canadian authorities became concerned that Roy Gardner, American train bandit and Harry Houdini doppelganger, had become an expatriate. A lone robber held up a Dominion Express Company train as it rolled through Saskatchewan en route to Moose Jaw and looted the safe. The job had the hallmarks of Roy Gardner: a train was involved, and the bandit worked alone.

Without hard evidence, however, this was speculation. The editors of the *Saskatoon Daily Star* opined, "We doubt that Roy Gardner the Oregon bandit had a hand in the Moose Jaw express robbery. You see, it is customary for Roy to report his activities to a San Francisco newspaper, which as yet has received no communication from him to that effect."

The Moose Jaw robbery went unsolved, and Roy Gardner was yet to be found.

CHAPTER THIRTY-SIX

Islas de Todos Santos, Baja California

October 1921

While one theory had Roy Gardner robbing trains in Canada, others suspected he hijacked a boat and sailed into the waters of Mexico, the United States' neighbor in the opposite direction. A fishing crew on the *Colleen* picked up a stranded boat, *Spindrift*, near Todos Santos in Baja California. Its lone occupant was a shaken Norwegian sailor named Anton Krugh.

The crew of the *Colleen* towed the *Spindrift* back to San Diego. Krugh reported he was hijacked on the Los Angeles docks, where the *Spindrift* maintained its primary port. The armed hijacker ordered Krugh to navigate the vessel to Honolulu. By the time the boat got out into the rough, open sea, it lost its course and an unsecured boom swung and hit the hijacker in the back of the head. He fell into the tumultuous ocean and drowned. Krugh said the man never revealed his name during this ordeal, but Krugh hypothesized that it was Roy Gardner.

Investigators searching for Roy Gardner added Davy Jones's locker to their list of possible locations.

CHAPTER THIRTY-SEVEN

Napa, California

October 1921

For Dollie, there were no more cheerful letters from Roy once he escaped from McNeil Island. Instead she waited for phone calls that also never arrived. She waited for a postcard like the one she received from Vancouver, Canada, the first time Roy made his escape from the authorities. But now there was nothing.

Dollie felt like bait. All she wanted was to see Roy, or at least to know he was safe, but her presence was an enticement to lure her husband into the bear trap of police surrounding her Napa residence. She existed in a murky purgatory where she had a husband but felt like a widow. Jean, now four years old, had so many questions that Dollie could not answer.

More than anything was the all-encompassing hardness of it all. Some friends and family expressed support, but so many people mocked and criticized her for the actions of her husband. Then there were those who denounced Dollie's efforts to portray Roy as a good man despite the off-script bad streak of the past year and a half. In Roy's narrative published in the *San Francisco Bulletin*, Roy said he was staying with a friend. Which friend? Was it the police officer Louis Sonney from Centralia, who took a liking to Roy and mailed her fifty dollars for her own troubles? She didn't know, and she didn't know how to ask without possibly jeopardizing Roy. She looked for a job to have something to disappear into and started working at a department store in San Francisco.

On one of the evenings she was in San Francisco, Roy arrived unannounced at Dollie's sister's house in Napa's Gordon Valley. According to Dollie's sister, Martha, Roy arrived on a stolen motorcycle and stayed for only fifteen minutes. In this brief time period, he hugged Jean and most likely told Jean embellished stories of his life on the road, with certain chapters censored. And then he was gone, a human ghost story. This was to be Dollie's life: her married last name a rumor, her spouse an apparition.

Later in the month, Dollie received a letter from a forty-two-year-old railroad switchman named Percy Leaverton. Leaverton offered to serve Roy's time so that Roy could return home.

"I have never done much in this world, I'd like to do something really big. I know that people will say that I am just a nut, but they criticized Christ when he was on earth," he wrote. Leaverton explained that he had been living by himself since his parents were murdered when he was a teenager. Leaverton said that the Gardners were "three in this world. I am alone. If a pardon could be arranged, I would think that I had accomplished something by taking Roy's place in the penitentiary."

In nearby Oakland, Reverend Goette announced a Roy Gardner-themed topic for his Sunday sermon at the Olivet Congregational Church: "The Price of Life: A Live Dog and A Dead Lion," with a discussion on the question of "Roy Gardner's Repentance, Is It Genuine?"

CHAPTER THIRTY-EIGHT

Phoenix, Arizona

November 16, 1921

The department store Santa Claus broke the news to Dollie that they arrested Roy Gardner while he attempted to rob the Santa Fe *No. 170* train outside Phoenix, Arizona. As Santa scampered among the clerks with extra editions of the San Francisco newspapers under his arm in lieu of a sack of toys, Dollie had been preparing store displays in anticipation of opening. The store Santa wore his costume, and Dollie was most likely wearing her own veil of secrecy, not revealing to her coworkers who her husband was.

As her coworkers guffawed and gossiped about Roy's capture, Dollie made her way outside on unsteady legs to get fresh air. Outside in the commotion of San Francisco's commercial district, not far from where Roy was first arrested back in 1910 after running off with Glindemann's diamonds, Dollie heard the newsboys hollering the news. She broke down crying. The previous night she dreamed that Roy was safe in in Mexico.

The real Roy had been about 180 miles from the Mexican border preparing for his climactic bout of 1921: the former Kid Fitzsimmons, weighing in at 190 pounds, going toe-to-toe with Herman Inderlied, Santa Fe railroad clerk weighing in at 215 with a height of six foot two. It was a heavyweight clash of the titans with Inderlied holding a size advantage, but Roy had the element of surprise, as he had cased the trains near Phoenix for days. Inderlied pulled off the surprise win, however, for he wasn't the usual clerk that was supposed to be there on the Tuesday evening of the Phoenix-Los Angeles mail run. Roy had assumed that a different, smaller man would be working in the mail car, but he forged ahead. Plus, he had a .25 pistol to balance the scales. Roy had no intention of using the pistol, and its chamber was filled with wooden bullets, which could cause a commotion, but they wouldn't kill a man. Per Roy's style, the gun was just a prop to enable him to complete the robbery.

The first round went in Roy's favor. He successfully hid himself in the train's mail car before Inderlied's arrival. Inderlied entered and locked the door to keep trouble out. He was busy with the evening's work when the masked Roy surprised him, pointed the gun at Inderlied's stomach, and ordered his hands up. Inderlied refused, so Roy pushed him back, prodding the gun closer to his stomach, and he backpedaled until he was against the wall. Roy ordered Inderlied to get to the floor and started to tie his hands, but then the clerk turned the tables. Inderlied was quiet and unassuming by nature despite his large size, but he had no patience for Roy on this particular evening, so he grappled the bandit down to the floor and wrested the pistol out of Roy's hand. Then Inderlied sat on Roy. The knockout blow could be described no more gracefully.

With Roy pinned to the ground, Inderlied shouted for help and two marine guards on an adjacent car came to assist. With the arrest made, Roy identified himself as "R. P. Nelson," using Dollie's maiden name as an alias. The attempt at deception was futile, however, as Roy's now-infamous forearm tattoo tipped off the officers. As before, his tattoo souvenir of his Army days created more legal problems in Roy's later life than the initial act of desertion. Roy admitted to his captors that they had their man.

If Reverend Gouette in Oakland was still pondering the question, "Is Roy Gardner's repentance genuine?" Roy provided the answer. No.

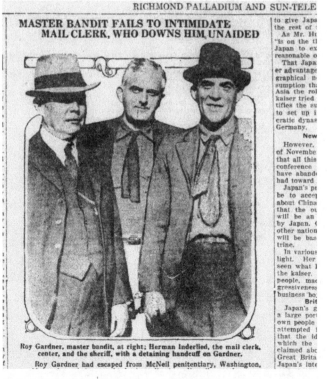

Mail clerk Herman Inderlied, center, thwarted Roy Gardner's robbery attempt on the Santa Fe *No. 170* train outside Phoenix, Arizona, in November 1921.

* * *

Once in custody, Roy filled in the gaps of his life since his getaway from McNeil Island. After swimming to Fox Island, he stole a rowboat, which he took to the mainland, and caught a train back to Centralia, as if he were playing the movie of his life in reverse. Despite his recent notoriety, Roy managed to get some new clothes and from there walked a few miles to the next town, Chehalis. He helped a man whose car was stuck in the mud, and after completing the good deed, the man offered to buy Roy a meal in town. While eating at the Gem Restaurant, the proprietor held court and talked excitedly about the McNeil Island escape and how he was convinced that he had seen Roy a few months prior when Roy was on the lam the last time in Centralia. The owner didn't seem to recognize that the real Roy Gardner was dining in his own restaurant at that very moment.

Recounting the episode, Roy said, "He told me a lot of things about Roy Gardner that Roy Gardner didn't know, but I felt it a wise move for me to disappear from there, which I did as soon as the meal was over."

After his close call in Chehalis, Roy made his way to Raymond, Washington, where he stayed for a few days, with the assistance of George Wilbur, to allow his gunshot wounds to further heal. Roy stole a car, or in his words "took a possession of a Columbia Six automobile," and made his way to Vancouver, Washington, where he abandoned it before crossing the Willamette Bridge on foot into Portland. Roy jumped a train to Oregon City, and then stole a Harley Davidson, which he took to Medford. He stayed near Medford for a few days and found work picking apples on a ranch outside the city. His female coworkers often spoke of the notorious Roy Gardner of the newspapers, and one even claimed she went to high school with him, insinuating that they dated. Roy chuckled at her boasting, for he had never seen the woman before, but the incident motivated him to move along.

He rode the Harley Davidson down California's spine: Red Bluff, Redding, Marysville, Sacramento, and then back to the Bay Area, where he stopped in Napa to visit Jean. Roy made a point during this recap with the reporters to thank his sister-in-law, Martha Silda, for her steady nerves and composure. He stopped briefly in San Francisco before continuing south on the motorcycle, making it all the way to San Juan Capistrano before the hard-driven motorcycle broke down.

From here he rode the rails hobo style down to San Diego and looked up a woman who sent him a letter while he was in McNeil, one of hundreds of "mash" notes Roy said he received from all over the US during his ten-week incarceration. He called the woman on the phone and said he was a friend of Roy Gardner's, and that Roy wanted him to let her know that Roy was safe in Mexico.

Then Roy did disappear south of the border into Mexicali but struggled to get work and returned to the US. He roamed through the lunar landscape of the

American Southwest with its Joshua trees and foreboding rock formations until he reached Arizona. He traveled eastward from Yuma, Arizona, until he dropped anchor in Phoenix, where he stayed for about three weeks prior to the attempted train robbery. Roy was sunburned from his days of travel, and his hair was dyed an unnatural hue, an attempt to disguise himself while on the lam.

For his arraignment at the federal courthouse in Phoenix, Roy was handcuffed and escorted by Marshal J. P. Dillon and a phalanx of guards, through a court-house bursting at maximum capacity with oglers and newspaper photographers. Roy stopped to chat with spectators and reporters, often smiling and laughing.

Upon re-meeting his adversary, Herman Inderlied, Roy shook the clerk's hand and said, "Well, you've earned your $5,000. No hard feelings for what I did, old man?" Inderlied still appeared shell shocked by the whole spectacle, and he was frequently asked why he resisted when a pistol was thrust in his belly during the robbery attempt. Roy answered on Inderlied's behalf.

"The next time somebody tells you to stick 'em up, you stick 'em up. You'll never come through again like you did this time. The next time won't be Roy Gardner," a reference to Roy's habit of not actually shooting his pistol during his robberies.

The taciturn Inderlied provided more thoughts in written format, which appeared in newspapers.

"I'm not a hero. I just shot off the hip, as it were," he wrote. "I see now that if Gardner hadn't been the man he is I would have been under the daisies at this moment. My wife is certainly grateful to Gardner. We're going to call on Gardner at the jail. I want him as a friend. I feel proud to have a man like that as a friend. Don't worry. I'm not going to buy any high-power limousines if I am given the reward for Gardner's capture. I have a boy to educate and he's going to get the best there is."

United States Commissioner J. B. Henke announced that Roy's bail had been set at $100,000.

"I think I can make it," Roy said, which aroused chuckles from the courtroom spectators.

Once back in his cell, Roy was allowed to converse with reporters, and he greeted them as if he were the father of the bride in a wedding receiving line. One reporter described him as a "cheerful creature," with laugh wrinkles around his eyes.

"Sorry to have you meet me in such attire," Roy said with a laugh as one reporter started their interview.

Someone asked if he ever drank alcohol to steady his nerves before a robbery, and Roy responded in the negative, adding that it "requires a clear head to be a robber." The reporter replied that Roy's thwarted robbery attempt of the Santa Fe didn't demonstrate much clearheadedness as he ended up in handcuffs after being sat on by Inderlied.

"Yet it might be that if I hadn't been clearheaded I'd be occupying a slab in the morgue right now instead of this nice, comfortable cell," Roy said.

A reporter pressed Roy on his written claim to President Harding that he was vowing to abandon the bandit's life.

"Did I promise that? Oh, I must have put that in the postscript!" Roy answered. When questioned further, Roy added with more earnestness that he meant to keep that promise when he wrote the letter, but that "there are always circumstances." Roy reopened the topic of his brain injury but took the story further, saying his mind was controlled by spirits from beyond.

As the interviews concluded, Roy reached through the bars to shake everyone's hand. After the round of handshakes, the reporters may have confirmed that everyone still had the rings on their fingers.

* * *

With Roy now a fixed target in the county jail after the Santa Fe *No. 170* train robbery attempt, a pawn shop owner came forward to say that a man he believed to be Roy had earlier attempted to pawn a woman's wristwatch connected with an unsolved robbery of a separate mail truck in Maricopa, thirty miles south of Phoenix. During the Maricopa robbery in early November 1921, a bandit broke into a locked mail train and grabbed a hodgepodge of envelopes and parcels, most of which had no monetary value, except for a registered mail item containing a wristwatch.

In addition, a Phoenix teenager named Maria Munoz lodged an accusation against Roy. On October 21, 1921, Munoz was walking home from school when a man approached her saying he was a police officer and that she was under arrest but didn't specify why. The man escorted Munoz away from her route to a nearby cemetery and sexually assaulted her. A teenage boy walking in the vicinity intervened to stop the aggressor, and a passing car also pulled over to intercede on Maria Munoz's behalf. The attacker ran off, and Maria went to the police station to meet with actual police officers to report the incident. At the time of the report, the attacker was identified as a generic "John Doe."

There were no other developments in identifying the assailant until Maria saw Roy's photo in the paper after the Santa Fe *No. 170* train robbery attempt. When she revealed her belief that Roy was the assailant, authorities brought her to the county jail where he was being held to do a face-to-face identification.

When Roy first heard the new accusation of sexual assault, he initially answered, "Fair enough," an odd answer for such a serious allegation. But he then clarified with more emphatic and consistent denials. Maria Munoz's accusation made the news for about two days, then became overshadowed by stories of Herman Inderlied's heroics during the train robbery.

The authorities perhaps had a chauvinistic belief that if Roy was bound for Leavenworth anyway, why bother with getting a formal conviction on the sexual assault charge. The absence of any extensive follow-up to Maria Munoz's accusation may have been a cold by-product of legal bureaucracy. Roy was already embroiled in the federal crimes of robbing the US mails and escaping from a federal penitentiary. The federal business would need to get wrapped up before the assault accusation, a state charge, could be pursued.

Maria Munoz's accusation, however, was still listed as "pending" in a Phoenix newspaper profile of Roy in 1923, over a year and a half after the sexual assault. That profile was an exception, as almost all newspaper stories on Roy from 1922 onward made no reference to the sexual assault accusation.

An editorial in *The Pasadena Post* advocated the reinstatement of a previous law that sanctioned capital punishment for train robbers. The writers acknowledged that this likely wouldn't happen, so the next best thing, per the editorial's conclusion, was that the "stretch of years ahead must present such an aspect of dreariness, that he (Roy Gardner) ought to be grateful to be hanged." This editorial never once mentioned Maria Munoz's accusation of sexual assault, which went public a few days prior to the editorial's publication.

The underwhelming follow-up to Mexico-born Maria Munoz's accusation may also have been a reflection of law enforcement's prejudice. Munoz's assault came five months after the attack on the Black community of Greenwood in Tulsa, Oklahoma, in what some historians later described as America's Kristallnacht. Entire blocks were wantonly burned, and an unknown number of residents, possibly as many as 300, were shot dead or immolated in the inferno. In the immediate aftermath of the Tulsa tragedy, visiting journalists described the human misery as comparable to the genocide in Armenia or Germany's invasion of Belgium during the First World War.

The Tulsa Massacre generated attention and outcry for a few days but was then largely swept under the carpet and relegated to whispers and rumors until the tragedy was reexamined decades years later by investigative journalists, historians, and forensic scientists. The lack of sustained follow-up to Maria Munoz's sexual assault allegation may have been a product of a similar willful societal blindness.

At the time of Maria Munoz's accusation, students at an Oakland high school presented their superintendent with a petition asking that their valedictorian, Yuki Furuta, be stripped of the honor as she was of Japanese ancestry. Local rabbi Rudolph Coffee provided a counter argument that the twenty-eight students who signed the petition flunked their lesson in character building, and it was mainly through his efforts that the petition had its legs kicked out. But the petition, signed by almost half of the graduating class, nonetheless provided a barometer of the atmosphere non-white teenage girls existed under in the 1920s.

Roy Gardner was neither cleared nor convicted of the allegation of sexual assault. Roy would go to prison one way or another, but Maria Munoz would not get closure or justice. If Roy Gardner was innocent, then a guilty man went on with his life without any repercussions for his actions.

Upon hearing of these new accusations, a tearful Dollie said, "I don't know what to think. I can't believe this hideous thing. And I won't believe it until Roy tells me it's true. I can't work. I can't do anything. I am going to Arizona tonight. I must see Roy. I do not say that Roy is above falling victim to the blandishments of a woman, but I can not believe that he would attack a girl. Not Roy. He is not that sort."

CHAPTER THIRTY-NINE

Phoenix, Arizona

November 20, 1921

Dollie arrived in Phoenix to visit Roy the week of Thanksgiving. The last time she saw him in person was on their June wedding anniversary in the San Francisco County jail.

After Dollie's arrival, a reporter wrote, "Marshal Dillon admitted afterward that when she stood before his desk and told him she was Mrs. Roy Gardner and that she desired a pass to enter the county jail to see her husband, he had to think twice before he had erased from his mind his preconceived idea of what Gardner's wife should look like." The same reporter described Dollie as "unusually attractive."

Dollie's first impression of Roy was that he looked "haggard" and she made a nervous joke about his dyed hair.

"Peroxide seems to become me, doesn't it, dear?" he replied.

Dollie made another comment about Roy using her maiden name for his alias upon his arrest.

"Well, I had a right to it. You took my name, didn't you?" Roy said.

After the ice breakers, Dollie cut to the chase. *Did you sexually assault the teenager?*

"Nothing to it all," Roy said. "No more than that stone wall there. You know I wouldn't do anything like that."

"Why didn't you go into Old Mexico and stay there? Why didn't you be good?"

"I didn't have a chance."

"You did have a chance, said Dollie. "In your letter to President Harding you promised to be good. I'm going to talk plainly to you. I don't approve of this, not at all."

They continued to talk about Jean and Dollie's job at the department store. Roy inquired about Dollie's biscuits. After departing, Dollie consulted with Roy's lawyer, and then went to a cafe where she fielded questions from more reporters, with whom she engaged in an open and polite manner.

She explained, "I have done everything in my power to influence him for the good, but the excitement of his criminal life breaks down every resolution he makes. He has always done everything he could for me and Jean, and I will always be loyal to him. He has never stolen for the money alone, for he has never made a cent from all his operations, but he has done it, as far as I can figure out, because he is just a little over balanced mentally."

A reporter described Dollie as "slim, delicate woman, whose childish face is still strangely free from all lines of suffering."

Dollie went on:

> Many people have asked me why I don't divorce Roy, and start life over again, and I can't say that I haven't given it some thought. You see, I'm only twenty-four. But how could I leave him? What would he do if he didn't have me? Why, I've just got to stand by him no matter what happens. Roy has made me unhappy, yes, but never enough so to make me forget how happy we were together. And when I saw him standing there behind the bars today I cannot tell you the feeling that came over me. All the resentment I had faded. He looked so helpless; just like a big overgrown boy, who knew he had done wrong and begged forgiveness. He didn't look much like the Roy I knew. I must get him some clean clothes and see about a haircut for him, tomorrow. No, I simply couldn't forget Roy. You see, I've got a picture in my own mind of Roy coming free from prison, and what our life together would mean when he could go straight. So no matter what he has done or may do, I cannot get his picture out of my mind. I think it is what I live for because whenever I think of never having Roy with me again . . .

Dollie paused, then concluded, "He is just my Roy."

CHAPTER FORTY

Phoenix, Arizona

Thanksgiving 1921

Roy was now looking at seventy-five years in prison: twenty-five for the mail truck robbery in San Diego, another twenty-five for the Roseville train robbery, and an extra twenty-five for the attempted Phoenix train robbery. The powers that be were determined to pin the Maricopa robbery on him as well.

His three escapes wouldn't win him any favors with prison officials, either. The prison cooks at Leavenworth were keeping a plate warm for him, but before being shipped off to Leavenworth he would remain in Phoenix county jail awaiting his trial and formal sentencing to conclude the spectacular Roy Gardner year of 1921.

With the trial pending, law officers restricted Roy's visitors to Dollie, who remained in Phoenix for the trial, and his lawyer, Carl Davis. There would be no more direct interviews with reporters, and no more curious onlookers.

One guard reported that "several women have appeared and stated they were anxious to see him. They were referred to the marshal's office but never returned."

Despite Roy's grim future, the jailer described Roy as the "most jovial prisoner in jail" who was on friendly terms with the other prisoners. He accepted any prisoner's offer to sit in on a card game, and a fellow inmate told a reporter that Roy excelled at the game penny ante. In the absence of reporters Roy would hold court with fellow prisoners and guards alike.

Despite Roy's pleasant and gregarious nature with the guards, everyone knew his escape history and it was reported that "the sheriff's office will breathe easier when Gardner is taken from their custody by federal officers."

Roy's lawyer, Carl Davis, disclosed his trial strategy: that Roy was insane as a result of his head injury from the Bisbee mining accident in 1908. Davis ordered X-rays to be taken of Roy's skull in anticipation of the trial. Taking it one step further, Roy doubled down by insinuating that the silver plate in his head was a beacon for ghosts and spirits. Roy was often compared to Harry Houdini, but the two diverged on this topic; Houdini despised ghost-inciting spiritualists as charlatans.

If not the head injury or ghosts, Davis could have blamed Roy's behavior on jazz, a phenomenon which Herbert Booth Smith, a Los Angeles pastor of the time, described as "musical bolshevism, having the same disorganizing effects on the nervous system as moonshine liquor."

Both Roy and Dollie explained to reporters that insanity was a characteristic in Roy's family, and Roy said that his mother was a spirit medium who taught Roy about seances. Roy also claimed his mother died in an insane asylum.

Reporters tracked down Roy's father, who was still in Oklahoma City. Roy's father said their family had denounced Roy years ago and had been out of contact. In response to Roy's description of his mother as a spirit medium, Roy's father said the extent of their family's spirituality, mother included, was limited to infrequent visits to a Methodist church. Roy's father clarified that Roy's mother died of natural causes and was never in an insane asylum.

A Prohibition-era writer for California's *Hanford Sentinel* said, "Roy Gardner says that 'Spirits made me a bandit.' The kind of spirits that people absorb these days are enough to make anybody a bandit."

CHAPTER FORTY-ONE

Phoenix, Arizona

December 5, 1921

Judge William Sawtelle presided over Roy's sentencing in Phoenix to determine his Leavenworth Prison sentence. For the first round of attack, the prosecutor, US Attorney Thomas Flynn, focused on the Maricopa train robbery from a month prior. A locksmith took the stand to say that a man, whom he now knew to be Roy due to the media fireworks, approached him in late October about making a key that would fit into a Southern Pacific lock. At the time of the request the locksmith didn't connect the dots as to Roy's real identity, and the locksmith obliged to make the key. This same key was later found in one of the rooms where Roy was boarding in Phoenix.

A postal worker took the stand to confirm that a woman's wristwatch was sent by registered mail from Salt Lake City, but the watch never made it to its intended recipient, a relative of the sender. The watch did, however, make an appearance at Kelly's Waffle Kitchen in Phoenix, where Roy presented the watch as collateral for a few meals and a down payment on a room at the nearby Bachelor Inn, both businesses being owned by the same proprietor. With that, the state rested its case against the "bandit of bandits," as a Santa Ana newspaper described Roy.

For the defense, Roy's lawyer brought forward a string of witnesses, including Dollie; Louis Sonney, the arresting officer from Centralia; and Roy's brother-in-law, Robert Nelson. The witnesses testified that they thought Roy was insane and was prone to laughing "hysterically without cause."

Dollie, too, emphasized the story she'd told over the past year of Roy being a solid and honest provider prior to the 1920 San Diego robbery, and that he'd increasingly become prone to debilitating headaches.

An expert "alienist" took the stand to say that Roy "sincerely desired the funds to pursue the process of spiritual development that would fit him better for the hereafter. His crimes were beginning to oppress him."

Another witness who served time with Roy at San Quentin said that Roy would sometimes fall down, froth at the mouth, and need to be carried away on a stretcher. This description, however, would be more appropriate for an epilepsy diagnosis than the insanity being argued.

The prosecution countered with Dr. L. L. Stanley, resident physician at San Quentin. Dr. Stanley said Roy never received any medical treatment matching what the San Quentin inmate witness described.

Roy's lawyer countered with Dr. Ray Ferguson, superintendent of the Arizona Insane Asylum, by asking him questions pertaining to the Maricopa robbery: "Are you able to form an opinion that the act of November 3 was committed under an insane delusion?"

Dr. Ferguson responded, "I am." The doctor said that in his opinion, Roy should be committed to an insane asylum rather than Leavenworth.

Dr. Mary Neff, an expert in mental and nervous diseases, also corroborated that many patients admitted to asylums had a preexisting condition of a traumatic brain injury similar to the one Roy experienced in the Bisbee mine cave-in. The defense presented records from the Copper Queen Mining Company confirming that Roy fractured his skull in late March of 1908.

* * *

The final witness for the defense was Roy Gardner himself.

"In a low, controlled voice, he told the story of his life from early infancy," an article reported. "His testimony was counted upon his counsel to add materially to the insanity theory upon which his fight to escape the penitentiary is being waged."

Any lingering doubts around who committed the Maricopa robbery evaporated when Roy himself took the stand and admitted that he did it. He said he was under the control of two spirits, one named "Warecka" and the other named "White Feather," and that he only obeyed the laws of the spirit world and the laws of earth were irrelevant to him. He explained that the crime of murder was the only felony shared in common with his spirit guides and *terra firma*.

Prosecutor Flynn questioned Roy during cross-examination.

> Prosecutor: "Were the affairs at San Diego, Roseville, and Phoenix carried out by you after consulting with spirits?"
> Roy: "Whatever I've done has been done by my physical body."
> Prosecutor: "Have you a mind?'
> Roy: "Certainly."
> Prosecutor: "What spirit control did you consult?"
> Roy: "Warecka always advised against it."
> Prosecutor: "Did you consult with your controls at McNeil Island?"

Roy: "White Feather."

Prosecutor: "Is White Feather a good control?"

Roy: "Good and bad He said that I would not be injured nor would I pass on. Either he was under another control or he gave me a bum steer, for I was wounded."

During his December 1921 trial, Roy Gardner presented the theory that two warring spirits from beyond were locked in battle for control of his mind. His wife, Dollie, testified on his behalf to vouch for the side effects of his head injury from a mining accident. The headline mistakenly identifies Roy as a college graduate.

After Roy completed his testimony, Judge Sawtelle ordered Roy to explain where the missing packages from the Maricopa robbery were stashed. Roy refused to divulge this information, saying he made a "deal" with one of the deputy marshals presently serving as sentry in this very courtroom. Judge Sawtelle threatened to hold Roy in contempt of court but admitted that this wouldn't make a difference with Roy facing seventy-five years. At the end of the day's court proceedings, Roy apologized to the judge like a contrite schoolboy.

George North, assistant editor of the *San Francisco Bulletin*, took the stand for the prosecution to say that when he interviewed Roy during the incarceration at McNeil Island, Roy made no mention of any beliefs of spirit controls. Furthermore, North said that shortly after the Phoenix arrest, Roy telegrammed him to say that upon learning that Postmaster General William Hays declared that there would be no compromise with mail bandits, Roy came to terms with the futility of his written appeal to President Harding.

North implied that Roy felt he had nothing left to lose at that point and made the conscientious and willing decision to return to the bandit's life.

* * *

Despite Roy's admission of guilt for the Maricopa robbery, the jury remained deadlocked on how to proceed given the brain injury defense. The charge was dismissed.

Roy then withdrew his "not guilty by reason of insanity plea" for the robbery attempt in Phoenix and pleaded guilty.

The guilty plea, without any qualifications, ensured that Herman Inderlied received the full government reward of $5,000. Roy may have admitted guilt to be a gentleman in defeat, but he may also have wanted to get out of the state of Arizona as soon as possible to avoid more questions around Maria Munoz's accusations and the hangman's noose.

Roy was sentenced to seventy-five years for robbing or attempting to rob the US mails three times: the San Diego mail truck robbery, the Roseville train robbery, and the Phoenix train robbery attempt. Preparations were made to ship him off to Leavenworth Penitentiary in Kansas. The Phoenix robbery attempt, one reporter opined, would be Roy's Waterloo.

CHAPTER FORTY-TWO

USP Leavenworth, Kansas

Christmas 1921

The Rock Island *Train No. 4* took the cigar-smoking, newspaper-reading Roy Gardner from the Southwest deserts toward the flank of the Missouri River in the lingering days of 1921. A Kansas snowstorm operated with a brutal efficiency to prevent Roy from leaping off the train again. Even if he did manage to make a run for it, he was equidistant from both the Atlantic and Pacific Oceans, and the Mexican and Canadian borders offered no horizon for escape. The Midwest plains surrounded Leavenworth with a land moat to keep Roy in.

A man finding work in the town of Leavenworth would either be a prison guard, a convict laborer in the prison industries, or a soldier. The penitentiary housed three thousand inmates, a city within a city, and adjacent to the penitentiary was an army base, where prisoners stayed through the 1890s and ultimately worked to build the new penitentiary. The walls for the new prison were sunk forty feet into the earth. It was a prison built by prisoners, some of whom completed their labors with a ball and chain ironed to their ankle.

By the 1920s, Leavenworth was a drain that caught the entirety of the criminal population: murderers, dope peddlers, horse thieves, and rapists all thrown into one incarcerated society. Sprinkled within these ranks were about forty political agitators and pacifists who ran afoul of then-President Wilson's Sedition Act, and their status remained in limbo three years after Armistice Day. The train taking Roy to USP Leavenworth would travel past the prison cemetery and the bones of men who never made it out.

Roy and his cordon of guards made their way beneath the machine gun tower and arrived at Leavenworth's "Big Dome" administration building under a black, Kansas winter sky with icy flurries cutting across their cheeks. Certain lights from within the prison were never turned off, and from the outside these brightened windows gave the otherwise dark building an appearance of a solemn jack-o'-lantern. Towers with armed guards marked the distance of the prison boundaries at regular intervals.

The spotlit clock tower of the military base could be seen from the prison. The clock served as a constant reminder to the men in prison that the contours of their own humanity were now broken down into units of time. In more pleasant seasons, manicured lawns softened the approach to the main prison entrance, but barbed wire dominated the landscape. To gain a better understanding of the United States Penitentiary at Leavenworth, one just needed to know its nickname: The Big L.

Warden William Biddle would control Roy's fate. The warden was an autocratic king and mercurial god ruling over his domain of three thousand incarcerated men. While Warden Biddle was relatively new to Leavenworth Penitentiary at the time of Roy's arrival, most of his adult life centered around employment at the adjacent military base. The warden was a proud American who threw his full support behind the doughboys crawling through the Argonne Forest of France during the Great War.

Roy crammed as much information from his newspaper as he could before his arrival. This would possibly be his last chance to get uncensored news for a while. The year 1921 achieved grim milestones including the bloodshed, looting, and burning of Tulsa, Oklahoma's Black Wall Street and the labor battles of West Virginia. In both conflicts, airplanes became weapons in the arsenal against civilians, a trend that anticipated the misery airplanes would wreak in the next World War.

The end of 1921 saw the third year of civil war in Russia, which left millions starving and a decimated transportation network with winter's arrival. With so much internal destruction and chaos, the Soviet Union's primary export became the paranoia that the red menace hatched in Moscow would bleed into all corners of the planet.

Germany struggled to pay its reparation obligations from the First World War, and throughout the year the United States and Japan engaged in tense diplomatic standoffs over size limits on their respective navies.

"The Japanese military party is hostile to the United States," one writer concluded almost twenty years to the day in advance of the attack on Pearl Harbor. The pieces were being set for the babies born in 1921 to be the soldiers of the next World War.

During one performance at Sacramento's Orpheum Theater, vaudeville performer Bob Hall, who was known for cobbling together song lyrics using audience members' spontaneous topic suggestions, stitched together a tune using the suggestions of "Prohibition, the Ku Klux Klan, disarmament, and Roy Gardner." These were the topics on the collective mind at the end of 1921.

As Roy read the newspaper on the Rock Island *No. 4*, a person on the platform might have mistaken him for a normal passenger, aside from the heavy presence of guards in the observation car. He arrived at Leavenworth at 9:40 p.m., with the winter darkness already well established. Despite the bleakness of his surroundings, he joked with the guards and explained that his small bundle containing his belongings would be sufficient for his "temporary stay." Upon receiving his week's ration of tobacco, the chain-smoking Roy said that the amount should be enough to cover his time at Leavenworth.

Warden Biddle presented Roy with six letters he had already received from "sentimental women," and instructions to report to the prison tailor shop for his initial work assignment.

Roy could joke that he was only planning on passing through Leavenworth, but Christmas in 1921 felt similar to Christmas in 1920: he was separated from his family and alone in the vast, dead landscape of a Midwest winter. The key difference was that in 1920, he was on the lam in Davenport, Iowa. He was hunted but still had the freedom of movement and could make his way back to California. For Christmas 1921 he was United States Penitentiary Leavenworth Inmate #17060.

As an escape artist, Roy put up some good numbers: three escapes from US incarceration and incarceration-related transport and one international escape. If this were a game, he won more often than not against the US marshals and prison officials, but the deck was stacked. He may have frequently made fools of his captors, but they got to go home to their families each night.

The newspaper stories and attention from reporters fed Roy's ego, but this thrill corresponded with more and more people becoming familiar with his outlaw story. Ultimately, he was playing blackjack against a dealer who might lose a few hands here and there but would never actually lose house money.

Roy was playing with a deck that only had fifty-one cards. He would need a new game. He would need a new strategy.

PART THREE
1921–1936

"Grief is the price paid for love."

—*Colin Murray Parkes* (no relation to William Parkes)

CHAPTER FORTY-THREE

Los Angeles, California

December 26, 1921

* * *

PANTAGES
AMERICA'S GREATEST VAUDEVILLE CIRCUIT
Seventh Street at Hill
APEARING IN PERSON
MRS. ROY GARDNER
*With a narrative of interesting information about the life and career of her
bandit husband
and exclusive films in which he re-enacts his adventures.*
*SEE THE ROY GARDNER RELICS IN THE PANTAGES THEATER
LOBBY*

* * *

While Roy chipped away at his seventy-five-year prison sentence at Leavenworth one day at a time, Dollie worked through her own string of dates throughout California: Los Angeles, Long Beach, and San Francisco. She booked herself on the vaudeville circuit to showcase the good side of Roy that Dollie knew best. The only trouble was that although Roy might have been good 51 percent of the time, he packed a lot of action into the balance of his bad side. Aiming to get Roy out of prison before his 110th birthday, Dollie added a second persuasive element to her shows: explaining that what Roy really needed was a brain operation.

Los Angeles winters are pleasant, but the critical response to Dollie's first Los Angeles performance was frosty.

"Mail Car Bandit Makes Tawdry Hero," the *Los Angeles Times* announced in its review headline.

The critic explained, "Making a hero out of a criminal is always a doubtful sort of business," but acknowledged Dollie's point that Roy never killed anyone in his escapades. The writer also pointed out that bandits like Roy were responsible for the recent development of armed marines on trains, and asked, why shouldn't we all just become highwaymen?

The critic conceded, "It is easy to feel much sympathy with Mrs. Gardner." The knife in the heart arrived later: "The bad taste of such exhibitions as this is just as subversive of theatrical standards as it is of moral ones." The critic also blasted the singing acts of the vaudeville bill as "fair to middling," and said the "Christmas pantomime is very poor."

The Los Angeles Evening Post-Record was more gracious to Dollie's week-long run at the Pantages Theater, concluding, "Roy Gardner has an able aide in this charming and determined girl-wife of his."

Caustic reviews aside, the show must go on. Dollie entered 1922 with a series of performances at Long Beach's Hoyt's Theater with the next leg of the tour continuing to San Francisco.

CHAPTER FORTY-FOUR

McNeil Island, Washington

Late December 1921

After arresting Roy in Centralia back in the spring, Louis Sonney hung up his badge. He wasn't finished with Roy, however. Sonney founded the "Roy Gardner Picture Company," a cinematic venture whose first order of business was to film reenactments of Roy's escapades. Sonney and his crew were scheduled to film some scenes on McNeil Island in the icy opening days of winter when one of their automobiles slipped off the ferry transporting them across the Puget Sound and plunged thirty feet into the depths. Anticipating Stanislavski's system of Method acting, two of Sonney's actors escaped out of the sinking car and battled hypothermia-inducing temperatures of the Northwest currents before they managed to clamber back to the safety of the boat. They were ready to play Roy Gardner.

As Dollie finished her week-long series of vaudeville shows in Los Angeles, Sonney, too, began his own Roy Gardner lecture circuit, starting in Washington state. He complemented his talks with his newly created film reenactments. As Dollie was leaving Hollywood, Sonney would soon be arriving.

Louis Sonney remained a long-term friend of Roy Gardner after arresting him in Centralia, Washington, in June 1921. Sonney ditched his police badge and pivoted to Hollywood, where he became a salesman of lurid and crime-focused cinema.

CHAPTER FORTY-FIVE

Long Beach, California

January 9, 1922

In the opening weeks of 1922, Dollie Gardner faced a new hurdle in Long Beach: a women's civics group protesting her scheduled shows.

City manager Charles Hewes came to her aid and said, "We could not prevent Roy Gardner himself from coming here if he were out on parole, and under such circumstances he might even appear on the stage, and if his performance was not objectionable in itself, the city could not interfere."

As a concession to the women's group, Hewes said he would appoint four policewomen to monitor moral conditions on the beaches and in dance halls, ensuring that the bathing suit ordinance was enforced.

Dollie met with local reporters to address the protests, saying that she was committed to the vaudeville tour for no longer than ten weeks and that her performances were just a means to an end.

"I am doing it because I need the money and to help Roy. I have a little girl to consider," she said.

Dollie, described as "pleasant faced," said that Roy was scheduled to meet with a "lunacy commission" at Leavenworth. The wording of Roy's medical report after the Bisbee mine cave-in said he experienced a "compound depressed fracture of the skull," but the word preoccupying Dollie on the post-surgery document was "improved." She pledged to advocate on Roy's behalf until more medical interventions could change his status to "cured."

Dollie reiterated that she was not "stage struck" and wanted to be with Jean, who was staying with relatives in the Bay Area. The vaudeville circuit "is lonely for me," Dollie concluded to the reporter.

CHAPTER FORTY-SIX

Bay Area, California, and Spokane, Washington

Late January 1922

Dollie's tour continued with performances in San Francisco and Oakland. The accompanying acts on the bill shuffled between performances: at times Fred and Tommy Hayden's "Artistic Oddities" made an appearance, and a singing group calling themselves the Glasgow Maids rounded out the program on other dates.

Performing for the hometown crowds created no problems of note, but a snag like that in Long Beach occurred once Dollie and her vaudeville group continued up to Washington, the scene of so many of Roy's escapades.

Spokane city commissioner Maurice Smith declared, "Putting her on the stage is simply exploiting the career of her husband and is a dangerous thing. It makes criminality a virtue, holding it up for approval for the public and certainly has a detrimental effect." Other commissioners, described by local newspapers as "City Dads," agreed with Smith. The compromise was that city leaders would view Dollie's first Spokane appearance before deciding if they would ax the rest of the week's shows.

Judge J. B. Lindsley made his conclusion after watching Dollie's act: "Strict censorship is long past due." He added that Dollie's accompanying films were "neither artistic, entertaining, amusing nor instructive."

If anyone still couldn't read between the lines of the judge's ruling, he continued, "The exploitation of the pretended good character of a notorious criminal with pictures intended to reproduce him in motion in some connection with his crimes is an offense to the moral sentiment of all decent, clean thinking people, it is corruptive of the morals of the young and immature and is satisfying only to morbid minds. I know of no law conferring a right to cater publicly to such curious and morbid minds."

The theater manager protested, but ultimately lost. Spokane residents wanting to see some vaudeville on a Saturday night would still get a chance to see the Aerial Rooneys opening for La Zar and Dale, the Ethiopian Hunters, but they would not get to see film footage of a smiling Roy Gardner walking from jail to a Phoenix courthouse while handcuffed.

The Spokane Federation of Women's Organizations joined the City Dads in lauding the decision to ban Dollie from speaking and presenting films about Roy. Two hundred miles west of Spokane, the mayor of Yakima, Washington, canceled Dollie's upcoming performance as well.

Seattle's city council president, Robert Hesketh, maintained the censorship streak and also barred Dollie's shows. Roy Gardner did all that he could to get out of the state of Washington, and most of its leaders made the de facto commitment that his wife, Dollie, would never get back in, at least not in a vaudeville act.

CHAPTER FORTY-SEVEN

Vancouver, British Columbia

February 14, 1922

Dollie received a valentine from the Canadian theater community when compared to the controversy and hullaballoo that graced her tour south of the Canadian border. There were no threats of censorship or shutdowns for any of her mid-February vaudeville shows in Vancouver, and she was loudly applauded after speaking at the Canadian satellite of the Pantages Theater. Canadian news articles emphasized Dollie's intention to raise money for Roy's brain surgery rather than glorify his criminal acts.

The bill for Dollie's Canadian shows included the "boyish and sparkling Gladys Walton" who appeared in the photoplay *Playing with Fire*, a film full of "clean fun" per one review.

Dollie's Vancouver shows let some steam out of the prior controversy, and she was allowed to return to Tacoma, Washington, to give a brief presentation on the condition that she didn't present any films. A newspaper critic for the *Tacoma Daily Ledger* wrote, "The simple directness that Mrs. Roy Gardner employs at Pantages has won her friends. In her own intimate, vivid story of what she is trying to do for her husband she has won deep sympathy. The applause she receives at every performance shows the reflex of an audience toward her."

Dollie stressed again that she had "no desire to remain on the stage. I am thankful, however, for this

Mrs. Roy Gardner

Dollie Gardner described her life on the vaudeville circuit as a lonely endeavor, and in time returned to the San Francisco Bay area to begin training as a nurse with a specialization in mental health. This would remain her vocation until her retirement.

opportunity of telling my story and earning money to help my husband, but I am anxious to be again settled quietly with our little daughter. That suits me better and someday again I hope to have a home of my own."

CHAPTER FORTY-EIGHT

Los Angeles, California

March 1922

* * *

La Petite Theatre
Ocean Park
BIG SENSATION
THE FIRST MOTION PICTURES OF THE WORLD'S FAMOUS
BANDIT
ROY GARDNER
3 REELS OF ACTION, Showing His Wonderful Escapes
SEE THE BANDIT KING MAKE HIS GETAWAYS
His Captor, Louis Sonny, Will Appear in Person to Tell You How He Captured the
Famous Bandit

* * *

It was called the Petite Theatre, but the oversized Louis Sonney went big, and his efforts paid off with sold-out shows and crowds flowing onto the sidewalks. Whereas Dollie kept her presentations brief and focused on the appeal for brain surgery, Sonney pulled out handcuffs, shot demonstration pistols, and positioned an enlarged copy of the Centralia arrest photo of Sonney and Roy at the theater's entrance.

Sonney did it. He escaped a life of working in the lightless depths of Washington mines and found his purpose in the darkened interiors of Hollywood theaters instead.

Dollie's vaudeville tour returned to the Los Angeles area at the same time Sonney debuted his cinematic recreation for Hollywood, but the two competing Roy Gardner offerings expanded the overall crowd size rather than canceling out the other's ticket sales.

"Great crowds surged to the Burbank all day Sunday," the *Los Angeles Evening Post-Record* wrote of Dollie's return, and more shows were added to meet demand. When Dollie had started her tour in Los Angeles three months prior, the critics were tepid and questioned her motives, but now the Los Angeles press described Dollie as a "courageous woman," and press for a Venice show included the description, "Direct from her Los Angeles sensation."

In the spring of 1922, both Dollie Gardner and Louis Sonney toured their respective Roy Gardner-themed shows across the West Coast, often arriving in the same city at the same time. Rather than being competitive, however, their performances supplemented each other, and sell-out crowds became the norm.

Roy Gardner had become a brand. An ad for Harley-Davidson motorcycles boasted that Harleys were "Roy Gardner's Choice" when he made his way down Oregon and California after his McNeil Island escape. The Harley-Davidson ads made sense for the motorcycle's deepening image as the preferred choice for nonconformists. Schaefers Bros. skin care products engaged in a head-scratching move, however, when they used Roy's name to pitch their brand, given that newspaper accounts consistently described Roy as sunburned at the time of his 1921 Phoenix arrest.

Sonney and Dollie appeared to have a cordial relationship and didn't seem to bear any resentments toward each other's respective Roy Gardner touring circuit. He remained consistent in his offer to give Dollie part of any reward he might receive as the arresting officer who finally saw Roy installed at McNeil Island. Sonney also maintained friendly written correspondence with Roy at Leavenworth and mailed him five dollars a month to help with cigarettes.

While Dollie's vaudeville lectures stressed her hope to get a brain operation for Roy which would "cure" him of his Mr. Hyde-like impulses, Sonney's films emphasized his own heroics in capturing Roy. Their respective shows served as complements rather competition.

Dollie filed an injunction, however, against the Arizona Picture Company, which she claimed was using the same Roy Gardner newsreels that caused such an uproar over her act in Spokane. These films were being shown in Los Angeles theaters independent of Dollie's vaudeville performances, and Dollie's injunction said she was the sole proprietor of the films and the Roy Gardner name. It was unclear how the Arizona Picture Company obtained their copies.

While Dollie's attempt to stop the Arizona Picture Company was motivated by finances and her desire to maintain autonomy over her husband's fate, she wasn't the only one attempting to throttle the Los Angeles region's entertainment options. On the same day the local newspapers announced her injunction, Pasadena civic leaders were seeking to end the "shimmy" in addition to imposing restrictions on "toddling" and "flirting" at dance halls.

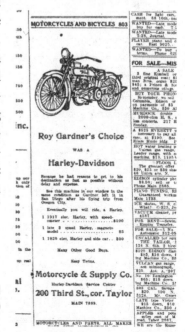

By 1922, Roy Gardner's name was being used to help sell products ranging from Harley-Davidson motorcycles to skin cream.

CHAPTER FORTY-NINE

USP Leavenworth

June 1922

When the escape-prone Roy Gardner arrived at United States Penitentiary Leavenworth in the opening days of winter, he joked with guards that he would only need a few things, as his stay was going to be temporary despite his seventy-five-year sentence. With the onset of humid summer rains and the hot weather that traditionally wreaked havoc with Roy's head and health, he nonetheless remained a convict in good standing during his first six months at Leavenworth. Roy invested faith in the legally sanctioned route of parole, if he could only get the brain operation. Roy explained that his brain injury was the reason he "robs mail trains like a small boy robs the jam shelf in the pantry."

The one successful escape from Leavenworth had occurred over ten years prior to Roy's arrival. Leavenworth Penitentiary was a city within a city, complete with its own train network to facilitate the transport of supplies within its walls. In 1910, two Leavenworth convicts, one with a pistol and the other wielding a stolen ax, commandeered the train and forced the engineer to go full steam into a closed prison gate. The train was transformed into a battering ram.

Once they smashed through the prison walls like a fist breaking a nose, the escaping convicts separated and made their way on foot through the Kansas plains. The pistol-packing convict was eventually recaptured, and his pistol was revealed to be carved from wood, an independent study project not sanctioned by the prison wood shop instructor. Frank Grigware, the convict with the ax, made his way to Canada, where he changed his last name to Fahey and successfully ran for mayor of the town where he took residence. Grigware/Fahey's escape balanced the ledger of the universe, as there is strong evidence that he was sent to Leavenworth for a robbery he didn't commit. In response to Grigware/Fahey's escape, the Leavenworth authorities permanently sealed the busted gate and downsized their internal prison trains to minimize the damage if any future convicts tried to ram a train through the walls.

With Roy keeping his promise to be "good" in Leavenworth, Dollie continued to do lectures and film presentations on the vaudeville circuit throughout

California. One critic in Pomona described her act as "positively one of the most extraordinary pictures ever shown anywhere."

She'd come a long way from fair to middling. She was on the brink of cobbling together enough money to have a medical specialist examine Roy's case. Roy formally presented his consent to have brain surgery to the Unites States Attorney's office. Such was Roy's confidence that the request was also sent to none other than Heber Votaw, president of the Board of Paroles of the Department of Justice in Washington, DC. This was the same Heber Votaw who had VIP seating at the McNeil Island Labor Day baseball game.

While Dollie made a good in-person impression and Roy's name was a good brand for selling motorcycles associated with outlaw culture, Roy was still primarily viewed by the public as just that: an outlaw. A June 26, 1922, editorial in the *Los Angeles Daily Times* spoke extensively of the murderous new regime in Russia. While Vladimir Lenin and Roy Gardner had little in common, Roy's name was nonetheless invoked in the Russia editorial as an example of the futility of compromising with crime.

Winning over theater critics on the West Coast was one thing, but officials in Washington, DC, would ultimately determine Roy's fate, and by extension, Dollie and Jean's.

CHAPTER FIFTY

Maricopa, Arizona

July 1922

Hiram Juan, an Arizona teenager belonging to a local Native American tribe, noticed an odd bundle of scattered papers beneath a mesquite tree just outside Maricopa. The papers could have belonged to some type of camper, but staying in the desert for long in the summer heat would have been suicide. Juan investigated the half-buried, sun-bleached items further.

The pouch had a US MAIL identification stencil on the side, and most of the papers were letters ripped from envelopes addressed to Salt River Valley and Prescott, Arizona. Juan had found the last of Roy Gardner's loot from the November 1921 train robbery. The mail pouch was returned to the Post Office, and the letters were forwarded to their intended recipients. A local newspaper in Holbrook, the county seat of Navajo County two hundred miles to the northeast of Phoenix, announced that it finally received the check payment from an optician who had placed an ad in the newspaper eight months prior.

Post Office Inspector J. L. Cooper sent a letter to the editor of the *Holbrook News* explaining to local citizens, "The enclosed mail was recently recovered near Maricopa, Arizona, it having been stolen from the mail car on the night of November 2, 1921, by Roy G. Gardner, the notorious mail bandit. It is greatly regretted that you have been inconvenienced by this delay, but there is some satisfaction in knowing that Gardner is now serving a twenty-five-year sentence in the United States Penitentiary at Leavenworth, Kansas."

It was settled. After committing three high profile robberies, Roy Gardner, "the prince of bandits," could only boast of claiming seventy-five years at Leavenworth and a free waffle breakfast at the Bachelor Inn for his troubles.

CHAPTER FIFTY-ONE

Fresno, California

August 1922

Louis Sonney continued his own Roy Gardner-themed vaudeville tour through California during the summer county fair season in central California. Sonney's act now included rope throwing and trick shooting. He declared, too, that part of his proceeds would contribute to deferring the costs of Roy's brain surgery. To promote a Fresno gig, Sonney presented a Leavenworth letter he received from Roy to the local press:

> My Dear Louie:
> Yours of the 27th received. Sure glad to hear from you, also many thanks for the five spot. My cash was getting low and as long as there are no mail trains in here, I was wondering where my smokes were going to come from.
>
> I have finished writing my story and now I have to send it to Washington to be censored. I wrote it in 35 chapters about 40 thousand words. If they operate on me before the book gets back from Washington I will have written instructions that in case of my death the book be sent to you and if I live through it all right, I will send the book to you myself. I have one offer now of one thousand dollars for the story from the International News Syndicate, but I believe you can get that much more for it and at the same time reserve the moving picture rights. They demand moving picture rights and all.
>
> I believe the picture rights are worth one thousand dollars by themselves. Anyhow use your own judgment and get all you can out of it. If I do get out you are certainly to share 50–50 with me in all the money we make.
>
> Write me often, Louie. I love to hear from you.
>
> Always your friend, Roy Gardner

* * *

A few weeks later, Sonney presented another letter from Roy to reporters. The letter explained that the prison medical staff confirmed via X-rays that a segment of Roy's skull was pressing down an eighth of an inch into his brain. Their conclusion was that this needed to be remedied, and Roy's request for brain surgery was approved.

Sonney announced that he was going to contribute $250 toward the Kansas City specialist who would take on Roy's case. Sonney's vaudeville circuit paused for the moment, as Sonney caught a train to Kansas to be by Roy's side.

CHAPTER FIFTY-TWO

Washington, DC

October 1922

. . . Except the brain surgery was never approved. Warden Biddle announced that prison medical staff determined that it would be too risky and would serve no benefit. From Washington, DC, Attorney General Harry Daugherty officially declined Roy's request for the surgery.

CHAPTER FIFTY-THREE

USP Leavenworth

November 1922

A tearful Dollie journeyed to Leavenworth to visit Roy. For almost a year, she toiled on the vaudeville circuit, an isolating journey fraught with public shaming, but it would be a relatively small price to pay if the reward was the eventual reunion of her family. What was intended as an eight-week tour expanded into the entirety of 1922 as reviews became more positive and the press narrative coalesced around the appeal for a brain surgery for Roy. The authorities now seemed to kick the legs out of Roy's strategy after the initial hope. Dollie arrived at Leavenworth as the maple trees shed their leaves and the snapdragons and moss roses wilted; colorful summer souvenirs now left to the mercy of autumn.

Reporters followed Dollie's arrival and Roy participated in the vaudeville performance by using the concrete floor of his prison cell as a stage. He opened his monologue,

> I know crime . . . I should know crime, for I probably am America's most daring criminal, at least so my prison record says.
>
> I am not boasting of that fact. I am heartily ashamed of it. And to prove my sorrow, I am offering my brain, my life if necessary, to prove that crime can be prevented and to demonstrate to America that the jail system of the United States is built on wrong principles. Crime is a disease, just as smallpox, influenza or any other ailment. There should be hospitals and doctors for criminals instead of jails and jailers. That will solve the problem of crime.
>
> While my body is sound, one of the best among the nearly 3,000 prisoners confined here, my mind is a decaying, rotten thing. I can be cured, just as the great majority of my cellmates in Leavenworth can be cured. I want to prove that.

Although Roy appealed for a new brain surgery, he said that his surgery after the mine cave-in set the foundation for his current troubles: "Almost immediately after that operation I became a criminal. I wanted to plan crimes, to outwit others and take what was not rightfully mine."

Roy concluded by saying, "If some brain specialist will come to me, take me as the subject of a serious scientific investigation, probe deep into the disease tissue of my brain and cut them out I am quite positive that Roy Gardner, the bold, bad bandit, would be immediately transferred into an honest, upright man."

Roy anticipated the upcoming trend of lobotomies while failing to predict that this practice of the mid-twentieth century would eventually be consigned to the same category of regretful medical procedures as the application of leeches.

Louis Sonney continued to tour and present his movie, *The Smile Bandit*, venturing into the new market of Corsicana and Fort Worth, Texas. *The Smile Bandit* would also appear at the Black-owned Grand Central Theater in Dallas, and it was promoted in the *Dallas Express*, a newspaper championing African American rights and causes.

For Dollie, however, the touring circuit was finished. She had done what she could do, and it was time to go back to Napa. She would begin her training as a nurse at St. Luke's Hospital in San Francisco with an emphasis on studying mental health issues. For the third Christmas in a row, Jean would not have Christmas with her father, but at least Dollie was back home.

CHAPTER FIFTY-FOUR

USP Leavenworth

1923

Warden Biddle explained that Roy was put in solitary or "the dungeon" just as much for his own protection as anyone else's. Roy had remained a convict in good standing for over a year, buoyed by the hope that the authorization for brain surgery would grant him a pardon and he'd be able to walk out of prison through the front gates.

But when prison doctor Albert Yohe and Attorney General Daugherty officially declined Roy's request for the surgery, he alternated between despair and rage, culminating in threats against the prison guards and the doctor.

"Someone is going to get killed and I am going to get loose!" Roy reportedly yelled, and he drafted a letter to Dr. Yohe criticizing his medical qualifications, in addition to questioning his qualifications as a human being.

The warden feared Roy would make a reckless dash for the wire and get shot in the back as he dangled on the prison fence. In solitary, he'd be contained with his own anger. Another Leavenworth convict, Ben Clegg, described Roy as "having a bolt or two loose" during this period. While Roy may have been patiently waiting to get approval for surgery, he also may not have tried to escape from Leavenworth during his first year due to the hard reality that no opportunities presented themselves.

Louis Sonney became the primary torchbearer for Roy's cause once Dollie returned to the Bay Area to focus on raising Jean and training as a nurse. Sonney announced from Los Angeles that he was about to board a train for Washington, DC, to make the appeal directly to President Harding, a man who by that time could have benefited from a broad spectrum of counsel, as the vapors of scandal brought on by corrupt associates began to asphyxiate his presidency.

Sonney explained, "Roy Gardner never killed a man. He always was square. He turned back to the government every penny he stole, something like $300,000, and all property that he has taken has been recovered. That's why I am willing to spend $1,000 to help him get the operation."

A nearly destroyed registered mail pouch washed up on the banks of the American River in Sacramento to punctuate Sonney's point. Although the pouch itself was cut open, its lock was still intact, and the sack was believed to be a casualty of Roy's Roseville train robbery. While Roy himself didn't return the mail pouch, Mother Nature would be his surrogate to bring his evidence to the authorities.

If Sonney planned a layover in Leavenworth to say hello to his old friend Roy, he would be turned away by warden's orders as Roy continued to make his situation worse. After isolating Roy in segregation, which prison staff mistakenly believed would allow Roy to cool off, Deputy Warden S. M. Lee invited Roy into the warden's office to have a "fatherly talk." Roy responded to the fatherly talk by throwing punches and was dragged out of the office by a cordon of guards, then exiled into permanent solitary confinement or "the hole."

When discussing the plight of about forty political prisoners incarcerated at Leavenworth as a result of violating the Sedition Act, Warden Biddle told a reporter that prisoners put in "the hole" sometimes were left with a big rock for a cellmate. These prisoners could only get their next meal of bread and water once they broke the big rock down to smaller rocks. If convicts resisted, guards would chain their hands to the door to force them into a long-term standing position.

Per Warden Biddle's orders, Roy was prohibited from seeing or talking with anyone, Dollie included, and even the guards bringing him his meals became an impersonal hand slipping a plate through a briefly opened door.

The darkness and isolation of solitary could cause a man to think about everything and nothing all at once. There was a time in Roy's life where he was stranded in the wide-open Sonoran Desert with the sun blasting his eyes. Now he was enveloped by four walls squeezing in with nothing but darkness. There were memories of speeding down the back roads of northern California on a stolen Harley-Davidson motorcycle with shafts of sunlight piercing through cracks in the canopy of the redwood trees before his brief stop in Napa to hold his daughter. His current confinement clashed with sprinting down California until the motorcycle died in San Juan Capistrano, the site where flocks of swallows return from their migrations every year. If Roy could have willed it, he would have leapt into the air and taken flight with the swallows, but instead he sneaked on the flatbed of a train heading toward the Mexican border.

Roy may have reflected upon the entirety of his existence or nothing at all, for the blackness and quiet of "the hole" was the equivalent of floating in an outer space vacuum. After days on end in isolation, the nerve endings in Roy's eyes began to deteriorate for lack of anything to do.

Roy told the press he convened with ghosts, which most likely was a ruse; he likely talked to the walls to make imaginary friends out of necessity. His mind would need to become as vast as the Sonoran Desert to pass the time. For a few moments he may have been able to imagine hugging Dollie and Jean, but these conjured dreams would likely dissipate with thoughts of regret and what-ifs. *What if I never went to Tijuana? What if I never went int the Roseville cigar store to play poker? What if I had snuck on the steamer to Australia?*

The vast open expanse of the Mexican desert almost killed Roy, and now the universe was presenting him with an all-confining and saturated darkness that was also going to kill him one nerve ending at a time.

Once a day the guard's hand slid open the square door within the door to toss in Roy's ration of bread and water. Roy refused to eat his meals, however, and the bandit of all bandits was increasingly described as "haggard."

After being taken out of solitary, Roy was thrown right back in after he was caught supplying a shiv to another convict who was serving time for murder. The prison staff believed the shiv's intended target was a guard. The handmade knife was whittled from a spoon and hidden in a sock. It seemed Roy was determined not to earn any credits for good behavior. He was on a path to serve all 27,375 days of his seventy-five-year sentence.

CHAPTER FIFTY-FIVE

Dixon, California

Winter 1924

In the mid-1920s, Sacramento promoted itself as the "heart of the world's richest garden." A few miles west of Sacramento lies Dixon. Roy Gardner's brother-in-law, Manuel Silva, concluded that Sacramento might have been good for agriculture, but Dixon was the spot to set up a whiskey still in a rented house. Silva was fined for his offense, and there was one more outlaw added to the ranks of the husbands of the Nelson sisters of Napa.

CHAPTER FIFTY-SIX

Phoenix, Arizona

September 1924

Although Dollie left the vaudeville circuit, she began taking nursing courses with an emphasis on mental health issues to improve her understanding of Roy's case. With this knowledge, she returned to Phoenix two years after Roy's sentencing trial to resume the behind-the-scenes legal proceedings that could win an approval for Roy's brain surgery. She petitioned Judge Sawtelle, who had seemed sympathetic to Roy's situation during the 1921 sentencing. Judge Sawtelle granted Dollie an affidavit that she planned to take to Washington, DC.

Although no longer on stage, Dollie fielded reporter questions from the Jefferson Hotel in Phoenix.

"When Roy Gardner was convicted of mail robbery and sentenced to McNeil Island, I swore I would stick to him to the end and after four and one-half years of waiting I am still willing to stick with him and aid him in every way possible," she explained. "Never once during all these long years, which have seemed a nightmare, have I thought of securing a divorce."

Dollie added that Jean is always asking for "daddy."

While Dollie fulfilled the role of Roy's homespun lawyer, he was either working against her efforts or reinforcing her hypothesis of insanity with his ongoing assaults against Leavenworth prison staff, which landed him a permanent seat in solitary confinement. His neighbor was Robert Stroud, the eventual "Birdman of Alcatraz" and murderer of a Leavenworth guard.

CHAPTER FIFTY-SEVEN

The West Coast

Spring 1925

Twenty-five years before Sal Paradise and Dean Moriarty took a 1949 Hudson Commodore across America in Jack Kerouac's *On The Road*, there was Louis Sonney in his 1922 Buick sedan. The Buick logged 140,000 miles to assist Sonney in promoting all things Roy Gardner. The Buick, Sonney boasted, survived the badlands on impassable roads, sank floorboard-deep into mud, and navigated snowstorms all the while needing no more than $30 in repairs over the course of three years. With his arrival in each new state, Sonney placed a pennant on the Buick's doors like a luggage tag. Soon the Buick was covered in thirty-six state tags and its appearance in the small towns of America created the opening salvo for Roy Gardner Pictures. Roy Gardner, one of the last great train robbers, was in prison, and the circus train of the past was replaced by the automobile. The twentieth century had landed.

Police and thieves created most of the trouble for the Buick. Sonney received a ticket in Fullerton for failing to stop at an intersection, and thieves broke into the parked car in Los Angeles in order to steal a box of handcuffs and a convict suit.

"Why would any burglar want that stuff?" Sonney pondered.

The car itself, in addition to various Roy Gardner-related paperwork inside, was stolen once but mysteriously reappeared a few hours later with a handwritten note from the thieves: "It is too bad that this car belongs to Roy Gardner, otherwise we would have been across the line. We put six gallons of gas in it. Your friend, One Guy."

With the Buick safe and back on the road, Sonney's act expanded to include Montana Jack, a handcuff and straitjacket escape artist who incorporated a pet rat into his act. In each small town, Sonney invited local police officers to participate in his handcuff and straitjacket challenges. Sonney was a large man to begin with, and he took to wearing an oversized ten-gallon sombrero.

Despite the added theatrics, Sonney always stressed that his show was to help fundraise for Roy's brain operation. A writer for the *Selma Enterprise,* a newspaper based in Fresno County, California, mused that Sonney's "same appeal was made in Selma some two or three years ago. Evidently Roy's head if cracked as claimed must have a crack in it wide enough to permit the entry of a great many dollars and dimes and quarters."

Sonney countered by explaining to reporters that Dollie was down to eating two meals a day in order to help save for the operation. The authorities played tug-of-war with their hopes: one day authorizing more X-rays to be taken of Roy's skull only to conclude later that the surgery would be too risky.

If Dollie was down to two meals per day, Roy wasn't eating at all as part of his hunger strike, which now incorporated a protest of the segregated conditions at Leavenworth and the mistreatment of the African American prison population. In his first robbery in San Diego, Roy covered his face in shoe polish to create an identity misdirection which could have resulted in the unjust conviction of an innocent black man. Now Roy was fighting for racial equality, a position that didn't have many white allies in the mid-1920s. Roy, in addition to two African American convicts, supposedly hadn't eaten in thirty-two days. Roy also claimed to be going blind, a result of either malnutrition or the sustained darkness of solitary confinement. Warden Biddle responded that Roy was just a "grandstander" who was sneaking food on the sly.

Dollie always worried that Roy would make an escape attempt and get shot. Now she was worried that he was starving himself to death.

CHAPTER FIFTY-EIGHT

USP Atlanta

October 1925

Roy Gardner made it out of Leavenworth.

He didn't cut the prison wire and make a run for it, and he didn't overpower the guards with smuggled weapons. Roy Gardner made it out of Leavenworth through Warden Biddle's signature.

Roy Gardner was John Snook's problem now. Snook, the warden of United States Penitentiary at Atlanta, received Roy as part of a quiet transfer that was kept secret from the press until its successful completion. Roy won the war of attrition with Warden Biddle through his assaults on the guards, hunger strikes, and proxy wars waged by his surrogates, Dollie and Louis Sonney, who kept Roy's name in the newspapers even though Roy himself was hidden away in Leavenworth.

On top of that, there was the crowding. Leavenworth was over capacity. Six years of Prohibition created a new class of criminal armed with Tommy guns and fast cars. There was less whiskey in people's bloodstreams, but more blood on the streets. America's added prohibitions of the 1920s created the need for more prisons. Warden Biddle had already transferred 115 Leavenworth convicts to a new prison in the Nevada desert.

The convicts transferred to Nevada were residents of Pacific Coast states prior to their incarceration, but Warden Biddle chose not to include Roy in this group. All of Roy's escapades and infamy occurred in the West, so Warden Biddle would decapitate his West Coast notoriety by sending Roy as far east as possible, to the United States Penitentiary at Atlanta. Roy was now Atlanta's Inmate #18453. By the mid-1920s, he was accumulating more prison numbers than President Harding had scandals.

Once the transfer was completed without incident, Warden Biddle said, "We examined Gardner and found him in such a mental state that a transfer was deemed advisable. The report of the physicians was to the effect that Gardner should be transferred either to St. Elizabeth's Hospital in Washington DC, or to some other prison."

With his departure from Leavenworth, Roy declared that he was ending his hunger strike and officially resumed eating again.

Louis Sonney told a Los Angeles reporter, "When Gardner pleaded guilty in Phoenix, they promised him the operation to cure him. Then they stuck him in Leavenworth, trying to break the exaggerated idea he had of himself by solitude. Nearly killed the man. Now they're going to give him a chance. He's out of the hell hole of Warden Biddle's. He's going to get the medical attention he needs now. They are going to lift the scar tissue that is pressing on Gardner's brain over a quarter of an inch in depth and covering an area as large as a quarter dollar."

Atlanta Warden John Snook was less than one year on the job at the time of Roy's arrival. Snook had inherited a mess. The previous Atlanta warden, A. E. Sartain, resigned in disgrace when it was revealed he took upwards of $5,000 in bribes from convicts in exchange for plum prison jobs, such as chauffeuring the prison physician. Drug smuggling flourished during his watch, and he was further accused of pressuring George Remus, the Bootlegger King of Cincinnati, to make incriminating but false statements in court against Sartain's congressional enemies. As a final kick to the teeth, investigators accused Sartain of only receiving his position in the first place because he was a crony of the previous attorney general, Harry Daugherty, who had resigned in disgrace among the many falling dominoes of corruption surrounding former President Harding before his death in 1923.

Snook brought a hard-nosed and scrappy resume to Atlanta. He served as US Marshal in Sitka, Alaska, during the Yukon Gold Rush, where he helped bring down the Soapy Smith Gang, a band of Arctic mobsters led by a P. T. Barnum disciple, who hoodwinked victims into buying bars of soap selectively wrapped in paper currency as a lottery prize. Incognito members of the gang always ended up as the cash winners. Snook had turned around another troubled institution, the Idaho State Penitentiary, which had fourteen escapes in one year before Snook became the proverbial new sheriff in town and clamped that number down to zero.

With over 3,000 prisoners, Atlanta exceeded the overcrowded Leavenworth. In addition to the usual assortment of bandits and murderers, the Atlanta Penitentiary also imprisoned the former governor of Indiana and Elbert Robinson, the "Negro Ponzi," described by one victim as a "suave bunion trimmer from Nashville." Robinson duped his victims into believing he was due to receive ten million dollars in a patent infringement lawsuit for his "hard iron wheel," which even Henry Ford supposedly had his fingerprints on. All Robinson needed was some up-front cash for legal fees, which he promised credulous marks he would repay in interest. He may not have reinvented the wheel, but he utilized all manners of wheels to skip out of town with his victims' money.

After his transfer from Leavenworth, Roy became absorbed into the normal day-to-day life of the convict population at Atlanta without any immediate incidents of note. Upon his arrival at the Atlanta Penitentiary, Roy started work in the "duck shop," the primary prison industry, where inmates spun canvas for the government and military. Output from the duck shop also supplied the mail service with canvas pouches, which in Roy's case put the penance in penitentiary. In time, however, Roy earned his way into the auto shop, where he worked as a welder and eventually became foreman, a position similar to his pre-prison career. In the short term, he thrived and gained momentum doing "good time."

When Roy's former California nemesis, US Marshal James Holohan, was selected to be the new warden of San Quentin, Roy sent him a flattering and congratulatory letter. Gone were Roy's threatening missives toward Leavenworth staff.

In addition to getting promoted out of the duck shop, Roy also steered clear of the junk ward, the cold turkey detox set aside for inmates withdrawing from heroin. Roy may have been addicted to cigarettes, but he sidestepped the trap door of narcotics dependency, a legacy of Warden Sartain's tenure.

Atlanta seemed to reform Roy into a model prisoner, and he patiently waited for any news about the brain operation—until he was caught sawing through the bars of a prison window when he was supposed to be attending chapel. There would be no more chapel service after being thrown in solitary confinement for his transgression. Upon being released back into the general prison population, Roy made a point of sending a letter to Warden Snook, like a handshake from a vanquished athlete showing grace in defeat.

"Warden, this is the hardest pen in the United States to get away from," he wrote. For Warden Snook, these words from the bandit of all bandits would be a trophy for his bookcase.

If Roy's mind was a battlefield between the two opposing spirit forces of White Feather and Warecka, then his first three years at Atlanta would be a cerebral No Man's Land where neither side could gain an advantage.

Institutional corruption and drug addiction within the crowded convict population plagued the US Penitentiary at Atlanta in the 1920s. New warden John Snook did his best to mitigate these issues, but his list of problems would increase with the arrival of Roy Gardner in 1925.

CHAPTER FIFTY-NINE

Napa, California

Summer 1926

In the July 13, 1926, front page photo of the *Oakland Tribune*, Dollie and Roy look like characters from *The Great Gatsby*. Dollie wears a fashionable hat and her natural beauty, so often noted by reporters, is evident. Roy wears a suit and tie and casts a friendly grin combined with a thoughtful look of concentration. He appears to either be listening to a friend's humorous story or plotting his next caper. They are two separate photos placed together.

At the time of the story, Dollie and Roy's tenth wedding anniversary had recently passed. The newspaper had their two smiling photos placed together, but in real life the two had never been more geographically separated. Roy was incarcerated in the Atlanta penitentiary, while Dollie remained in Napa with Jean, who would soon be turning nine. Their letters, which Dollie continued to describe as "cheerful," were their only lifeline. Had a copycat mail bandit perpetuated Roy's exploits into the mid-1920s by grabbing mail sacks from trains and tossing the unneeded pouches into ravines, then Roy and Dollie's connection would have been completely severed.

The *Oakland Tribune* headline said that Dollie "Forgets Sorrow in Mercy Work," and the body of the article went on to explain that she had finished her nursing training and started work at Napa General Hospital. Through "easing the suffering of others, Mrs. Roy Gardner is seeking to forget her own sorrow," the article explained. In time she would become a nurse at Napa State Hospital, known as the Napa Insane Asylum when it first opened in 1875.

Dollie elaborated to the reporter by saying, "I want only peace of mind and surcease from notoriety now. I shall devote myself to my little daughter, Jean, and strive to keep her life from being marred by Roy's unhappy career of crime." She concluded, "I will never give up hope that someday we will be reunited. When that day comes we will take little Jean, go into a strange place and begin life over again."

CHAPTER SIXTY

USP Atlanta

July 1928

Warden Snook wasn't feeling well during an oppressive heat wave of an Atlanta summer, so he stayed home one day in late July when over 3,000 convicts were packed into the greenhouse conditions that maximized moisture and stifling misery. Three thousand men sweated amidst the odor of their wet and cranky bodies. The heat with no solace created a paradox where a man wanted to either lie down as still as possible or lash out at someone just to have something to do. The heat made many of the men dizzy, and in Warden Snook's case, it gave him stomach cramps. He stayed home to convalesce in a fetal position in a sweat-drenched bed.

Captain Parker stood sentry in the Atlanta Penitentiary recreation yard where 1,700 convicts from Cellhouses A and B were allowed a small respite from their cells outside before the switch to allow the remaining balance of the population a chance to get onto the yard. Everyone was in a bad mood, and Captain Parker strained to decipher if individual bursts of yelling were the seeds of fights about to break out or convicts just complaining in general. There was a lazy anger to the atmosphere, and Captain Parker wanted to go home like Warden Snook.

In the far distance beyond the throngs of convicts, Captain Parker observed Roy Gardner and another convicted train robber, Joe Urbaytis, hoisting up a long piece of lumber that appeared to be taken from the new powerhouse construction site. The two convicts leaned the piece of lumber against the far wall of the prison as if they were medieval knights placing a modified ladder against an enemy castle in preparation for invasion. In Roy and Urbaytis's case, they were planning to evacuate from their own fortress.

Captain Parker went over to investigate this suspicious development. He called over guards Bunce and Finn to assist. The guards walked as fast as they could to advertise that they meant business, but they also moved slowly as not to overexert themselves in the July heat. Bunce barked out a question at the two convicts, and Urbaytis responded by clipping him on the back of the head with the handle of a contraband pistol.

Within an instant, the heat no longer mattered. The prison alarm wailed in a lazy, dull roar, and individual officers screeched their own whistles. The gun guard in Tower Four immediately took aim and prepared to squeeze off a round at the convicts, but Roy and Urbaytis pulled in Parker, Bunce, and Finn as hostages.

Hostages created a new wrinkle in the escape attempt, as they weren't part of the original plan. Roy crab-walked Parker down a back corridor, toward a rear door. The remaining correctional officers on scene raided the penitentiary armory in preparation for a shoot-out and chased after Roy, while Urbaytis hung tight with Bunce and Finn to wait for Roy to create an opening.

Officer Nixon stood point in front of a barred door leading out of the recreation yard. Nixon was unarmed save for his billy club. Pointing a contraband pistol to make his command clear, Roy ordered Nixon to unlock the barred door, and the guard complied.

Roy shuffled along with his hostage, but he soon encountered another locked door. Taking advantage of the delay, Captain Parker tossed away his keys through the bars. Roy was cornered with a throng of guards closing in, including guards arriving on the other side of the locked door he was attempting to break through. Roy took a few wild potshots at the guards, but the game was rigged. Roy was the Bloodless Bandit, and he wasn't going to kill his hostage, Captain Parker. The hostage was a gambler's bluff.

Roy had no forest to vanish into. There were no dairy barns to take shelter in. There was only an army of guards and a locked door. Roy surrendered and was promptly thrown in the Hole. No one was hit in the shoot-out, and the lone injured party was Captain Bunce, when Urbaytis hit him on the head with the revolver handle.

The hundreds of convicts in the exercise yard were promptly moved back into their cells for lockdown, and the interruption of their yard time on a sweltering summer day caused a unanimous chorus of hollering and clanging. The inmates in Cellhouses C and D doubled the chorus's intensity when they realized they would lose their turn in the exercise yard due to the escape attempt.

From outside the penitentiary walls the yelling and sporadic gunfire created rumors of a mass riot, and local Atlanta police arrived to help clamp down the chaos. Warden Snook's chief complaint on the morning he called in sick was intestinal distress, and this was *before* he heard news of the near riot and escape attempt involving gunfire. Despite doctor's orders to remain home, he rushed back to the penitentiary to get his hands on the steering wheel. He collapsed a few days later after interrogating over thirty inmates to try to get to the bottom of how guns were smuggled into the penitentiary.

* * *

A few months after the foiled July break-out, a convicted Detroit bootlegger listed as Peter Hanson on his admission paperwork arrived at the Atlanta Penitentiary to become Convict #20260. Although Detroit was a thirsty city, it turns out there was no actual bootlegger named Peter Hanson. Convict #20260 a.k.a. Peter Hanson was sent to Atlanta at the direction of the Assistant Attorney General of the United States, Mabel Walker Willebrandt.

The pencil of Convict #20260 produced no love letters to a long-suffering wife. Instead he wrote in an odd and coded language to his friend, Thomas C. Wilcox, who headed the Detroit office of the Department of Justice.

Another convict became suspicious of this new prisoner and leaked their hypothesis to the press. After a little digging, reporters determined the Department of Justice was adding to the already overcrowded prison population with a government informant, whose directive was to keep tabs on the warden. The government had sent a spy, alias Peter Hanson, who became a snitch, who was ratted out.

Warden Snook said he had no idea the Justice Department was sneaking around on his turf, and Wilcox declined to comment on a reporter's question that he was "trying to get something on Snook."

After a brief stay at Atlanta, "Peter Hanson," convict #20260, was quietly transferred to Leavenworth.

It was eventually suggested that Roy and Urbaytis's contraband pistols were smuggled inside of cotton bales intended for processing in the duck shop. Warden Snook complained that the overcrowded conditions at Atlanta, where facilities held 3,780 convicts in space initially intended for 1,712 men, made it nearly impossible for correctional officers to uncover every plot. He suggested that a separate "junk farm" be created for drug addicts, to ease crowding and prevent violent criminals from mixing with people needing more tailored medical attention.

Assistant Attorney General Willebrandt disagreed with Snook's assessment and the two officials never achieved consensus. The controversy around the planting of government agents within the prison dogged Willebrandt, and she countered by saying that Snook continued the corrupt tradition he inherited of rewarding high-profile prisoners with special treatment. The more lurid tabloids suggested that Snook may have even been carrying on amorous relations with the wife of an Atlanta convict.

Snook resigned from his post by April 1929, after a prolonged fight with Washington, DC, officials. In the court of public opinion, however, Snook came out looking okay, as even an everyday citizen didn't have much tolerance for snitches.

CHAPTER SIXTY-ONE

Napa

Summer 1929

About a year after Roy's failed Atlanta escape attempt, Dollie had a "complete breakdown" per the local newspapers, and she was committed to bed rest at a sanatorium near French Camp in Napa. It was clarified that she had a slight case of tuberculosis but describing Dollie as being in a state of "breakdown" might not have been far from the truth.

In an earlier interview, Dollie explained that the Christmas of 1918 was the high-water mark of her domestic bliss with Roy and Jean—a moment now over ten years in the past. When Roy was first convicted for the San Diego robbery, the marshal's prediction was that Dollie would only stick by Roy's side for three years, and she had already beat that bet by six. But a hard situation was always getting harder. Roy's behavior was putting him geographically farther and farther away from home, and the latest escape attempt involved active shooting where any number of people could have been killed. No parole board would assess Roy as doing "good time." He seemed determined to spend the entire seventy-five-year sentence behind bars, and a significant chunk of that time in the Hole.

Dollie was transferred to a second hospital, San Joaquin General in Modesto, for further rest and convalescence. Despite all of this, Dollie spoke to a reporter from her hospital bed and described Roy as "the best husband and father that ever lived. I'll always love him. His robberies were the result of insanity. Oh, we write all the time, he writes to Jean, too, nice funny letters that she loves and cheerful, happy letters to me. But I can always tell about Roy, it's his disposition to plan and scheme and a year ago when he tried to escape, I knew it. I read it between the lines in my letters months before he tried. I can tell."

The reporter explained how Dollie became tearful at this part of the narrative, but she continued by explaining that she had considered moving close to Leavenworth during Roy's Kansas incarceration, but this plan just made Roy restless in Dollie's account, so she remained in Napa.

"He was a good husband, a better husband never lived, and it was like a thunderbolt out of the sky when he first robbed the train at San Diego. Now it's been nine years, long ones, too, believe me, and Roy shows it. His hair is snow white. He's only forty-three years old, but he looks fifty-five. Lord, but I've done everything I could to get him free. Fought with 'em all and it's no use. The doctors admit that he isn't right, he has a tumor in the center of his head and to operate would kill him. But to hope that he will ever be pardoned, no, I'm sure there's no hope of that 'cause he's tried to escape too many times."

Dollie brushed aside a tear and smiled. "But Roy will never give up, I tell you. He didn't rob for money, just for the thrill. Why, he doesn't have a thin cent of any of that money he took, didn't really want it, and he knows that if he ever escaped from prison, he'd have to go back sooner or later, but he loves to try. He isn't mean when they do get him. Last year he just laughed. Sure he had those guns with him, but I don't think he would kill."

Dollie concluded her hospital bed interview by saying, "There isn't any more that I can do for him. He loves to see me and little Jean. He's terribly anxious for her to have an education and I am going to see that she does, but as far as a Gardner home again—gee, I'm afraid it just can't be done."

CHAPTER SIXTY-TWO

USP Atlanta

September 1929

Roy may have continued to write "cheerful" letters to Dollie, but to Louis Sonney he sent off letters of a different sort, written in invisible ink to get past prison censors. Roy and Sonney developed a communication system where if Roy instructed Sonney to read the letter "carefully" Sonny would press a hot iron to the paper to reveal the full scope of Roy's narrative.

Roy wrote in invisible ink, "I have been in solitary confinement ever since those sleepy guards allowed guns to come into the prison under their very noses. I realize if I stay in solitary much longer, I will blow my top and therefore I have made up my mind to come out either dead or alive, probably dead. I have not eaten a bite since the 7th of this month and never will. I prefer death to insanity any old time."

CHAPTER SIXTY-THREE

St. Elizabeth's Hospital, Washington, DC

Autumn 1929

The Department of Justice finally authorized Roy to be transferred from Atlanta to St. Elizabeth's Hospital for the Criminally Insane in Washington, DC, for a psychiatric evaluation. Louis Sonney boasted that his personal advocacy to President Hoover motivated the development. The outcome of the doctor's assessments would determine Roy's fate.

With his departure from Atlanta, Roy resumed eating. After a few months of evaluation, the doctors announced their conclusions: Roy Gardner was sane, he did not need a brain operation, and he was to be returned back to the Atlanta Penitentiary. Sonney responded to this development by saying, "I now do not have a leg to stand on."

The Great Depression had begun.

CHAPTER SIXTY-FOUR

USP Leavenworth

Winter 1930

Roy Gardner was ordered back to Atlanta, but Atlanta didn't want him. A rule of thumb in customer service says that 10 percent of the people cause 90 percent of the problems, and Roy was a 10 percenter. The Department of Justice began discussions to create new federal penitentiary to add to the ranks of Leavenworth, McNeil Island, and Atlanta, to ease the stress of the growing prison population that just kept increasing with Prohibition and its criminal offshoots hiccupping into its second decade. In addition, there was now an unprecedented economic downturn creating a new element of desperate men.

Officials in Washington, DC, considered the creation of a new prison where the worst behaved criminals from the three existing penitentiaries would be skimmed off the top—or bottom depending on one's viewpoint—and housed in a new location that would serve as a penalty box for the already incarcerated. The overall prison population would decline at the three established penitentiaries, and the convicts trying to just get by and do their "good time" wouldn't get ensnared by the small percentage of violent and disruptive convicts.

This new penitentiary was still in the idea phase, so for now Roy was sent back to Leavenworth in a bulletproof train car while heavily manacled, with three armed marshals supervising the transfer. As the prison train passed through St. Louis, workhorses left for dead in the streets succumbed to the ravages of a snowstorm pummeling the Midwest. Roy was returning to Leavenworth just as he had arrived, during a snowstorm. He recently had his forty-sixth birthday, on January 5, and he had sixty-six more years to serve on his prison sentence.

CHAPTER SIXTY-FIVE

The West Coast

The Great Depression

Upon returning to Leavenworth, Roy shifted into doing "good time," as it was his only card left. He would always be known for his spectacular breaks from the McNeil Island-bound prison trains, and then from McNeil Island itself, but that was almost ten years in the past, and his escape attempts at Atlanta succeed in only landing him in the Dungeon. His hunger strikes didn't change anything, and his appeals for a brain surgery went up the chain of command and were ultimately answered with a resounding "no."

Louis Sonney continued to tour, but he, too, needed a new angle. He had saturated the country in the 1920s by pitching himself as the man who captured Roy Gardner, but his shtick was getting old, and the impact of the Roy Gardner story was evaporating like a California creek bed waiting for the rainy season. By 1930, a mechanic in Oregon who by coincidence was named Roy Gardner advertised his services in the local newspapers. His name appeared in big, bold letters, but he didn't feel the need to explain or attempt to capitalize on sharing the same name as Roy Gardner, the famed fugitive of old. Roy Gardner, the Smiling Bandit, now had his head down and was quietly doing his time at Leavenworth.

Enter "Sonney's Historical Museum," a motley rogues' gallery of life-sized wax figures including Pancho Villa, Black Bart, Billy the Kid, and Eva Dugan, the first woman to be hanged in Arizona. The show was officially presented as an educational exhibit for crime deterrence, but Sonney leaned hard on the titillation factor, as evidenced by the inclusion of a modern day "bluebeard," a man who despite ugly features successfully seduced and married eighteen women in France during the Great War, all before he murdered them.

To keep things on the respectable side of the spectrum, Sonney included wax figures of George Washington and Abraham Lincoln. But Sonney also displayed the actual mummy of a bandit named Elmer McCurdy who was shot dead in Oklahoma in 1911. The mummy would experience a zig-zagging purgatory through various carnival circuits before eventually receiving a proper burial by century's end.

As Sonney transported his wax figures from Arizona to California for his temporary exhibitions, his truck on more than one occasion was pulled over by police, who mistakenly thought the arms and legs poking out the sides of the truck were "foreigners" that he was smuggling into the country.

Sonney relished in clarifying the mix-up, as it gave him free publicity before he entered his next town. He may have even shown the local police officers his new bulletproof vests, one of the highlights in his menagerie of crime artifacts. Despite the inclusion of the dead Elmer McCurdy, Sonney emphasized that his show was "Endorsed By All Welfare Leagues Wherever Presented" in his printed advertisements.

While Sonney was no longer using the public arena to clamor for Roy Gardner's release from prison, the two still continued to correspond, and Roy cited Sonney as his best friend.

Dollie and Roy maintained their own weekly letters to each other, but Dollie slowly formed her own life independent of Roy. Her name appeared in the local Napa newspaper without any mention of Roy when she attended the wedding of a Napa State Hospital coworker. Jean's fifteenth birthday celebration also made it into the Napa newspaper, and again Roy's name wasn't included. Dollie and Jean were bit by bit creating their own lives autonomous of Roy as they made it through life's milestones. Roy continued to do time.

CHAPTER SIXTY-SIX

Washington, DC

1933

It would be America's own Devil's Island. Attorney General Homer Cummings and Board of Prisons director Sanford Bates envisioned a maximum-security, minimum-privilege penitentiary. The new penitentiary would house a relatively small prisoner population, but it would have a much higher ratio of correctional officers, all of whom would be selected for experience and proven to be beyond corruption. Prisoners would include grandstanders like Al Capone and other crime bosses, who would no longer be able to control their empires from behind bars.

There would be no commissary. There would be no gambling. Each prisoner would merely become a number. Everyone would be equal in their anonymity. The common denominator would be that they were the worst of the worst going in, but the men at this new penitentiary would be a collection of carbon molecules doing time. Nothing more.

Gangsters, bootleggers, and bank robbers had controlled the Roaring Twenties, while local city halls and police departments appeared too corrupt and impotent to control anything. Men like George "Machine Gun" Kelly engaged in a series of high-profile kidnappings for ransom, adding to the sense of chaos as the floor of the global economy dropped.

The relatively new FBI, led by an eager J. Edgar Hoover, and the Justice Department had to regain the upper hand. This new penitentiary was part of their strategy. If bullets didn't end a criminal's career—as would soon be the case for John Dillinger—then a prison sentence at this new penitentiary would slam the door and erase their persona from public view. Reporters would have almost no access to information about the prison or its inmates, and visitors would be strictly limited. Authorities allowed, and perhaps even encouraged, fear mongering rumors on the topic of the new penitentiary to spread in the criminal underworld. This new prison would be about control, with little thought given to reform.

Roy Gardner caught wind of these rumors through the convict grapevine. In a case of selective hearing, he focused on the fact that this new prison would be in San Francisco. If Roy could get transferred to San Francisco, he would be closer to Dollie and Jean, and thereby see them on a regular basis. Roy Gardner would be the only convict to volunteer to go to Alcatraz in its twenty-nine-year tenure as a US Penitentiary.

CHAPTER SIXTY-SEVEN

Alcatraz

September 1934

Within the grinding depths of the Great Depression, San Francisco longshoremen went on strike in the summer of 1934 as part of a larger strike along the Pacific Coast to protest dangerous work conditions and a bribery system where new workers had to pay to get job assignments. The best route for getting a job on the waterfront, however, was waiting for another worker to get injured. Police responded to the strike with billy clubs, tear gas, and bullets. On what became known as Bloody Thursday, two strikers were shot to death on Market Street, and thirty-two other strikers received non-fatal gunshot wounds.

The ongoing assertion of law and order continued when the largest group of inaugural convicts arrived at Alcatraz in September 1934. The military had determined that Alcatraz's previous function, as an island stockade, was too expensive and challenging to operate. So the federal Bureau of Prisons took over the island fortress. The exterior of the penitentiary was in full view along the San Francisco waterfront, but its inner workings would remain a secret.

The main group of transferred convicts took a circuitous train journey from Leavenworth to throw off reporters. They left Leavenworth at four in the morning in a rainstorm. The shackled convicts and shotgun-wielding guards traveled in a bulletproof train with blacked-out curtains. Bystanders might have mistaken it for a funeral train. Its final land-based stop was Tiburon, a small, bayside town whose name translates to *shark* in Spanish. Rather than transfer the convicts off the train and onto a boat for the final leg of their journey to the island prison, the train itself was taken off its tracks and placed on a special barge. The weight of the train pushed the barge to a precarious position, just a few inches above safe sailing, but the men eventually made it to Alcatraz without facing the cruel and unusual punishment of drowning while handcuffed and trapped.

Whether by design or accident, opening the new penitentiary in early September was a con pulled by prison officials, as the month of September represents the brief moments where San Francisco has weather resembling summer. The still, warm, late-summer air emboldened an armada of law-abiding citizens to take to the Bay to enjoy the sunshine in their own boats, while others took the auto ferry to Sausalito for a journey into the Marin hills. Pelicans in formation guided the revelers across the currents that for a brief moment offered a smooth glide from one side of the Bay to the other, in contrast to the usual whipsaw of water rushing in and out of the Golden Gate like a dam bursting. The sight of these revelers may have induced anguish in the new Alcatraz arrivals by offering a glimmer of regular life being snatched away—or the pleasant weather could have lulled them into complacency.

Poseidon's fist would arrive soon enough. Alcatraz could have been nicknamed the "Salt Crystal" rather than "The Rock." During most of the year saltwater attacked everything: sea water assaulted the prison dock at high tide and made its way into the plumbing pipes of the island's structures. The skeleton of the prison's architecture became afflicted with the rust and corrosion of relentless sea spray and fog. Nagging westerlies from the Pacific perpetually slapped the penitentiary walls and windows. Sea gulls hung motionless in the sky as they fought blasts of wind, and the breeze carried sea gull poop in unpredictable directions to create an added insult to inmates trying to find solace in limited time outside in the recreation yard. The stench of fish, sea water, and bird guano permeated the island.

In Roy's Alcatraz admission photo, he looks like a world-weary Lee Marvin. Gone is the rogue's smirk and boast that no prison could hold him. In 1921, he looked like a Hollywood cowboy, waving and blowing a kiss to his fans. By the time of his Alcatraz arrival, he looked like a train-hopping hobo elder, dispensing advice as to which Northern Pacific train agent or "bull" was to be avoided.

The one hundred and six new arrivals were stripped, showered, and marched naked up Alcatraz's main corridor, usually referred to as Broadway. Roy was seven men ahead of Machine Gun Kelly in this nude procession of the damned. Al Capone, now only called "Eighty-Five" by the correctional officers, had arrived a few weeks prior with a smaller group of convicts from Atlanta Penitentiary. The policy of Alcatraz would be that all of its new prisoners would arrive from other prisons.

"Break the rules and you go to prison. Break the prison rules and you go to Alcatraz," became an institutional mantra.

A hundred naked prisoners marching down the main corridor could have induced a raucous cheer of tension-shattering hollering and catcalling, but the boots of the correctional officers, marching in harmony with the shuffling of convicts' bare feet on the cold floor, made the only sound.

As one of his first orders of business, Alcatraz's first warden, James Johnston, initiated the Rule of Silence, a restriction held over from nineteenth-century penitentiaries, where talking was prohibited within the cellhouse. This included no conversation with anyone in neighboring cells while locked within one's own. Any convict mistakenly viewing the Rule of Silence as one meant to be broken was in a for a rude awakening once they were thrown in Alcatraz's "Spanish Dungeon," a wet, cold, and absolutely dark holdover of Alcatraz's military days. Convicts would call a stay in the dungeon being "in the water," as the floors were uneven, and dampness from the rain and fog trickled down the sides of the rock walls and pooled. A convict's own urine added to the pool after a few days of fumbling to take care of their body's needs in the darkness of a cramped cell.

Warden Johnston emphasized that his philosophy had no foundation in barbarity. He advocated for relentless discipline and scheduled repetition to mold a demographic that had proven their inability to work within structure. With this philosophy, Warden Johnston called for the disuse of the Spanish Dungeons, but they remained in service as receptacles for the worst of the worst of the worst until 1938, when the updated D Block or "Treatment Unit" isolation cells were completed.

The Rule of Silence may have been petty and infantilizing, but the enforcement was the point. There would be no exceptions at Alcatraz.

Alcatraz inmate Robert Luke, AZ #1118, who grew into law-abiding stability after completing his prison obligations, confided that he struggled to fill the Alcatraz pages of his autobiography as every new day at Alcatraz was just like the last. Add in San Francisco's maritime climate, where July mimics January, and the convicts quickly felt like Sisyphus pushing the same boulder up the same hill day after day, experiencing the tedium of a drug addict chasing their daily fix without the benefit of the drugs' pain-numbing qualities.

An Alcatraz inmate of the Depression-era penned a poem with the conclusion: "Now Alcatraz from Frisco is one mile out in the Bay, but Frisco from Alcatraz is years and years away."

At least Dollie would be able to visit soon, or so Roy thought. Warden Johnston imposed a prohibition on all visitors for a convict's first three months at Alcatraz. No exceptions. Roy had false hope that Alcatraz's proximity to Napa would engender frequent visits with Dollie and Jean. Instead, he was tortured by the thought that the same foghorns he heard sounding on the Bay were the same foghorns Dollie might hear. If he caught glimpse of a cloud formation through the barred windows of the dining hall, Dollie might be looking at the same set of clouds. Her presence would remain an abstraction, however. Dollie, too, likely felt restless. She hadn't seen Roy in person in six years. Now he was a heartbeat, something she could feel but not actually see.

CHAPTER SIXTY-EIGHT

Alcatraz

November 1934

Continuing his tradition going back to Warren Harding, Roy submitted an appeal to the current president, Franklin Roosevelt:

In April 1920, I held up and robbed a mail truck in San Diego. I was arrested four days later, sentenced on a plea of guilty by Judge Trippett to 25 years at McNeil's Island. En route to prison I escaped and was a fugitive 13 months.

In May 1921, I robbed a mail car on the Pacific Limited near Roseville and was sentenced on June 1 by the late Judge William C. Van Fleet to 25 years at McNeil's Island.

I entered McNeil's Island prison June 16, 1921, and escaped September 5, 1921.

In December 1921, I entered a mail car at Phoenix, Arizona, with intentions to rob. The mail clerk refused to submit to robbery and although unarmed, he attacked me and I was forced to surrender to him or shoot him. The mail clerk was 100 per cent man and I was a cheap crook. The result was inevitable.

I respectfully pray that I be granted a commutation from 25 to 20 years for the following reasons: A 20 year sentence means 13 years and four months imprisonment. I never killed or injured any person, I have no affiliation with the underworld, never associated with gangsters or criminals, committed all my crimes single handed and now feel sure I am 100 percent rehabilitated after 13 years incarceration. I feel that I have paid sufficient penalty for my foolishness.

I am now 50 years of age and if I am to make a success of my life I must start pretty soon. Through study and work in prison I have become an expert electrician and I intend to devote the remainder of my life to electrical work.

I now have six years of a perfect prison record to my credit and I feel sure my rehabilitation is now complete.

I do not want to serve these last three years because I fear I may become bitter and develop an animosity toward society that would undo what I have accomplished up to the present time. At present I feel that society should be satisfied with the penalty I have paid.

I have seen a number of long term prisoners develop social animosity during the last few years of their term and go out with hatred in their hearts for laws and society. I do not want to risk developing that attitude, therefore I pray that you will commute my sentence from 25 to 20 years.

I have been told unofficially that I would eventually be paroled. After considering a parole from all angles, I am forced to the conclusion that I am not a fit subject for parole.

After serving 14 or 15 years in prison a man is completely out of touch with the social and economic world and he is sure to humble and wobble around before he regains his social equilibrium.

In my case a minor wobble or stumble would result in the revocation of my parole, and then the Parole Board would fall heir to bitter criticism for releasing a notorious criminal on parole. My life would also then be a total wreck.

Grant me this last chance to rejoin my wife and daughter and also prove to the world that I am still a man among men.

Respectfully submitted,
ROY GARDNER

Roy's letter also listed prominent people who would support his request, including federal judge William Sawtelle and Sanford Bates, the director of the Federal Bureau of Prisons. Bates's sympathy might explain how Roy's letter made it past Alcatraz censors in the first place. Roy didn't include Louis Sonney as part of his crime narrative recap.

While Roy had high-profile supporters, San Quentin warden James Holohan dissented, saying, "Roy Gardner has a weakness for robbing mail cars and if he ever gets out, he'll stick up the first car he sees."

The letter was also forwarded to US Attorney H. H. McPike, who said, "Roy Gardner hasn't a chance." McPike reminded reporters that Roy's letter failed to mention the Maricopa train robbery and the Atlanta escape attempt involving smuggled guns.

CHAPTER SIXTY-NINE

Alcatraz

December 4, 1934

On the same day that the newspapers announced with misguided optimism that Germany and France signed a peace agreement and the Nazis vowed equal treatment for Jews in the Saar region, Dollie and Jean set out to visit Roy at Alcatraz. His three-month probation period had expired. It would be Dollie and Roy's first face-to-face visit in six years.

Dollie struggled with what wear for this reunion. She wanted to wear something pretty, as it was a special occasion, but it was also an event tinged with sadness. If she wore something too nice or suggestive, it might seem like this was an outfit she wore all the time—perhaps even purchased by another man. The truth was that Dollie mainly just wore her nurse uniform at the Napa State Hospital. With the Great Depression grinding into its fifth year, Dollie valued her job more than ever. Prohibition had finally ended, but Dollie couldn't afford to spend time in saloons or hotel bars. She had work to do.

During their journey to visit Roy, Dollie and Jean's ferry would pass within sight of the work crews setting the foundation for the millions of tons of concrete and miles of cabling and steel that would be used to create the Golden Gate Bridge. In an alternate reality, Roy could have been one of the men helping construct what would eventually become San Francisco's most cherished icon. Instead he was doing time on San Francisco's other notorious landmark, Alcatraz.

On the island her visitor pass would be reviewed by the guards with a scrutiny appropriate for someone trying to cross a hostile country's borders during wartime. An Alcatraz inmate joked that not even Santa Claus would be able to visit Alcatraz in December because he wouldn't be able to get a visitor pass. Once cleared, Dollie and Jean would be driven beneath the watchtowers and kept under heavy escort. The truck driving them to the top of the hill would strain its gears as it made the hairpin turns that traversed the equivalent of a thirteen-story building as they made their way to the main cellhouse. The slow, grinding drive would likely exacerbate a visitor's nerves.

The guards viewed all human beings not wearing correctional officers' uniforms as a threat, and they brandished rifles and machine guns as a warning. Officers searched her bags, and she had to pass through the "snitch box," or metal detector. Fortunately for Dollie and Jean, nothing they were wearing set the metal detector off. (Al Capone's mother once set the alarm off simply because her undergarments had a metal clasp, thus delaying her visit and creating a commotion until the guards could find the cause.)

The Visitation Area was small, and one could argue whether a meeting there met the criteria for a face-to-face visit, as a thick bulletproof glass separated any visitor from their host. The window was smaller than a chess board. During Dollie's visits with Roy pre-Alcatraz, she was allowed to sit with him and hold his hand. At Alcatraz, they conversed through phone receivers and strained to hear each other clearly. The doors of adjacent prisoner cells boomed and echoed as they were periodically opened and closed. A correctional officer stood nearby to advertise that their conversation was being listened to. If the conversations steered into politics or news, whether it be international or just anything pertaining to the world of Alcatraz, then the visit would be cut short and ended. By design, Dollie and Roy most likely made stilted small talk about friends, the weather, and the types of food Dollie was making at home. By the time they had a chance to ease the situational awkwardness, the allotted two-hour visiting time was finished.

Dollie and Jean could visit again on January 1. Convicts were allowed one visit per calendar month. No exceptions.

"I wish I had never gone there," Dollie would later explain. "It seemed like going into another world. I still love Roy, and I'll love him until he dies, but I cannot stand the strain seeing him today and thinking of him as he was fifteen years ago."

Roy, too, would retreat to his cell in silence to ponder what just happened. The echoes of the correctional officer's footsteps moving across the cement floor to complete one of their innumerable head counts paradoxically induced both agoraphobia and claustrophobia all at once. Roy would describe these nights of depressed isolation and brooding as "hellnighting."

After their demoralizing first Alcatraz visit, Roy and Dollie's ship sank a little deeper. In response to Roy's public appeal to President Roosevelt, Attorney General Homer Cummings hinted he would entertain the possibility of a commutation, but he would seek other counsel before making any decision. In mid-December, one of Cummings's close advisers, US Attorney Pierson Hall, declared that Roy should serve the entirety of his sentence, with the soonest consideration for early release not until 1961, when Roy would be in his mid-seventies.

Undaunted, Dollie continued to write to US Attorney H. H. McPike, to request copies of federal records that could aid Roy's early release.

Jean was now a teenager at Napa High School and became a writer and editor at the school newspaper, partially motivated to be a gatekeeper on any gossip people might spread about her outlaw father. She might have held fuzzy memories of their life before his incarceration, and perhaps she even still had the teddy bear he sent from Mc Neil Island for her third birthday. But at present, Roy was a mirage, housed at the new island prison that local editorial boards railed against for fouling the Bay Area landscape and putting citizens at risk. His presence was everywhere, but nowhere.

CHAPTER SEVENTY

Napa, California

June 1935

For the fifteenth year in a row, Dollie marked her wedding anniversary without the physical presence of her husband. She had a new timeline, the number of anniversaries without Roy. A clock or a timepiece is the customary gift for a fifteenth anniversary, and for Dollie, this custom represented a cruel joke and bad reminder. She sat on the sidelines of the Roaring Twenties, a devoted wife to her incarcerated husband, and now she was aging into the Great Depression.

A few weeks after her solo wedding anniversary, Dollie celebrated her thirty-eighth birthday with appendicitis and a trip to the hospital. Roy, of course, was not there to bring her flowers, but Dollie likely had many coworkers drop by to wish her well, with groups of nurses from Napa State Hospital bringing flowers to Dollie on behalf of their departments. Dollie's work was increasingly becoming a source of her autonomy, independent of Roy.

William Parkes, a staffer at Napa State Hospital, might have brought his own card and flowers, or perhaps thinking that too untoward, he could have signed his name with other staff members. He may have dropped by because whether she had appendicitis or not, William was in the habit of saying hello when their paths crossed at work. He had a crush on her.

Dollie likely appreciated the attention. She was married, of course, but her marriage was dominated by isolation, loss, and hardship. She never knew whether she was married, a widow, or floating in some type of marital purgatory. A compliment from a man made her feel good.

William Parkes had a funny but charming accent. Like Roy, he had been wounded in the leg, but in William's case, he was hit with shrapnel while serving under the Union Jack during the Great War, as a sergeant with the South Wales Borderers. William was short in stature, but he still manned a machine gun, and he cited his smaller size as helping him to "reconnoiter" better than the taller men.

After the war he made his way to the Bay Area, lured by its pleasant weather and sense of growth and possibility, an optimistic counterpoint after donating his blood on the European continent, which seemed hellbent on killing itself.

Once in California, he joined the San Francisco Barbarians, the local soccer team. As proof that his recuperation from his war injury was complete, William's teammates nicknamed him "the speedy little Welshman" and they won the state championship in 1922 and 1923. Possessing firsthand experience of what it took to recuperate from a major leg injury and become a champion athlete, William began to work as an occupational therapist at Napa State Hospital.

Dollie may or may not have spoken about Roy to her coworkers, but her wedding ring made William approach with a respectful distance. Still, he made Dollie laugh, and he was a nice man, which was sometimes just enough to help her get through a sad day.

Or perhaps William Parkes only knew about Dollie's marriage through a local newspaper story, in which a woman sought a judge's approval to annul her marriage. By coincidence, the woman's husband was also named Roy Gardner. The judge granted this request, and the marriage was dissolved. Dollie later explained to local newspapers that this story was not about her, and she wanted to publicly clarify the situation as she was fielding many inquiries from friends.

Through Dollie's clarification, reported in the newspaper, William would have learned for certain that Dollie had a husband and she wasn't annulling her marriage, but Dollie's husband was a phantom. William was probably too polite to ask Dollie directly, but through some roundabout questioning of coworkers he may have figured out that Dollie's husband had been incarcerated for the past fifteen years and was currently a resident of Alcatraz, alongside Al Capone and Machine Gun Kelly. For Dollie's husband, a release date was still unclear.

CHAPTER SEVENTY-ONE

Alcatraz

Winter and Spring 1936

A rumor spread that Roy Gardner saved Al Capone from a prison assassination. In January 1936, after Alcatraz marked its second New Year as a federal prison, upwards of 100 Alcatraz convicts—over a third of the prisoner population—staged a strike to protest its harsh conditions, including the despised Rule of Silence that landed many a man in the Dungeon, often due to a brief and accidental lapse. The striking convicts refused to attend their prison work details, including tasks such as kitchen duty and maintenance, which helped the island function. Unbowed, Warden Johnston threw the strike leaders in the Dungeon and the protest dissipated. Once the strikers were allowed back to their usual work details, four of the strike organizers supposedly inched toward Al Capone in the prison laundry.

Capone had refused to participate in the strike. His sentence for tax evasion was comparatively short, and he wanted to keep his head down and do "good time" so he could complete his prison obligations before his fortieth birthday. Additionally, by the time of his arrival at Alcatraz, the symptoms of syphilis—in a period preceding the large-scale use of antibiotics to alleviate them—had started to impact Capone's psyche. His Alcatraz tenure was marked by increasing disorientation and antisocial behavior, such as throwing excrement-filled bedpans. Eventually, he would receive a medical discharge, as his issues were beyond the scope of Alcatraz's infirmary.

Whatever the reasons for not participating in the prisoner strike, he hadn't participated. And now he would pay.

Four convicts blanketed Capone from behind as he worked in the laundry. Without warning, one of the convicts launched a heavy iron window weight at the back of Capone's head. Roy was also working in the laundry at the time, and his eyeline faced the four convicts. Roy had no allegiance to Capone, but for this split second, Roy saw a man about to get seriously hurt, if not killed, and instinct took over. Roy lunged at Capone and knocked him out of the way of the incoming missile. The iron fastball hit his arm instead of his head as Capone hit the deck.

Realizing the gravity of the situation, Capone maneuvered behind a table to avoid an encore attack.

By now correctional officers were on scene to quell the commotion. The four involved convicts, fresh from the Dungeon after instigating the strike, were sent back to the Dungeon for the assault. Capone was sent to the infirmary to have his injured arm attended to.

Capone was reassigned to the prison library, a job that entitled him to be the film projectionist for inmates in good standing, who were permitted to see warden-approved movies. The story of the assault made the newspapers, but its foundation in truth was blurrier than a movie on Capone's first day as a projectionist. Significantly, convicts wouldn't have casual access to a heavy weight that could be used as a weapon. But for a few days the newspapers ran with Roy's alleged exploits.

Roy may have saved Capone from a prison assassination, but he wasn't able to save his marriage from the isolation and uncertainty of a prison sentence. By mid-April, he received a letter explaining that Dollie was pursuing an annulment of their marriage. This time annulment wasn't a mere coincidence involving a different man with the same name. Dollie Gardner, formerly Dollie Nelson, was calling it quits. The letter from Dollie was a paper cut to Roy's heart.

Some predicted Dollie wouldn't last three years when Roy was first put in prison. Instead she lasted fifteen years and had been Roy's champion. But even Dollie had her limits. Roy's strategy of volunteering to go to Alcatraz so he could be closer to Dollie had backfired. Dollie wasn't just filing for divorce, she was seeking an annulment, which to Roy felt like she wanted to invalidate the entirety of their relationship. She based her annulment request on grounds of fraud, saying that Roy never told her he was a San Quentin ex-convict during their initial courtship.

In time, Roy would write and publish a book about Alcatraz entitled *Hellcatraz*. He would describe the convict's struggle with their own nocturnal thoughts, alone in their cell after the lights went out, when the only sounds were the snores of sleeping men and the mournful clanging of the buoy bells out on the San Francisco Bay. But while some men snored, others stayed awake to have gibberish conversations with the walls. With the arrival of midnight, other convicts began sobbing after a day's worth of false macho posturing in front of the other men. Roy described this as "hellnighting."

Roy usually had some hope, even while imprisoned. He could figure out an angle for escape, or he could bank on the prison authorities allowing a brain surgery. If not that, then a brand-new president might have a different clemency philosophy than his predecessor.

More than anything else, the thread of hope was Dollie. In 1920, he managed to reinvent himself in Iowa while on the lam, but for what purpose, without his wife and child? So he returned to Napa as a fugitive, a risky and bold move that Dollie described as a grand and romantic gesture at the time. But now she was suggesting that none of that had ever existed. The past twenty years had been an apparition.

Alcatraz was nicknamed "The Rock," but it had become Roy's mausoleum.

Roy's injury from Dollie's news became complete once he learned of William Parkes. After absorbing the initial blow, Roy could step back, if only to a limited degree, and objectively view the situation. His ongoing request for a commutation gained no traction, and authorities implied he would be incarcerated until at least 1961, twenty-plus years down the road, when Roy would be in his mid-seventies.

Dollie would soon be turning forty, not old per se, but she had spent the bulk of her twenties and thirties waiting. Waiting and waiting for no reward. She was overdue to move forward. Dollie described William as a sober and good man. Besides, Jean was old enough now, too, that she would soon be out on her own and wouldn't necessarily have to live with an interloping stepfather.

Roy officially gave Dollie's relationship with William Parkes his blessing, and things remained outwardly amiable. However, he quietly removed Dollie from his approved visitor list and continued to do his own research on "hellnighting."

CHAPTER SEVENTY-TWO

USP Leavenworth

August 1936

Roy volunteered for Alcatraz with the intention of shoring up his relationship with Dollie and getting the attention of the new president, Franklin Roosevelt. These plans fell apart. Dollie and William Parkes wed in July 1936 at an Episcopal church in Napa.

Roy's tenure at Alcatraz was a disaster given his goals, but he unexpectedly succeeded where he had rarely found success before: he became a model prisoner. In what could have been a case of the farmer letting the fox guard the hen house, Alcatraz staff asked Roy, a welder by law-abiding trade, to construct a room-sized cage in the basement's loading dock area, beneath the kitchen and dining hall. Roy designed the cage so that the receiving door could be opened to allow the delivery of produce, while still be closed to prevent convicts from escaping. Entrusting Roy with this task demonstrated a change in how the authorities viewed Roy, and how Roy viewed himself.

Roy was now in his fifties. He'd leave the fighting, striking, and jailbreaks to younger men, and several picked up Roy's torch during his two years at Alcatraz. Inmate Joseph "Dutch" Bowers made a brazen daytime jump over a fence near the prison garbage incinerator and was fatally shot in the back by a guard. This was Alcatraz's first listed escape attempt, but many believe that the mentally unstable Bowers, who had a history of suicide attempts, became confused by a guard's instructions or that he may have intentionally committed what would later be termed "suicide by cop."

Others left no ambiguity about their deaths by suicide, such as Inmate #47, Edward Wutke, who bled to death in his cell after slashing his elbow and neck with a blade modified from a pilfered pencil sharpener.

From certain vantage points, the convicts at Alcatraz could see the construction of the Golden Gate Bridge. Its progress marked the passage of time. If the cards had landed differently, Roy could have been a foreman on one of the bridge's construction crews. Instead he was a foreman in the prison mat shop. He helped convert old tires into rubber mats for the Navy's use.

Theodore Cole and Ralph Roe also worked in the Alcatraz mat shop, located in the Model Industries Building on the edge of a surf-battered, vertical drop into the San Francisco Bay. Cole and Roe used a contraband blade to methodically saw away at bars on one of the windows and covered up their progress at the end of each shift with putty. In time they worked through the bars. On a mid-December morning, when a thick fog made the island of Alcatraz look like an apparition and the Bay looked like the River Styx, Cole and Roe made their escape. They scrambled down the side of the cliff before plunging into San Francisco Bay at ebb tide. Dead or alive, the two were never seen again.

Ralph Roe, born in Missouri like Roy, may have invited Roy into their escape plan, and as the foreman of the mat shop, Roy may have had an inkling of what the two were up to. By the time of their December 1937 escape, however, Roy had already disappeared from Alcatraz. Almost one month after the wedding of Dollie and William Parkes, Roy was transferred out of Alcatraz. Warden Johnston cited "good behavior" as the justification.

Although Roy had volunteered for Alcatraz, his prison biography of escape attempts and disruptive behavior made him a perfect candidate for its mission statement: a prison for those who break the prison rules. But Alcatraz was a middle chapter for most of its alumni. Once a man demonstrated that he could walk the Alcatraz line, the authorities would transition the convict back to a different prison.

Like a weary pitcher getting pulled from the game after getting shellacked by the other team's batters, Roy was on another prison train, too old and tired to try to escape. On his way out of Alcatraz, Roy would say hello to newly arrived Alvin "Creepy" Karpis, the FBI's Public Enemy Number One, who accumulated a hat trick of crimes including bank robbery, kidnapping, and possibly murder. Roy was one of Alcatraz's first inmates, but Creepy Karpis would stay longer on Alcatraz than anyone else, at twenty-six years.

The authorities transferred Roy, now a bachelor in his fifties, back to Leavenworth Penitentiary.

PART FOUR
1938–1940

"I hold no malice toward any human being."
—*Roy Gardner*

CHAPTER SEVENTY-THREE

USP Leavenworth

June 1938

As the summer sun scorched Leavenworth, Kansas—in addition to the entirety of the Dust Bowl in the nagging, lingering days of the Depression—Louis Sonney drove away from the town's namesake penitentiary with a man in the passenger seat. The season of humidity, lice, and cockroaches was upon USP Leavenworth. Sonney was not a getaway driver aiding and abetting a fugitive, however. He was just a citizen giving a ride to another citizen. But the citizen was Roy Gardner.

Roy Gardner had served his time. James Bennett, director of the Federal Bureau of Prisons, granted Roy early release due to ten years of sustained good behavior since the 1928 Atlanta debacle. There was also an error in semantics as to whether Roy's twenty-five-year sentences would run "consecutively" or "concurrently," and "concurrently" won.

At Alcatraz, the authorities conveyed that Roy's release wouldn't occur until at least 1961, but Roy cleared the odds by twenty-three years. It was a muted victory, however, as Dollie had walked away before the change in Roy's fate. She waited fifteen years for Roy to be released, longer than most wives would have waited. The irony that she would have only had to endure two more years cast a gray cloud over what should have been a jubilant occasion, as Roy made his way west to California.

"I'm very glad Roy was released. We will always be good friends," Dollie said to reporters. Her words were those of a diplomat, but they are also the most dreaded words to a person who's still in love. Dollie would remain a friend, but she had a husband. And that husband was not Roy. These were the facts as Roy left Leavenworth.

On Roy's Alcatraz admission paperwork, he listed "Napa" as his home, but now he was a bachelor. He would return to San Francisco, like he had so many times in his life. Whether incarcerated or free, San Francisco was Roy Gardner's center of gravity.

Dollie was gone, but there was still Sonney. As Charles Bukowksi wrote in *Notes of a Dirty Old Man*, "If you want to know who your friends are, get yourself a jail sentence."

At the time of Roy's arrest in 1921, Sonney promised Roy he'd send five dollars a month and that he'd have a law-abiding job ready for Roy when he got out. For two hundred and four months, Sonney sent the five dollars, and in June 1938, he showed up at Leavenworth to pick up the now-free Roy. Alongside the gate was a stray dog that ran up to Roy.

"You miss dogs in prison," Roy mused to Sonney, patting the dog's head.

During the Depression, Sonney remained busy producing lurid movies that magnified the melodramatic horrors of narcotics and Sing Sing Prison. Despite his exploitative approach toward all things drug addled and incarcerated, he consistently demonstrated sincere friendship toward Roy.

Upon their return to California, Roy began working as a co-promoter for Sonney's film company. Alcatraz was two miles from San Francisco's downtown newspaper offices, but the island was a media Siberia per Warden Johnston's strict orders. Former Alcatraz inmates who could pull back the curtain were a rare and hot commodity during the penitentiary's Depression years, and Roy was ready for the spotlight.

Reporters had written, perhaps erroneously, about how Roy saved Al Capone's life by the prison laundry when Roy was still a convict, but as a free citizen who could now meet face-to-face with reporters, Roy was quick to emphasize that Capone was hated by most convicts on Alcatraz, himself included. Now that he was free, Roy took to wearing tweed jackets and glasses. He looked like a professor, creating a stark contrast to his tale of getting into a fistfight with Al Capone by the dining hall, caused by Roy giving Capone a hard time for appearing bleary-eyed and depressed after a night of restless sleep. Of course, Roy's teasing very well could have been a projection of his own mental condition after learning of Dollie's annulment.

"What's the matter? Can't take it?" Roy said as he ribbed the sullen Capone, and Capone took a swing. Roy may have either tackled Capone or pulled him away from the sight line of an approaching guard in the gun gallery. The two men avoided any disciplinary report and the telling of the story may have lasted longer than the fight itself.

"He is a worthless husk of a man for his mind is gone," was Roy's final assessment of Al Capone. This statement could also have been the whispers of the demons inside Roy's own damaged skull. These demons had trespassed within his mind during seventeen years of incarceration, and they invited their friends to drop by once Roy become imprisoned at Alcatraz and his marriage fell apart.

The completion of the Golden Gate Bridge during Roy's final stretch at Leavenworth served as an appropriate reminder that Roy, now a free man, was entering a new era. So much of the news had been restricted during Roy's incarceration, and he spent time in the library catching up. He learned of Hitler's bombing and destruction of Guernica during the Spanish Civil War, and Japan's invasion of China. Hanging over everything was the intractable Great Depression.

With Sonney's assistance, Roy rented a room at the Hotel Governor on Turk Street. The area formed a stale crust around San Francisco's bustling downtown, but it was a step up in accommodations compared to the cellblocks on Alcatraz's C-D Street. The Hotel Governor was a seven-minute walk from the Glindemann Jewelry Store on Market Street, the scene of the crime that landed him in San Quentin, which in turn lit the fuse that would immolate his marriage. In an appropriate nod to Roy's aging circumstances, the Glindemann Jewelry Store also shared office space with an optometrist by the time of Roy's 1938 return.

Upon his release from Leavenworth, Roy told reporters that he wanted to visit Jean in Napa. The last time he saw her outside of a prison was when she was four years old and Roy arrived wind-weathered and road-dusty on a stolen Harley-Davidson. Now she was twenty years old, and Roy wouldn't have to strain his ears to listen for approaching police. There would be no time limits and there was no need to feel nervous, but the reunion with Jean would be filled with a different, more intangible awkwardness that Roy minimized with a steady ingestion of cigarettes, a habit that had aged him considerably over the decades. At Jean's house he would see photographs. These would be photographs that pertained to himself and his own family, but he very well might feel like a cat burglar, snooping around a stranger's belongings.

In the end, Roy didn't meet Jean at Napa, and he didn't attend her wedding, which occurred less than a month after his release from prison. It's unclear whether Roy was officially invited to her wedding or not, but he got to meet Jean and her new husband, Jack Janessi. Jack had modified his surname from the original Janofsky to avoid the rampant ethnic bigotry of the time period. Immediately after their Napa wedding, Jean and Jack went to San Francisco, so they could include Roy in the special occasion.

"Daddy?" was Jean's uncertain question upon seeing her father without a bulletproof glass divider separating them. After faltering chitchat, the trio drifted into free-flowing conversation for the next two hours, then Jean and Jack continued their honeymoon. Jean's new spouse worked for the US Forest Service in Napa. Roy could have discussed how the forests of the Northwest shielded him and provided a haven for his years on the run. He may have joked about the timing of her wedding, so close to his release from prison.

This was a bittersweet, but primarily happy, meeting for Roy. During his time on the lam he risked exposure by going back to see his family, and even if it took seventeen years, he was able to see his daughter. Jean may have felt a shame about her maiden name, Gardner, but she nonetheless sought out her father's company.

Roy was an ex-con, but Jean made a point of making sure her new husband met him.

He missed so many of Jean's milestones as she grew up, and he did not attend the wedding with Dollie nor walk Jean down the aisle, but she came to his apartment on Turk Street.

"Good-bye, Daddy," Jean said as she left, just as she did as a two-year-old on the phone with Roy, when he stood at the Sacramento train station, on his way to McNeil Island prison.

When Jean and Jack left, Roy may have wondered what to do with himself to fill the rest of the day. He could do anything now. There were the saloons and gin mills of the neighborhood where a whiskey bottle and the company of other men could help translate the murky feelings he was having into a coherent narrative, but he decided against this.

Perhaps he just stayed in his room thinking about the other convicts at Alcatraz just three miles away, as the cormorant flies. Though he was miles away, Alcatraz had an underground cable tethered to his mind. Roy would continue "hellnighting," whether free or incarcerated.

CHAPTER SEVENTY-FOUR

California

Summer 1938

When Roy first entered Leavenworth, back in the waning days of 1921, Dollie and Sonney went on their respective vaudeville tours to drum up support for Roy's brain operation.

The brain surgery never happened, but once Roy was released, he, too, took to the publicity trail behind a radio microphone, complemented with in-person theater stops. Roy's message on his shows was to inspire people to stay out of prison in the first place. Wherever Roy could get an audience, he would talk. During his tour, he made a stop at the Lions Club in Roseville, California, where he once stole $185,000 from the fast-moving Pacific Limited, only to have the loot scatter into the wind while he tried to figure out the train's emergency brake.

Roy's message for his audience: "Men who can think do not commit crimes."

"Calling All Cars," the dramatization of Roy's exploits, filled the California radio waves from KSFO in the Bay Area to KNX in Long Beach during the lingering summer days of 1938. The show wasn't intended to sensationalize Roy's daredevil escapes but to show how much he had lost for so little gain. Roy traveled to individual radio stations to elaborate and proselytize from behind the microphone, and he titled these lectures, "Crime Doesn't Pay."

"I'd blow my own head off before I'd return to crime," he told an audience in Visalia.

* * *

While making a stop in Yreka, near the Oregon border, Roy proclaimed that he wanted to shake the hand of Sheriff W. G. Chandler, a railroad officer at the time of Roy's first escape. Before Roy's repeated escapes made him a daily newspaper presence, Chandler had chased Roy in relative obscurity through the forests of Oregon until their game of whack-a-mole ended with Roy disappearing across the Canadian border en route to his reemergence in Iowa under a new identity.

Roy explained, "I have met and outwitted many officers in my time, including some of the best in the country, but I want to tell you, and with no qualifications, this man Chandler is the most fearless, efficient and persistent officer I ever met."

In response to Roy's request, Sheriff Chandler said, "He dodged me so long, it will be a pleasure to have him come voluntarily. Gardner was one of the craftiest and brainiest criminals of the present century. I have always considered that Gardner was no common criminal, but a brilliant man who for some reason got off on the wrong road. I will be glad to meet Roy Gardner again for this meeting will be vastly different than the last one."

During a lecture stop in southern California, Roy made a detour to Mesa, Arizona, to visit Herman Inderlied, the mail clerk who thwarted Roy's final train robbery attempt. Over the years Inderlied held firm to his plan of sending his son to college.

"We had a fine time and many a chuckle over that fight," Roy said of his reunion with Inderlied.

* * *

Roy's "Crime Doesn't Pay" tour became an ironic title when he signed a $20,000 contract with Universal Studios for the rights to his life story and a second movie project entitled *Hellcatraz*. He sat with reporters in Santa Ana during one of his tour stops, and upon being asked if he got to see any movies while at Alcatraz, Roy responded that the authorities occasionally allowed the prisoners to see a Shirley Temple or Roy Rogers film. The guards never showed any gangster movies, Roy explained, as "the audience would be too critical."

He reiterated his story that Al Capone was losing his mind on Alcatraz, and Roy again stressed that he himself would commit suicide before returning to a life of crime.

CHAPTER SEVENTY-FIVE

Nevada City, California

Christmas 1938

Flush with Hollywood money, Roy finished his tour and purchased property that included a ranch house in Nevada City at the base of the Sierras, not far from Roseville, the scene of his notorious train robbery. He would become a farmer.

Less than a month after making his purchase, however, a fire destroyed the house while Roy was still in San Francisco, over the Christmas holidays. It was a complete loss, with damages of $1,000 or the equivalent of $20,000.

Roy would remain at the Hotel Governor on Turk Street.

One night a woman fell past his window. He rushed down to street level, where he was the first to assist, but the fifty-year-old woman was already dead. She had fallen from a tenth story window of the Hotel Governor after a night of heavy drinking.

The year 1939 began with what felt like a curse, between the fire that destroyed Roy's nest egg and the woman who plunged to her death in front of him. On the other side of the globe, Hitler ratcheted up his war plans.

CHAPTER SEVENTY-SIX

The West Coast

Winter and Spring 1939

The United States Postal Service was never going to put Roy Gardner's face on a postage stamp, and their adversarial relationship deepened in the early days of 1939.

After the Nevada City fire destroyed Roy's investment in post-prison stability, he drifted down to Los Angeles to make appearances at both the Santa Anita Racetrack and Universal Studios, where *The Day of the Locust* author Nathanael West took the assignment to script Roy's life story. A few months earlier, Roy met a different writer, Ardith Homan, during one of his "Crime Doesn't Pay" lectures in Lodi, California.

Roy and Homan made an agreement that she would help ghostwrite Roy's life story, and his need for a ghostwriter became apparent when in March of 1939 she turned over a letter Roy wrote and mailed to her that was "too filthy" to appear in court records, according to US Attorney Carl Donaugh. Roy said the letter was sarcastic and written in a moment of anger after Homan requested additional money from Roy.

Around the time of the dispute with Ardith Homan, Louis Sonney also announced that he had "given up" on Roy over financial disagreements. Sonney said that he, too, was the recipient of Roy's written diatribes, and Roy was demanding to be paid fifty dollars a day, not just fifty dollars a week.

"I'm convinced that Roy Gardner hasn't changed," Sonney concluded. He added that the letters Roy had written to his long-time benefactor were "unprintable." The climax of the disintegration of their friendship occurred in a Los Angeles bank where the two got into a fist fight while waiting in line.

During his trip to Los Angeles, Roy inadvertently accumulated more material for a follow-up to "Crime Doesn't Pay," but the sequel could have been titled "Hollywood Doesn't Pay." Universal Studios recalibrated their contract so that Roy would now only receive $5,000, when he was initially promised $20,000, with much of the advance already gone with the Nevada City fire.

Roy took his frustration out by going to the Santa Anita Racetrack, and while his trip to the horse track didn't solve his financial headaches, he at least heeded his own "Crime Doesn't Pay" sermons and opted not to rob any mail trucks afterwards.

Roy placed his next bet on San Francisco's Golden Gate International Exposition, a colossal project on Treasure Island that served as an Art Deco foreshadowing of Disneyland. The Golden Gate International Exposition would be a last-ditch attempt to portray world harmony one year after the "Rape of Nanking" and a few months before Hitler's invasion of Poland. Roy paid for space at the Exposition to set up a stand for his "Crime Doesn't Pay" exhibit. Before he finalized the details, however, police officers arrested him in the diner next to the Hotel Governor for the Depression-era crime of sending obscene material through the US mail—in this case his angry letter to Ardith Homan. The officers cuffed him while he was eating breakfast.

"Why the irons?" Roy asked as they clicked the handcuffs. The officers reminded him that he was Roy Gardner, hence the precaution of the cuffs, but they allowed him to finish his cigarette and leave a tip for the diner staff.

Roy Gardner, former Alcatraz convict, spent a night in the more pedestrian San Francisco County Jail, and was released when he was able to post a $2,000 bond. His "Crime Doesn't Pay" exhibit was becoming a living and breathing work of performance art. Although free from a jail cell, Roy was ordered to face a judge in Oregon, where Roy had mailed the offensive letter during his lecture tour.

Oregon, the epicenter of so many of Roy's wild escapes in the 1920s, would be the scene of the fifty-something Roy soberly waiting for his federal court case in 1939. To pass the time, he scheduled a hastily arranged "Crime Doesn't Pay" lecture for a Portland audience.

As Roy waited, San Francisco was set to open the Golden Gate International Exposition on Treasure Island, the landmass that served as the mid-point and hinge of the newly completed Bay Bridge, which connected San Francisco and Oakland. Although Roy was still awaiting prosecution in Portland, he was allowed to return to San Francisco given the payment of his $2,000 bond and overall cooperation with the authorities.

Over the course of its 1939 run, the Treasure Island fair would draw in over five million visitors with its daily guarantee of "eighteen hours of fun." Roy had graduated from the island of "Hellcatraz" to Treasure Island's "Gayway," the Coney Island-inspired Midway filled with hollering barkers, food concessions, and a hundred opportunities to win prizes or lose money. A newspaper photo captured the opening of Roy's "Crime Doesn't Pay" exhibit, showing a scholarly looking Roy reading from his newly published book, *Hellcatraz*, to a group of seated young women.

Roy Gardner sold his book *Hellcatraz* at the 1939 Golden Gate International Exhibition on Treasure Island, an artificial island constructed within viewing distance of the notorious Alcatraz. The Golden Gate Expo aimed to facilitate global harmony, but the fair would close down ahead of schedule due to the opening salvo of World War II and bad weather.

Before he could get comfortable, however, he decided he needed to drive to Los Angeles to get some more items to complete his exhibit. While descending the Cuesta Grade near San Luis Obispo at dawn, Roy fractured four ribs and received facial lacerations when he collided with the back of a truck pulling a trailer, which Roy said didn't have taillights. Roy's passenger, Harry Lykke, a newspaperman from San Francisco, broke his collarbone and fractured his pelvis. The scale of Lykke's injuries would necessitate two months of hospitalization.

The car accident would be the beginning of Roy's automobile problems. Later in the fall, Roy would square off in a courtroom to face his longtime friend-turned-enemy, Louis Sonney. Sonney became acquainted with the expression "No good deed goes unpunished" when he gave Roy a car upon his release from Leavenworth, with the written promise that Roy would eventually pay him $620 for the automobile. The $620 never materialized, and when Sonney took Roy to court over the matter, Roy counterpunched with his own lawsuit, saying Sonney owed him an additional $2,900 for his labors as a salesman for Sonney's film production company.

In the end, neither man got what they wanted. Roy lost his investment in the Nevada City fire, and his habitual jaunts to the racetrack further chipped away at his wallet. He didn't have the money. Sonney had already done so much for Roy that he didn't owe him anything anymore. Alcatraz may have doomed Roy's relationship with Dollie, but his erratic and insulting behavior torpedoed his friendship with the man who had been his biggest advocate for over eighteen years.

CHAPTER SEVENTY-SEVEN

San Francisco

Summer and Autumn 1939

"The letter is vulgar, coarse and reflects the character of the defendant and the environment in which he has spent many years, but it is not criminal under this statute." This July statement from one of the jurors cleared Roy of the US Mail obscenity charge, but it was still a case of winning at losing. The money that Ardith Homan initially requested, which triggered Roy's impulsive and angry letter, paled in comparison to the fees Roy ended up paying attorneys to help clear the matter.

Roy had alienated people who could help him, and despite the popularity of the Golden Gate International Exhibition with its bottomless array of attractions—riding demonstrations by the Royal Canadian Mounted Police, performances of Shakespeare's *Taming of the Shrew*, marimba bands from Guatemala, and aviation displays that hinted at the reality of the gathering clouds of war— Roy's "Crime Doesn't Pay" exhibit was an example of crime truly not paying. He closed his booth and took a job with Tom Crowley's sightseeing boats, which were described as a "rubber necking" cruise operation that took people from the Port of the Trade Winds at Treasure Island to circle Alcatraz as close as legally allowed, with the newly hired Roy Gardner providing lurid commentary.

Although his book, *Hellcatraz,* didn't sell as well as Roy would have hoped, excerpts appeared in serial form in local newspapers throughout the summer to provide Roy with a bit of income. By early September, however, Hitler's invasion of Poland took over the news. The Great War of 1914–1918 could now be referred to as World War One, as World War Two had just begun. The Golden Gate International Exposition with its manicured gardens and namesake bridge as the backdrop would be a Technicolor Oz in contrast to the gray reality that would doom the earth for the next six years. The Golden Gate International Exposition's large overhead costs put the operation into debt despite drawing millions of people, while the unfolding war diverted resources and restricted travelers from Europe. A casual observer to the Exposition could be awed by the crowds, but the accountants noted that the Exposition fell well short of its attendance goal of twenty million visitors. The Exposition closed in late October, a month ahead of schedule, and the possibility of a springtime encore in 1940 became uncertain.

Roy was out of a steady and job and increasingly out of friends. His car crash in San Luis Obispo may have been due to the other truck not having proper lights, or maybe Roy just couldn't see well anymore. His eyes, strangled by the long-term and all-encompassing darkness in the Leavenworth and Atlanta isolation cells, were increasingly failing him. Prior to his falling out with Sonney, Roy confided to him his concerns about his worsening eyesight.

"But I'll never come around here with a tin cup in my hand," Roy said. "I'll beat nature to the punch."

In addition to his failing eyesight, Roy increasingly felt like he had one of Sonney's straitjackets tightening his chest, whether from his cigarette habit, his fractured ribs, or both. Although his world wasn't as small as a pool table-sized cell at Alcatraz, his life was shrinking to a short radius around the Hotel Governor, where the street preachers laid out their sandbags against the invading armies of sin.

CHAPTER SEVENTY-EIGHT

San Francisco

Thanksgiving 1939

A concerned parent might have thought that the film *Torchy Plays With Dynamite* was the one warning them about the perils of teenage marijuana use, but it was actually the second movie on the bill, *Tell Your Children*, that provided the goods on the cannabis scare. A dramatization of Roy Gardner's exploits, *You Can't Beat the Rap*, opened up the evening's cinematic events.

While teenagers apparently had no problem getting access to marijuana in *Tell Your Children*, the real Roy Gardner likely wouldn't find any marijuana for purchase when he walked into a San Francisco pharmacy Thanksgiving week of 1939, when the existence of Hitler and Stalin made it increasingly difficult to give thanks.

Although Roy couldn't buy any marijuana at the pharmacy, he had no problem buying a few pellets of cyanide and a jar of acid. The pharmacist reported that Roy was quite pleasant and chatty while making the ghastly purchase.

From the pharmacy, Roy went to the diner by the Hotel Governor, where the kitchen staff and waiters had become the dwindling source of companionship for Roy, and he was viewed as an amiable presence who always tipped well. He would need to ask the hotel manager for an extension on paying his rent for the upcoming month, but he would always make sure to leave a tip for the diner staff.

CHAPTER SEVENTY-NINE

Hotel Governor

January 10, 1940

The smell emanating from behind the door suggested a cigarette laced with some kind of narcotic, or perhaps a party attended by heavily perfumed streetwalkers.

The occupant smoked a lot of cigarettes for sure, but he was too old to mess around with prostitutes, and the room had been quiet all night and morning, thought Madelyn Langston, the hotel maid.

She couldn't place the smell, but it perhaps reminded her of burnt almonds. She passed by the room earlier in the morning and saw the "Do Not Disturb" sign hanging on the door handle, so she passed by and continued her cleaning rounds. She finished her other tasks by the afternoon and returned to Roy Gardner's room, where the sign still hung. It was getting late in her shift, and Mr. Gardner—he had asked her to call him Roy—always woke up at the same time each morning. She never found any empty whiskey bottles in his room, so she didn't think he was in bed with a hangover.

Maybe he left for the day and forgot to move the sign, she concluded. She gave a warning knock and announced herself. There was no response, so she knocked again, waited a few beats, and when there was no response, she entered. The strange smell became much more powerful when she opened the door, but Mr. Gardner's room was quiet and already straightened up as if Ms. Langston herself had already attended to it. A suitcase was packed and placed in a deliberate manner next to a chair with a suit neatly folded and resting on the back. On a table were pieces of paper with the names of the hotel staff, her name included, with half-dollar coins set adjacent to each name. Another sealed envelope rested on the suitcase, and everything was placed in an organized manner.

Then she saw the sign on the private bathroom door, which was closed. The sign read: "Do not open this door. Poison gas. Call police."

* * *

Police officers Jim Souscoff and Leo Martin arrived on scene and aired out the main room thoroughly before they opened the bathroom door, where they found Roy Gardner's dead body. On the bathroom sink was a water glass and the acid container Roy had purchased over a month earlier. Roy had dropped the cyanide pellets from the same pharmacy purchase into the liquid and draped a wet towel over his head while ingesting the fatal fumes.

The letter on his suitcase was addressed to local reporters and read:

> I am old and tired. I don't care to go on with the struggle any longer. There are no love affairs or disappointments. I'm just tired. I hold no malice toward any human being.
>
> I didn't think of checking out on the spur of the moment. I bought the poison two months ago. I hope all I have wronged will forgive me for it. If I had realized what the future held in store for me, I would have checked out in 1920 and saved my loved ones the disgrace and shame they have had to endure these many years.
>
> All the men who have served more than five years in prison are doomed, but they don't realize it. They kid themselves into the belief that they can come back, but they can't. There is a barrier between the ex-convict and society that can not be leveled. Every man on Alcatraz today would be better off if they would jump in the bay and start swimming for China.
>
> As a last request to the press, please do not mention my daughter's married name in connection with this, her in-laws do not know that she is my daughter, and it probably would wreck her happiness. Thanks, boys.
>
> Please let me down as lightly as possible, boys. I have always played ball with you, and now you should pitch me a slow one and let me hit it.

Roy also included instructions for his funeral arrangements which he directed to Robert Nelson, Dollie's brother living in Oakland.

He had $3.69 in his pocket, and his bank book indicated his last deposit was made back in August. His rent was overdue. Perhaps Roy Gardner had one final caper in mind to get himself out his current financial mess, but he decided otherwise. At earlier times in his life, he had held $175,000 in his hands and he was compared to Houdini. He still did seventeen years, however. That was while at the top of his game. Now he was old and tired.

CHAPTER EIGHTY

Phoenix, Arizona

January 11, 1940

Rawghlie Stanford, former governor of Arizona, sat in his law office in Phoenix while discussing the morning's news with his friend, Harry Cohn. Stanford knew Roy from Roy's Arizona escapades back in 1921, and Cohn, a Los Angeles resident, was familiar with Roy as well.

As they discussed the news of Roy's suicide, in walked a man that they recognized as Roy Gardner, who said his "hellos" and explained he wanted to discuss some legal business. Stanford commented to the visitor that he had just read of his suicide in San Francisco.

"That's the first I've heard of it; it must be slightly exaggerated," the visitor responded. In the summer and autumn of 1921, everyone had been looking in vain for Roy Gardner, and now, nearly two decades later, there seemed to be two of him. The mysterious arrival of the man looking like Roy Gardner in front of the former Arizona governor ensured that Roy received a few more newspaper articles of a spectacular nature the day after he was confirmed dead at the San Francisco morgue. In death he could still squeeze a double out of a single after getting his slow pitch. Soon enough, however, the newspapers would find other stories to write about.

CHAPTER EIGHTY-ONE

Alcatraz

Summer 2021

Visitors gradually returned to Alcatraz in the summer of 2021 after the global COVID pandemic paralyzed commerce and travel in 2020. The development of the COVID vaccine in the spring of 2021 allowed a cautious return to previous activities. Although 2,000 visitors a day to the prison-turned-park was much lower than pre-pandemic levels, the number of visitors in one summer day still surpassed the 1,576 total inmates processed at Alcatraz during its twenty-nine-year reign as a US penitentiary.

The topic of Al Capone dominates visitor inquiries to staff stationed throughout the cellhouse. Capone's monopoly on curiosity has a star power logic to it, but what of the other 1,575 convicts, all of whom had their own sorrows, tragedies, and absurdities as part of their biographies? Correctional officers once considered Charles Berta AZ #132 the toughest convict at Alcatraz. He was a season-ticket holder to the Spanish Dungeons, but he could never be broken. After Berta fulfilled his prison obligations, he returned to San Francisco to become a bartender on Mission Street.

Before he became Alcatraz inmate #209, John Carroll and his wife robbed jewelry stores and post offices throughout Montana until they were eventually caught and convicted. He went to Leavenworth. She went to a women's prison in Missouri.

Upon learning that his wife was dying from tuberculosis, Carroll persuaded a civilian superintendent at the Leavenworth shoe factory to ship him out in a moving crate with the promise that Carroll would share a portion of some buried loot he had hidden in New Orleans. The only promise Carroll kept, however, was to his wife. He wanted her to die peacefully at home rather than inside a prison, so he helped her escape. She died outside prison with Carroll at her side. He continued to rob jewelry stores and post offices but was eventually captured, earning a ticket to Alcatraz.

The summer and autumn of 2021 would be the one hundredth anniversary of most of Roy Gardner's escapes and train robberies that made him a steady presence in American and Canadian newspapers in the first chapter of the Roaring Twenties. One hundred years later his story merits a few paragraphs, maybe a few pages, in a few select encyclopedic books on Alcatraz history in the former penitentiary's museum store.

When Alcatraz visitors aren't asking about Al Capone, they tend to ask about ghosts. Supposedly, the phantom of Alvin Karpis, sometimes known as "Creepy Karpis," lurks in the Alcatraz dining hall. But why would Creepy Karpis, the convict who logged the most years on Alcatraz, return as a phantom to the place that caused so much grief? Once Karpis completed his prison obligations, he left the United States, and it could be safely argued that he broadcast his preferred location to spend his afterlife when he went to sleep in Torremolinos, Spain, the night of his death.

It is rumored that Al Capone's ghost can be heard plucking a banjo near the Alcatraz shower room, which was adjacent to the music room where the prison band, The Rock Islanders, rehearsed. Capone's ghost supposedly hovers around Alcatraz despite the fact that he died at his Florida mansion, ten years after his transfer off Alcatraz.

To answer the question as to whether Alcatraz is haunted, it might first be necessary to define what a ghost is. A ghost might not be the presence of a phantom, but the absence of a mortal human being, which in turn generates an emotional hunger. A haunted locale could be a purgatory of memories that a living person hasn't been able to make reconciliation with. In this case, the visitation room of Alcatraz might be its most haunted location. It is the graveyard of marriages—as was the case with Dollie and Roy Gardner. Dollie Gardner once visited her husband there, and now she doesn't.

In the early mornings before any visitors arrive to Alcatraz, a gentle light sifts its way into the cellhouse through the barred skylights to make the center corridor of Broadway Avenue feel like an empty church. There is a silence that doesn't suggest ghosts, but an absence. The only ghosts on Alcatraz are the shadows of the broken hearts, and the quiet is the reminder of everyone who is no longer there.

Epilogue

Although their friendship ended in a fistfight while waiting in line at a bank, **Louis Sonney** continued to entertain people with the story of how he arrested Roy Gardner in Centralia, Washington, back in 1921. Sonney remained in Los Angeles during the 1940s in support of his film production company. He had a stroke and died in Portland, Oregon, in 1949, while on a business trip. He was sixty-one years old. Elmer McCurdy, the mummified outlaw who was part of Sonney's wax museum show, received a proper burial in Oklahoma in 1977.

Shortly after Roy's death, **Dollie Parkes** filed a libel lawsuit against Universal Studios claiming that the Roy Gardner-inspired film, *I Stole a Million,* inaccurately portrayed her as an ex-convict and active participant in Roy's criminal exploits.

She continued to work at Napa State Hospital until her retirement in 1957. During her tenure, she became an authority and historian on the evolution of the hospital's mental health services. She started a recreation dance program for patients, in addition to establishing a low-cost resource called the Dollie Shop, later renamed the Dollie Parkes Clothing Center. Dollie and William Parkes remained married until she passed away in 1979 at the age of eighty-two. Her obituary made no mention of Roy Gardner.

Jean Janofsky, daughter of Dollie and Roy Gardner, was a co-plaintiff in Dollie's libel lawsuit against Universal Studios. Jean's husband, Jack, worked as a meteorologist and they lived in Missoula, Montana, and Redlands, California, before eventually settling in Los Angeles, their home for fifty years. They had a daughter, Gael, who still lived in Oakland as of 2023. Jean died of pneumonia in 1995 at the age of seventy-seven.

William Parkes entered an elite club of World War I veterans who lived beyond their 100th birthdays. He would be the last surviving member of his regiment. French General Consul Gérard Coste bestowed Parkes with the National Order of the Legion of Honor when he was 104 years old. He died in Napa, his home for seventy years, in 2002, at the age of 106.

Acknowledgments

The author would like to thank the following for their support and inspiration:

Brandon Allen, Fred Auda, Jolene Babyak, Bill Baker, Hannah Baldwin, Benny Batom, Alice Bennett, Kathy Bennett, Melanie Born, Kayla Brecheen, Susan Canavan, John Cantwell, Chupa, Jamie Clark, Lee Cline, Tim Costigan, Lisa Crane, Tad Crawford, Brent Cunningham, Johnny Davis, Jason De León, Kevin DeMattia, Joe Donohoe, Susanne Dyckman, Olivia Emerson, Michael Esslinger, Dan Fine, Kevin Finnerty, Kristi Friesen, Mel Gragirena, Cynthia Grant, Annemarie Heineman, Gael Janofsky, Sarah Janssen, Naomi Jelks-Glaser, Z'ev Jenerik, Steven Keena, Christopher Key, Greg Kim, Amy Kirby, Jonathan Lemon, Kim Madsen, Liam Martin, Patrick McAllister, Mike Mehaffy, John Moran, D'Marco Parrilla, Tom Ryan, Vanessa Sacks, Cynthia Schreiner-Smith, Edwin Serra, Hal Smith, Alex Soriano, Donna Spinola, Mary Beth Stone, Chris Tubbs, Joe Wicht, Wilburn Williams, Jill Winters, and Mary Yang.

It has been an honor and a privilege working with the staff and volunteers at Project Open Hand and the Golden Gate National Parks Conservancy.

An additional huge thanks to Mom, John, Dave, and Dad, all of whom are incredible storytellers who have taught me a few tricks.

And of course, a gigantic thank you to Sarah and Seamus. Their love and support during this process is immeasurable.

Notes and Bibliography

A note on name spellings: newspaper accounts of the time often used "Dolly" when referring to Dollie Gardner and "Sonny" when referencing Louis Sonney. The "Dollie" and "Sonney" spellings used throughout this book reflect the spellings used in their respective obituaries.

BOOKS

Asbury, Herbert. *The Barbary Coast: An Informal History of The San Francisco Underworld.* New York: Basic Books, 2002, originally published in 1933.

Beacher, Milton Daniel. *Alcatraz Island: Memoirs of a Rock Doc.* Lebanon, NJ: Pelican Island Publishing, 2001.

Bowen, Robert R. *San Francisco's Presidio.* San Francisco: Arcadia Publishing, 2005.

Bukowski, Charles. *Notes of A Dirty Old Man.* San Francisco: City Lights, 2001.

Davis, Bob and Brian Clune. *Ghosts and Legends of Alcatraz.* Charleston: The History Press, 2019.

De León, Jason. *The Land of Open Graves.* Oakland: University of California Press, 2015.

Ellsworth, Scott. *The Ground Breaking: An American City and its Search for Justice.* New York: Dutton, 2021.

Esslinger, Michael. *Alcatraz: A History of the Penitentiary Years.* Marina: Ocean View Publishing, 2003.

Esslinger, Michael. *Letters from Alcatraz.* Marina: Ocean View Publishing, 2015.

Fanning, Branwell, and William Wong. *Images of America: Angel Island.* San Francisco: Arcadia Publishing, 2007.

Flamm, Jerry. *Good Life in Hard Times: San Francisco in the '20s and '30s.* San Francisco: Chronicle Books, 1978.

Hinckle, Warren. *The Big Strike.* Virginia City: Silver Dollar Books, 1985.

Jackson, Joe. *Leavenworth Train: A Fugitive's Search for Justice in the Vanishing West.* New York: Carroll & Graf Publishers, 2001.

Johnson, Jenell. *American Lobotomy.* Ann Arbor: University of Michigan Press, 2014.

Jones, Gregg. *Honor in the Dust: Theodore Roosevelt, War in the Philippines, and the Rise and Fall of America's Imperial Dream.* London: Penguin, 2012.

Karnow, Stanley. *In Our Image, America's Empire in the Philippines.* New York: Penguin Random House, 1990.

Kennedy, Patricia. *Images of America: San Francisco, California*. Chicago: Arcadia Publishing, 2001.

Kerouac, Jack. *On The Road*. New York: Viking Press, 1957.

Lamaster, Kenneth M. *Leavenworth Seven*. Charleston: The History Press, 2019.

Lieberman, Daniel Z., and Michael E. Long. *The Molecule of More: How a Single Chemical in Your Brain Drives Love, Sex and Creativity—And Will Determine the Fate of the Human Race*. Dallas: BenBella Books, 2018.

Luke, Robert. *Entombed in Alcatraz*. USA: Robert Victor Luke, 2011.

Madigan, Tim. *The Burning: Massacre, Destruction, and The Tulsa Race Riot of 1921*. New York: Thomas Dunne Books, 2001.

Oaks, Robert F. *Images of America: San Francisco's Fillmore District*. San Francisco: Arcadia Publishing, 2005.

Parkes, Colin Murray. *Bereavement: Studies of Grief in Adult Life*. Oxfordshire, UK: Routledge, 2009.

Posnanski, Joe. *The Life and Afterlife of Harry Houdini*. New York: Simon and Schuster, 2019.

Ryan, Tom. *Roy Gardner: My Story/Hellcatraz*. USA: Douglas/Ryan Communication, 2000.

Shogan, Robert. *The Battle of Blair Mountain: The Story of America's Largest Labor Uprising*. New York: Basic Books, 2006.

Starr, Kevin. *Golden Gate: The Life and Times of America's Greatest Bridge*. New York: Bloomsbury Press, 2010.

Svenhold, Mark. *Elmer McCurdy, The Misadventures in Life and Afterlife of an American Outlaw*. New York: Basic Books, 2002.

Thomas, Gordon, and Max Morgan Witts. *The San Francisco Earthquake*. New York: Stein and Day Publishers, 1971.

Tuchman, Barbara W. *The Zimmerman Telegram*. New York: Random House, 1957.

Ungaretti, Lorri. *Images of America: San Francisco's Sunset District*. Chicago: Arcadia Publishing, 2003.

Ward, David A. *Alcatraz: The Gangster Years*. Berkeley and Los Angeles: University of California Press, 2009.

DISCOGRAPHY

Cash, Johnny. *Johnny Cash at San Quentin*. New York: Columbia Records, 1969.

Ronstadt, Linda. *Canciones de Mi Padre*. New York: Elektra/Asylum Records, Rhino, 1987.

Vargas, Chavela. *Colección de Oro*. Mexico: Discos Orfeón, 1999.

CHAPTER NOTES

PROLOGUE, San Francisco, January 1940
"Ex-Robber Arranged His Own Funeral." *San Francisco Chronicle*, 12 January 1940, p. 1+. Chestnut, James G. "Train Bandit, Old, Ill, Dies By Gas." *The San Francisco Call-Bulletin*, 11 January 1940, p. 1+.
McArdle, Kenneth. "Mail Robber Turns Room Into Lethal Cell, Executes Self." *San Francisco Chronicle*, 11 January 1940, p. 1+.
"Respite from Rain Today; More on Way." *The San Francisco Examiner*, 4 January 1940, p. 1.
Bay Area Census. http://www.bayareacensus.ca.gov/counties/SanFranciscoCounty 40.htm. http://www.bayareacensus.ca.gov/counties/SanFranciscoCounty50.htm.
"Alcatraz." *Lincoln News Messenger*, 13 July 1939, p. 3.
"S.F. Fair's Fate Still Undecided." *Red Bluff Tehama County Daily News*, 30 October 1939, p. 1.
"Director's Statement On Exposition Closing." *The San Francisco Examiner*, 29 September 1939, p. 19.
Dashiell Hammett Apartment, 891 Post St. https://www.markcoggins.com/891 -post-street/.
Baer, Arthur "Bugs." "The B Girl." *The San Francisco Examiner*, 10 August 1938, p. 22.
Baer, Arthur "Bugs." "White Slave's Story Brings Big Vice Raids." *The San Francisco Examiner*, 26 January 1938, p. 1+.
Baer, Arthur "Bugs." "All Russ Can Get Out of Finland is Ice for Headache!" *The San Francisco Examiner*, 4 January 1940, p. 1.
Baer, Arthur "Bugs." "Rush Your Help for Hard Pressed Finns." *The San Francisco Examiner*, 4 January 1940 p. 1.
Bindman, Lou. "Bindman's Selections, At Santa Anita." *The San Francisco Examiner*, 4 January 1940, p. 24.
"Seabiscuit, Kayak II to Pass Up." *The San Francisco Examiner*, 4 January 1940, p. 24.

PART ONE Opening Quote
United Press. "Says Gardner A Bad, Bad Boy." *The Sacramento Star*, 17 November, 1921, p. 7.

CHAPTER ONE, Vallejo and the Bay Area, The First World War
Wells, Evelyn. "Story of Roy Gardner, Told by Wife." *The San Francisco Call*, 18 June 1921, p. 1+.
McGee, Agnes. "Roy Will Always Plan Break: Says Mrs. Gardner; Wife of Train Robber at S.J. Hospital." *Stockton Independent*, 4 July 1929, p. 1.

"Marine Force Is To Be Increased, Will Go to Mare Island When Appropriation Bill Passes-Two Vallejo Weddings." *San Francisco Chronicle*, 2 June 1916, p. 6.

Obituary. "Robert P. Nelson." *The Napa Valley Register*, 16 January 1967, p. 4.

"A Sudden Death." *Napa Journal*, 18 September 1914, p. 5.

Reed, Alma. "My Life With Roy Gardner, By His Wife, As She Told It to Alma Reed, Chapter I." *Los Angeles Evening Express*, 23 June 1921, p. 1+.

"Police Seek Firebugs." *The San Francisco Examiner*, 16 May 1917, p. 8.

Saunders, Wallace. "The Ballad of Casey Jones." genius.com, https://genius.com /Wallace-saunders-the-ballad-of-casey-jones-lyrics.

Glassford, Alec. "South San Francisco Hillside Sign." foundsf.org, https://www .foundsf.org/index.php?title=South_San_Francisco_Hillside_Sign.

Reed, Alma. "My Life With Roy Gardner, By His Wife, As She Told It To Alma Reed, Chapter II." *Los Angeles Evening Express*, 24 June 1921, p. 23.

Reed, Alma. "My Life With Roy Gardner, By His Wife, As She Told It To Alma Reed, Chapter III." *Los Angeles Evening Express*, 25 June 1921, p. 2.

"Mary Pickford Speeds Up Bonds Sales," *San Francisco Examiner*, 8 October 1918, p. 13.

"Automobiles For Sale." *San Francisco Examiner*, 3 November 1918, p. 34.

Reed, Alma. "My Life With Roy Gardner, By His Wife, As She Told It To Alma Reed, Chapter IV," *Los Angeles Evening Express*, 27 June 1921, p. 21.

CHAPTER TWO, San Francisco and the Philippines, 1900–1906

Chesley, Kate. "First Transcontinental Railroad and Stanford forever linked." *Stanford News*, https://news.stanford.edu/2019/05/08/first-transcontinental-rail road-stanford-forever-linked/, 8 May 2019.

Tennyson, Lord Alfred. "The Charge of the Light Brigade." poetryfoundation.org.

Lepley, Robert E. "Roy Gardner, U.S. Mail Bandit, Was Excellent Soldier, Says Police Captain He Served With." *The El Paso Times*, 12 November 1922, p. 5.

Robinson, Douglas. "Song My Massacre Not Unique in United States Army History." *San Bernardino County Sun*, 23 December 1969, p. 15.

Rare Historical Photos. "US soldiers pose with the bodies of Moro insurgents, Philippines, 1906." 25 November 2021, https://rarehistoricalphotos.com/moro -insurgents-1906/.

CHAPTER THREE, Gallup, New Mexico, and Bisbee, Arizona, 1906–1908

Federal Bureau of Investigation. "A Brief History." fbi.gov/history/brief-history.

Crime Scene Forensics. "History of Fingerprints." http://www.crimescene-forensics .com/History_of_Fingerprints.html.

Broadhead Mine Explosion. "The Gazette's Special State News Service." *The Weekly Gazette* (Colorado Springs, Colorado), 7 August 1902, p. 3.

Bowen Mine Explosion. "All The News From All The World: Local." *The Weekly Gazette* (Colorado Springs, Colorado), 14 August 1902, p. 4.

C.F.I. Mine Explosion. "The Worst Disaster In Western Mining." *Arizona Republican*, 1 February 1910, p. 1.

Snake and Opportunity Mine. "Mining Activity of Hillsboro." *The Santa Fe New Mexican*, 16 May 1906, p. 8.

"Awful Explosion at Denn, More Than Ten Tons of Dynamite Explode." *Bisbee Daily Review*, 5 January 1907, p. 1.

"Only Those Who Can Show No Connection With IWW Organization Are Allowed to Remain in District." *Albuquerque Morning Journal*, 19 July 1917, p. 2.

"Life Story of Roy Gardner Is Told In Trial In Federal Court." *Arizona Republican*, 8 December 1921, p. 1+.

CHAPTER FOUR, Northern Mexico, The Revolution, 1908–1909

The Editors of Encyclopaedia Britannica. "Venustiano Carranza." britannica.com, https://www.britannica.com/biography/Venustiano-Carranza.

Ascarza, William. "1906 strike signaled change at the Cananea Mines operated by Col. Greene." *The Arizona Daily Star*, 3 June 2013, tucson.com.

"Ysabel May Have To Explain To Diaz." *El Paso Herald*, 4 June 1906, p. 1.

Rojas, Diana. "Hermosillo and Belo Horizonte make CDP A grade as two of Latin America's greenest cities." reutersevents.com, 3 April 2020.

La cárcel de Cananea. https://en.google-info.in/21743435/1/la-carcel-de-cananea.html.

Perry, Ray Sumner. "Roy Gardner As I Knew Him." *Oakland Tribune Magazine*, 17 December 1922, p. 5+.

Uenuma, Francine. "During the Mexican-American War, Irish-Americans Fought for Mexico in the St. Patrick's Battalion." smithsonianmag.com, https://www.smithsonianmag.com/history/mexican-american-war-irish-immigrants-deserted-us-army-fight-against-america-180971713/, 15 March 2019.

CHAPTER FIVE, The West, 1909–1910

"Says Rockefeller Responsible for Colorado Disorder." *The Fresno Morning Republican*, 30 August 1915, p. 3.

Gentile, Jay. "Weed Town, USA: How Marijuana Rescued the Town of Trinidad, Colorado." hightimes.com, 18 June 2018.

"M. Bannon Wins Championship from Texas-Three Fast Bouts." *Oklahoma City Daily Pointer*, 9 September 1909, p. 3.

"Jack Johnson." britannica.com https://www.britannica.com/biography/Jack-Johnson.

"'Stop That Fight' Says Governor Gillett." *The Fresno Morning Republican*, 16 June 1910, p. 1.

"$7,500,000 is Asked for World's Fair." *The San Francisco Examiner*, 17 June 1910, p. 1+.

"Sporting World Waits for the Fourth of July." *The Sacramento Bee*, 2 July 1910, p. 2.

"Letter of Governor to Attorney-General. It is Time to Stop These Outrages, He Says." *The San Francisco Examiner*, 16 June 1910, p.2.

"Mayor McCarthy is Real Mad." *Santa Cruz Evening News*, 16 June 1910, p. 1.

CHAPTER SIX, San Francisco and San Quentin, 1910–1913

"Tetrazinni to Sing in Street at Gate." *The Los Angeles Times*, 22 December 1910, p. 2.

"Daring Diamond Thief a Mystery to the Police." *San Francisco Chronicle*, 24 December 1910, p. 3.

Tikkanen, Amy. "San Quentin State Prison." britannica.com, https://www.britannica.com/topic/San-Quentin-State-Prison.

"Palace of Fine Arts to be Built of Concrete." *The Recorder* (San Francisco), 8 December 1913, p. 1.

PART TWO Opening Quote

"Quixotic Train Robber Looks and Acts His Part, Interviewer Finds." *Arizona Republican*, 17 November 1921, p. 9.

CHAPER SEVEN, Tijuana and San Diego, Spring 1920

"Plan for a New Monte Carlo." *Petaluma Daily Morning Courier*, 13 July 1919, p. 1.

"San Diego Wants No Nearby Monte Carlo." *Sacramento Bee*, 1 October 1919, p. 21.

Williams, Fred. "American Gambler Kings Await Turn of Political Cards in Mexico- Seeking the Tijuana Prize." *Stockton Daily Evening Record*, 18 August 1920, p. 11.

"Tijuana Races." *San Francisco Chronicle*, 21 April 1920, p. 11.

Reed, Alma. "My Life With Roy Gardner, By His Wife As She Told It To Alma Reed, Chapter VI." *Los Angeles Evening Express*, 29 June 1921, p. 30.

Kedrosky, Davis. "In the Shadow of the Slump: The Depression of 1920–1921." *Berkeley Economic Review*, 18 March 1921, https://econreview.berkeley.edu/in-the-shadow-of-the-slump-the-depression-of-1920–1921/.

"Quick Action Promised to Lower H.C.L. (High Cost of Living)." *The San Francisco Examiner*, 5 August 1919, p. 1.

"Utilize Land To Solve High Costs." *The Fresno Morning Republican*, 24 September 1919, p. 4.

Associated Press. "Big Postal Robbery by Lone Bandit." *Los Angeles Evening Express*, 28 April 1920, p. 1.

"Liquor Cache 20 Miles Out From Coast is Seized." *Los Angeles Evening Express*, 28 April 1920. p. 1.

Associated Press. "Red Peril Increases, Is Charge in Senate." *Los Angeles Evening Express*, 28 April 1920, p. 1.

Wooster, April. "From fezzes to secret rituals: A Field Guide to Shriners." *The Journal, The News Source for Downtown and Northeast Minneapolis Residents*,

30 June 2003, https://www.journalmpls.com/from-fezzes-to-secret-rituals-a-field
-guide-to-shriners/.

"Officers Recover Valuable Letters." *The Los Angeles Times*, 30 April 1920, p. 20.

"Alleged Mail Bandit Denies His Guilt." *Santa Ana Register*, 30 April 1920, p. 1.

"Admits Part In Mail Loot." *The Los Angeles Times*, 1 May 1920, p. 24.

"Capture of Carranza Now Officially Confirmed." *The Los Angeles Times*, 11 May 1920, p. 1.

CHAPTER EIGHT, Napa and San Diego, April and May 1920

Reed, Alma. "My Life With Roy Gardner, By His Wife As She Told It to Alma Reed. Chapter VII." *Los Angeles Evening Express*, 30 June 1921, p. 27.

Reed, Alma. "My Life With Roy Gardner, By His Wife As She Told It to Alma Reed. Chapter VIII." *Los Angeles Evening Express*, 1 July 1 1921, p. 27.

"Roy Gardner Indicted For Big Mail Theft." *Los Angeles Evening Express*, 8 May 1920, p. 28.

CHAPTER NINE, Los Angeles and Sacramento, June 1 to 5, 1920

"Long Term for Looting Mails." *The Los Angeles Times*, 25 May 1920, p. 30.

Reed, Alma. "My Life With Roy Gardner, By His Wife As She Told It to Alma Reed. Chapter IX." *Los Angeles Evening Express*, 2 July 1921, p. 7.

CHAPTER TEN, Oregon, June 7, 1920

"Federal Prisoners Bind Guards, Make Escape from Train." *The Sacramento Bee*, 8 June 1920, p. 4.

CHAPTER ELEVEN, Napa, June 1920

Associated Press. "Another Policeman Killed in Ireland." *Los Angeles Evening Express*, 14 June 1920, p. 1.

"Los Angeles Shaken Up by Earthquake." *The Daily Telegram* (Long Beach, California), 18 June 1920, p. 1.

Associated Press. "Escaped Chinese Prisoner Captured." *The Los Angeles Times*, 10 June 1920, p. 1.

"No Trace of Mail Robber Gardner is Found in Oregon." *Long Beach Press*, 15 June 1920, p. 2.

Reed, Alma. "My Life With Roy Gardner, By His Wife As She Told It to Alma Reed. Chapter X." *Los Angeles Evening Express*, 4 July 1921, p. 19.

Stoddard, Lathrop. "'Crisis of Ages' in War of Colored Races Versus White, Says Stoddard." *The San Francisco Examiner*, 20 June 1920, p. 17.

CHAPTER TWELVE, Parts Unknown, Summer and Autumn 1920

Pitt, Leonard M., "Los Angeles, CA. The 1920s and 30s." brittanica.com, https://www.britannica.com/place/Los-Angeles-California/The-1920s-and-30s.

"Roy Gardner Safe in Europe, Report." *Weekly Times Advocate* (Escondido, CA), 6 August 1920, p. 8.

CHAPTER THIRTEEN, Davenport, Iowa, Autumn 1920 to Winter 1921
Reed, Alma. "My Life With Roy Gardner, By His Wife As She Told It to Alma Reed. Chapter XII." *Los Angeles Evening Express*, 6 July 1921, p. 21.

CHAPTER FOURTEEN, Napa, May 11, 1921
Zagorsky, Jay L. "Rise and fall of the landline: 143 years of telephones becoming more accessible-and smart." The conversation.com. https://theconversation .com/rise-and-fall-of-the-landline-143-years-of-telephones-becoming-more -accessible-and-smart-113295. 14 March 2019.
Reed, Alma. "My Life With Roy Gardner, By His Wife As She Told It to Alma Reed. Chapter XI." *Los Angeles Evening Express*, 5 July 1921, p. 21.
Reed, Alma. "My Life With Roy Gardner, By His Wife As She Told It to Alma Reed. Chapter XII." *Los Angeles Evening Express*, 6 July 1921, p. 21.

CHAPTER FIFTEEN, Roseville to Newcastle, California, May 20 to May 24, 1921
"Mail Clerk Says Gardner is Bandit." *The Sacramento Bee*, 21 May 1921, p. 17+.
Rocklin/Roseville Car Accident. "Auburn Lions Club." *The Placer Herald*, 24 September 1938, p. 3.
"Daring Convict Escapes Again." *The Tacoma Daily Ledger*, 23 May 1921. p. 1.
Associated Press. "Robber Takes Great Chance and Succeeds." *The San Bernardino County Sun*, 21 May 1921, p. 1.
$5,000 Reward. "Lone Bandit Boards, Robs Mail Train." *Modesto Morning Herald*, 21 May 1921, p. 1.
"Blame Train Robbery to Fugitive Bandit, Authorities Believe Lone Man Who Looted Mail Car is Roy Gardner." *Norfolk Daily News* (Nebraska), 21 May 1921, p. 1.
"Some Slips And A Few Slaps." *The Californian* (Salinas, California), 23 May 1929, p. 2.
"Gardner Claims He Can Prove Alibi In Court." *The Sacramento Bee*, 27 May 1921, p. 1+.
"Bandit Gardner and Wife Make First Statements." *The Sacramento Bee*, 25 May 1921, p. 1.
"Jail Break Planned By Roy Gardner With Razor Blade Smuggled In Cell." *The Sacramento Bee*, 26 May 1921, p. 1.

CHAPTER SIXTEEN, Sacramento, May 29, 1921
Associated Press. "Gardner Admits Robbery." *The Los Angeles Times*, May 29, 1921, p. 1.
"Gardner Starts for Prison Tonight." *The Sacramento Bee*, 2 June 1921, p. 16.

CHAPTER SEVENTEEN, San Francisco, June 1, 1921
"Mrs. Gardner Loyal to Mail Bandit." *The San Francisco Examiner*, 26 May 1921, p. 3.

Associated Press. "Bandit To Try Escape Once More." *The Los Angeles Times,* June 2, 1921, p. 7.

"Holohan Voices Chagrin Over Bandit's Coup." *San Francisco Chronicle,* 12 June 1921, p.4.

CHAPTER EIGHTEEN, Sacramento, June 10, 1921

"Gardner Led A Party Around." *The Sacramento Star,* June 10, 1921, p. 2.

John, Finn J.D. "Brutal Oregon Boot made our state prison infamous." offbeatoregon. com, https://offbeatoregon.com/1403b.oregon-boot-cruel-unusual-punishment .html, 9 March 2014.

CHAPTER NINETEEN, Washington State, June 11, 1921.

"Officers Held Up, Robbed of $200 and Handcuffed." *The Sacramento Bee,* June 11, 1921, p. 1.

"Gardner's Freedom Won With Hidden Revolver; Deputies Depict Escape." *The San Francisco Examiner,* 13 June 1921, p. 1.

CHAPTER TWENTY, Castle Rock, Washington, June 11, 1921

"Posses In Pursuit of Fugitives." *The Tacoma Daily Ledger* (Tacoma, Washington), 12 June 1921, p. 1+.

"Gardner's Escape Cause of Much Comment Here." *The Sacramento Star,* 11 June 1921, p. 1.

"Roy Gardner, Mail Robber, Escapes Again." *The Oregon Daily Journal,* 11 June 1921, p. 1+.

"Mail Bandit Escapes from Two Guards." *The Long Beach Daily Telegram,* 11 June 1921, p.1.

"Gardner Outlined Plan of Escape to Movie Writer In Front of Guards." *The Sacramento Bee,* 13 June 1921, p. 2.

"Deputies Investigate Visits to Prisoner." *San Francisco Chronicle,* 12 June 1921, p. 4.

The Editors of Encyclopedia Britannica, "Mount Saint Helens." britannica.com. https://www.britannica.com/place/Mount-Saint-Helens.

CHAPTER TWENTY-ONE, Centralia, Washington, June 13, 1921

"The Traveling Salesman." *The Seattle Star,* 14 June 1921, p. 3.

Centralia. https://www.cityofcentralia.com/Page.asp?NavID=752.

Beda, Steven C., "Why the massacre at Centralia 100 years ago is critically important today." *The Washington Post,* https://www.washingtonpost.com /outlook/2019/11/11/why-massacre-centralia-years-ago-is-critically-important -today/, 11 November 2019.

Portland Beavers. "Pacific Coast League." *The Bellingham Herald* (Bellingham, Washington), 13 June 1921, p. 5.

"Bandit is Believed Circled." *The News Tribune* (Tacoma, Washington), 13 June 1921, p. 1+.

"Laughs at Locks and Law Officers." *Saskatoon Daily Star* (Saskatoon, Saskatchewan, Canada), 11 June 1921, p. 1.

"Mail Car Bandit Escapes Officers." *The Brattleboro Daily Reformer* (Brattleboro, Vermont), 11 June 1921, p. 1.

"Bandit Holds Up Officers: Makes Escape." *The Tampa Times*, 11 June 1921, p. 1.

Roy Gardner in Iowa Newspapers. *Quad-City Times* (Davenport, Iowa), 13 June 1921, p. 9.

"Roy Gardner's Pal is Retaken After Escape." *Des Moines Tribune*, 13 June 1921, p. 2.

"Last Night's News in Tabloid Form." *The Gazette* (Cedar Rapids, Iowa), 13 June 1921, p.6.

"Dalton, Ex-Outlaw, Advises Gardner to Surrender." *The Oregon Daily Journal*, 15 June 1921, p. 18.

"Mrs. Gardner Wishes Her Escaped Husband Luck." *The Oregon Daily Journal*, 11 June 1921, p. 2.

CHAPTER TWENTY-TWO, Centralia, Washington, June 15, 1921

"7,000 Pounds of Free Fish Available Here." *The Seattle Star*, 3 June 1921, p. 19.

"Woman's Curiosity Traps Mail Bandit." *Santa Cruz Evening News*, 25 June 1921, p. 3.

CHAPTER TWENTY-THREE, Centralia, Washington, June 16, 1921

"Bandit Gardner Is Captured Without Sign of Fight." *Reno Gazette-Journal*, 16 June 1921, p. 1.

"Woman Outwits Bandit Roy Gardner." *Oregon Daily Journal*, 17 June 1921, p. 6.

"Gardner Is Delighted That Chase Is at End." *The San Francisco Examiner*, 17 June 1921, p. 2.

"Man Had Been There 3 Days, He Says." *The Sacramento Star*, 16 June 1921, p. 1.

"Train Bandit Caught In Washington After Five Days' Search." *The Sacramento Bee*, 16 June 1921, p.1.

"Gardner Is Caught In Centralia." *The Oregon Daily Journal*, 16 June 1921, p. 1+.

"Roy Gardner, Mail Bandit, Is Captured Without Fight In Hotel At Centralia." *The Pomona Progress Bulletin*, 16 June 1921, p. 1+.

"Arch Bandit Recaptured in Centralia." *The San Francisco Examiner*, 17 June 1921, p. 1+.

CHAPTER TWENTY-FOUR, US Penitentiary, McNeil Island, Washington State, June 18, 1921.

Associated Press, "Gardner Had Chicken." *The Bellingham Herald* (Bellingham, Washington), 17 June 1921, p. 1.

"McNeil Island History." Department of Corrections Washington State, https://www.doc.wa.gov/about/agency/history/micc.htm.

"Bloodhounds on the Trail, Albert Bell Escapes from McNeil's Island Prison." *The Evening Statesman* (Walla Walla, Washington), 23 March 1905, p. 1.

"Was Hidden Under Hay." *Spokane Chronicle*, 25 March 1905, p. 1.

"Sylvia Pankhurst Freed." *Independence Daily Reporter* (Independence, Kansas), 18 June 1921, p. 12.

"Bandit 'At Home' On Island." *The News Tribune* (Tacoma, Washington), 17 June 1921, p. 1+.

A Prison Comrade of Roy Gardner, "Gardner Has Money Says Ex-Prison Pal." *Los Angeles Evening Post-Record*, 7 September 1921, p. 1.

Metcalf, Elliot, "Gardner, Bandit, Boxed in the N.W." *The News Tribune* (Tacoma, Washington), 8 September 1921, p.16.

"Gardner's Cache Pure Fiction." *Morning Register* (Eugene, Oregon), 19 June 1921, p. 7.

"Broadway Methodist South. What Should Roy Gardner Do To Become a Christian?" *The Chico Enterprise*, 18 June 1921, p. 5.

United News. "Gardner's Wife Is 'True Blue' Woman." *The Des Moines Register*, 18 June 1921, p. 3.

CHAPTER TWENTY-FIVE, The West Coast, Summer 1921

"Gardner Reward Not Yet Paid; Captors Must Wait for Cash." *San Francisco Chronicle*, 3 July 1921, p. 8.

"Await Money For Capture." *The Fresno Morning Republican*, 20 July 1920, p. 12.

"Northwest Notes." *The Beaver County News* (Milford, Utah), 6 July 1921, p. 7.

CHAPTER TWENTY-SIX, McNeil Island Penitentiary, July 1921

"No Home Runs in League at McNeil Island." *The Tacoma Daily Ledger*, 12 July 1921, p. 1.

"Operation Asked by Roy Gardner." *The Tacoma Daily Ledger*, 1 July 1921, p. 1.

"Surgical Cure of Rogues." *San Francisco Chronicle*, 4 July 1921, p. 18.

"Ring Down the Curtain." *Stockton Daily Evening Record*, 7 July 1921, p. 16.

"Captor Visits Roy Gardner." *The Tacoma Daily Ledger*, 19 July 1921, p. 10.

CHAPTER TWENTY-SEVEN, McNeil Island Penitentiary, Labor Day 1921

I.N.S., "Secy. Davis in Plea to Nation." *The Chattanooga News*, 5 September 1921, p. 1.

"Championship Swimming and Diving Events, Labor Day." *The Tacoma Daily Ledger*, 4 September 1921, p. 12.

"Train Robber, Famous for Clever Breaks for Liberty, Escapes from Federal Men." *Statesman Journal* (Eugene, Oregon), 6 September 1921, p. 1+.

"Daring Fugitive May be on Mainland; Hunt on Island is Failure." *The Seattle Star*, 6 September 1921, p. 1+.

"Had Guards 'Fixed.'" *The Bellingham Herald* (Bellingham, Washington), 7 September 1921 p. 8.

Star Staff Special, "Prison Pal of Gardner's Tells Star How Bandit Calmly Planned Escape." *The Seattle Star*, 9 September 1921, p. 1+.

"Man Hunt Will Extend Today to Mainland." *San Francisco Chronicle*, 7 September 1921, 1+.

"Bandit Roy Gardner Still is at Liberty." *The Sacramento Bee*, 7 September 1921, p. 1+.

CHAPTER TWENTY-EIGHT, San Francisco, September 7, 1921

"Monte Cristo's Escape Outdone by Roy Gardner." *New York Herald*, 25 September 1921, p. 81.

"Mrs. Gardner Sorry." *Medford Mail Tribune* (Medford, Oregon), 6 September 1921, p. 8.

Associated Press Night Wire, "Daredevil Swimmer." *The Los Angeles Times*, 7 September 1921, p. 3.

CHAPTER TWENTY-NINE, McNeil Island?, Mid-September 1921

Associated Press, "Posse on McNeil Island Gets Trace of Fugitive Through Mystery Shots." *Los Angeles Evening Express*, 8 September 1921, p. 1.

"Net Closing on Gardner Says Warden." *The San Francisco Examiner*, 14 September 1921, p. 1.

"United Press, "Hunt for Gardner More Like a Farce." *The News-Review* (Roseburg, Oregon), 15 September 1921, p. 1.

"Gardner Will Shoot If Trapped, Says Sleuth." *The San Francisco Examiner*, 9 September 1921, p. 2.

"Roy Gardner is Uninjured." *The San Francisco Examiner*, 18 September 1921, p. 14.

"Prohibition Making U.S. Liars' Nation." *St. Albans Daily Messenger* (St. Albans, Vermont), 19 September 1921, p. 1.

Crowe, James, "Gardner Not a Criminal at Heart; Adventurer Who Loves To be in Limelight." *The Seattle Star*, 9 September 1921, p. 1+.

Davis, Clare L., "Passed By the Censor." *Stockton Daily Evening Record*, 8 September 1921, p. 14.

"Police Nab 75 Men in Raid." *Los Angeles Evening Post-Record*, 7 September 1921, p. 1.

"S.F. Booze Party Kills Young Actress." *The San Francisco Examiner*, 10 September 1921 p. 1.

"Sacramentan Threatens Life of 'Fatty' Arbuckle." *The Sacramento Star*, 15 September 1921, p. 1.

CHAPTER THIRTY, McNeil Island, September 20, 1921

"No Trace of Bandit on McNeil." *The Tacoma Daily Ledger*, 16 September 1921, p. 3.

"Prisoners Get Liberties Back." *The Seattle Star*, 20 September 1921, p.4.

CHAPTER THIRTY-ONE, The West, Autumn 1921

"Pen Points By the Staff." *The Los Angeles Times*, 22 September 1921, p. 24.

"Has Roy Gardner Turned Attention to Circus Trucks?" *The Washington Standard* (Olympia, Washington), 23 September 1921, p. 7.

"Was Gardner Here?" *The Bellingham Herald* (Bellingham, Washington), 20 September 1921, p. 8.

"Bandit Victim Thinks Robber Was Gardner." *The San Francisco Examiner*, 21 September 1921, p. 4.

"Honeymooners Think They Met Bandit Roy Gardner in Nevada." *The Sacramento Bee*, 1 October 1921, p. 20.

"Is He In Butte?" *The Billings Gazette* (Billings, Montana), 27 September 1921, p. 2.

"Roy Gardner and Family From McNeil Island Are Visitors At State Fair." *The Sacramento Bee*, 10 September 1921, p. 14.

Monson, Jacob. "The Great Depression in Washington State." https://depts .washington.edu/depress/Raymond_Advertiser.shtml

"Gardner's Friend Has Disappeared." *Stockton Daily Evening Record* (Stockton, California), 28 September 1921, p. 1.

"Trying To Pick Up Gardner Trail." *Stockton Daily Evening Record* (Stockton, California), 28 September 1921, p. 1.

"Express Readers Give Their Theories on Gardner Escape." *Los Angeles Evening Express*, 26 September 1921, p. 29.

CHAPTER THIRTY-TWO, *The San Francisco Bulletin*, September 26, 1921

Associated Press. "Super-Bandit, Wounded Twice, Confined To His Bed, Begs for President Harding's Pardon." *Los Angeles Evening Express*, 26 September 1921, p. 1+.

"Escape Told in Letter to 'Bulletin.'" *Medford Mail Tribune* (Medford, Oregon), 26 September 1921, p. 1+.

"'Ridiculous' Says Warden About Roy Gardner's Letter." *Medford Mail Tribune* (Medford, Oregon), 26 September 1921, p. 1.

United Press, "'Friends Can't Help You Now,' Is Her Appeal." *The Sacramento Star*, 28 September 1921, p. 3.

"Offers Gardner Good Job If He's Pardoned." *The Sacramento Star*, 28 September 1921, p. 3.

CHAPTER THIRTY-THREE, Raymond, Washington, September 30, 1921

"Gardner's Pal in S.F., Detectives Believe." *Petaluma Daily Morning Courier* (Petaluma, California), 29 September 1921, p. 1.

"Roy Gardner Used Tablet In Raymond." *Albany Democrat-Herald* (Albany, Oregon), 30 September 1921, p. 1.

Associated Press Night Wire. "Friend of Gardner Can Not Be Found." *The Los Angeles Times*, 2 October 1921, p. 7.

CHAPTER THIRTY-FOUR, California, October 1921
"Stockton Boys Claim Gardner Drove to L.A." *Stockton Daily Evening Record* (Stockton, California), 3 October 1921, p. 1.
"Roy Gardner Is Seen Here." *The Los Angeles Times*, 3 October 1921, p. 24.
"The Famous Gardner Hoax." *Los Angeles Evening Post-Record*, 3 October 1921, p. 10.
Gatewood, Boyd W. "Gardner Trail is Found." *Los Angeles Evening Post-Record*, 6 October 1921, p. 1.
United Press Leased Wire. "Two Physicians Deny Treating Roy Gardner." *Santa Ana Register*, 8 October 1921, p. 4.
Editorial. *Stockton Daily Evening Record* (Stockton, California), 4 October 1921, p. 14.

CHAPTER THIRTY-FIVE, Moose Jaw, Canada, October 1921
"Did Roy Gardner, Escaped Convict, Commit Robbery?" *Calgary Herald* (Calgary, Canada), 20 October 1921 p. 1.
"The Daily Starbeams." *Saskatoon Daily Star* (Saskatoon, Canada), 26 October 1921, p. 4.

CHAPTER THIRTY-SIX, Islas de Todos Santos, Baja California, October 1921
"Link Gardner With Theft of Yacht From L.A. Harbor." *The Bulletin* (Pomona, California), 25 October 1921, p. 12.
"Think It Was Gardner." *The Los Angeles Times*, 25 October 1921, p. 8.

CHAPTER THIRTY-SEVEN, Napa, California, October 1921
United Press. "Famous Bandit Describes Escape, Flight." *The Sacramento Star*, 17 November 1921, p. 7.
"Would Serve for Bandit's Crimes." *Muskogee Times-Democrat* (Muskogee, Oklahoma), 6 October 1921, p. 2.
"Gardner's Repentance Will Be One Subject." *Oakland Tribune*, 22 October 1921, p. 11.

CHAPTER THIRTY-EIGHT, Phoenix, Arizona, November 16, 1921
"Santa Claus Told Mrs. Gardner of Capture." *Santa Cruz Evening News* (Santa Cruz, California), 19 November 1921, p. 1.
"Mail Car Bandit Captured In Phoenix Tuesday Night Is Notorious Roy Gardner." *Arizona Republican* (Phoenix, Arizona), 17 November 1921, p. 1+.
"Captor Tells Fierce Battle With Bandit." *The San Francisco Examiner*, 17 November 1921, p. 1+.
"Gardner Tells of His Travels Since Escape." *Arizona Republican* (Phoenix, Arizona), 17 November 1921, p. 8.

"Big Crowds Throng About Jail to See Noted Highwayman." *Arizona Republican* (Phoenix, Arizona), 17 November 1921, p. 9.

"Mail Bandit in Phoenix Says He Is The Fugitive." *The Sacramento Star*, 16 November 1921, p. 1+.

United Press. "Inderlied Glad He Was Not Murdered." *The Hanford Sentinel* (Hanford, California), 18 November 1921, p. 4.

"Held in $100,000 Bonds." *The Sacramento Bee*, 17 November 1921, p. 1+.

"Quixotic Train Robber Looks and Acts His Part, Interviewer Finds." *Arizona Republican* (Phoenix, Arizona), 17 November 1921, p. 9.

Associated Press. "Roy Gardner Is Accused of Another Mail Robbery." *St. Louis Post-Dispatch*, 18 November 1921, p. 3.

"Bandit Charged With Attack On Girl in Phoenix." *Arizona Republican* (Phoenix, Arizona), 18 November 1921, p. 6.

Associated Press. "Super Bandit Identified on Attack Charge." *The San Francisco Call*, 17 November 1921, p. 1.

"Phoenix Gaining Fame As Nemesis of 'Shadowed' Suspect." *Arizona Republican* (Phoenix, Arizona), 10 June 1923, p. 9.

"An Admirable Law." *The Pasadena Post*, 21 November 1921, p. 4.

"Civic Leaders Decry Protests Against Japanese Valedictorian." *Oakland Tribune*, 6 December 1921, p. 32.

"Mrs. Roy Gardner Refuses to Believe Girl Attack Story." *San Francisco Chronicle*, 18 November 1921, p. 5.

CHAPTER THIRTY-NINE, Phoenix, Arizona, November 20, 1921

"Roy Gardner's Wife Here Says She Will 'Stick.'" *Arizona Republican* (Phoenix, Arizona), 20 November 1921, p. 12.

Braddock, Cleo. "Wife's Faith Remains Despite Latest Crime of Roy Gardner." *Arizona Republican* (Phoenix, Arizona), 20 November 1921, p. 3.

CHAPTER FORTY, Phoenix, Arizona, Thanksgiving 1921

"Gardner Examined As To His Sanity at X-Ray Laboratory." *Arizona Republican* (Phoenix, Arizona), 27 November 1921, p. 8.

"Can't Break Jail, So Gardner 'Breaks' Inmates at Penny Ante." *Arizona Republican* (Phoenix, Arizona), 19 November 1921, p. 6.

"Spirits Control Me: They're To Blame, Says Gardner." *The San Francisco Call*, 17 November 1921, p. 1.

"Dr. Smith To Talk On 'Jazz Music, Whisky.'" *Los Angeles Evening Express*, 3 December 1921, p. 7.

"Life Story of Roy Gardner is Told In Trial in Federal Court." *Arizona Republican* (Phoenix Arizona), 8 December 1921, p. 1+.

"Gardner's Father Says He is Sane." *Stockton Daily Evening Record* (Stockton, California), 8 December 1921, p. 11.

"Pen Points." *The Hanford Sentinel* (Hanford, California), 1 February 1922, p. 2.

CHAPTER FORTY-ONE, Phoenix, Arizona, December 5, 1921

"Gardner In Court at Phoenix With Two Charges Over Him." *The Sacramento Bee*, 5 December 1921, p. 24.

"Insanity Line of Defense for Roy Gardner is Sprung In Trial." *Arizona Republican*, 7 December 1921, p. 1+.

"Alienists Declare Roy Gardner Insane." *Stockton Daily Evening Record* (Stockton, California), 9 December 1921, p. 1.

"Gardner Case to Jury Today." *The San Francisco Examiner,* 10 December 1921, p. 10.

United Press Leased Wire. "Gardner 'Stole to Rescue His Soul.'" *The Hanford Sentinel* (Hanford, California), 8 December 1921, p. 3.

"Alienists Tell Jury Gardner is Unbalanced." *Arizona Republican* (Phoenix, Arizona), December 9, 1921 p. 2.

"'30' Bulletins, Phoenix." *Santa Ana Register*, December 7, 1921, p. 1.

"Activities in Phoenix." *Arizona Republican* (Phoenix, Arizona), 8 December 1921, p. 2.

Associated Press. "Won't Say Where Loot Is Hidden." *The Tacoma Daily Ledger* (Tacoma, Washington), 8 December 1921, p. 1.

"Roy Gardner Is Not Insane Says Dr. T.H. Haines in Federal Court." *Arizona Republican* (Phoenix, Arizona), 10 December 1921, p. 1+.

"Arizona Law Makes Death The Penalty for Gardner's Crime." *Arizona Republican* (Phoenix, Arizona), 17 November 1921, p. 9.

"R. Gardner Is Given 25 Years More." *Bakersfield Morning Echo*, 13 December 1921, p. 1.

"Four On Stand Opening Day of Gardner Trial." *Arizona Republican* (Phoenix, Arizona), 6 December 1921, p. 9.

CHAPTER FORTY-TWO, USP Leavenworth, Kansas, Christmas 1921

"On His Way To The Federal Pen." *The Hutchinson News* (Hutchinson, Kansas), 15 December 1921, p. 13.

"Drove Home Through Snowdrifts." *The Sterling Kansas Bulletin* (Sterling, Kansas), 15 December 1921, p. 12.

Anderson, Paul Y. "Aspects of Prison Life Where Our War-Time Offenders Still Are Held." *St. Louis Post-Dispatch*, 10 June 1923, p. 9+.

Gibbs, Sir Philip. "Stoical Peasants Tighten Their Belts and Plant Seed Corn So that, Though They Die, There May Be Harvest Next Year for Those Who Live." *St. Louis Globe Democrat*, 11 December 1921 p. 17.

"Huns Ask Moratorium or Credit. German Mark is Now Practically Worthless." *Fort Scott Tribune and the Fort Scott Monitor* (Fort Scott, Kansas), 15 December 1921, p. 1.

Associated Press. "Northcliffe Hints At Singapore For U.S. Naval Base." *Honolulu Star-Bulletin*, 8 December 1921, p. 2.

Bailey, Roy V. "'Mystic' Act Is Hit At The Orpheum." *The Sacramento Bee*, 21 November 1921, p. 13.

"Gardner Threatens Only Temporary Stay in Leavenworth Prison." *Press and Sun Bulletin* (Binghamton, New York), 16 December 1921, p. 1.

Associated Press. "Gardner Pleaded Guilty; Expected Here This Week." *Leavenworth Times*, 13 December 1921, p. 1.

CHAPTER FORTY-THREE, Los Angeles, California, December 26, 1921

Pantages Ad. *Los Angeles Evening Express*, 26 December 1921, p. 33.

"Mail Car Bandit Makes Tawdry Hero." *The Los Angeles Times*, 28 December 1921, p. 32.

"Mrs. Roy Gardner Appears In Person At Pantages All Week." *Los Angeles Evening Post-Record*, 29 December 1921, p. 10.

Hoyt's Theatre Ad. *San Pedro Daily Pilot* (San Pedro, California), 5 January 1922, p. 5.

"'Bandit's Wife' To Appear at Pantages." *The San Francisco Examiner*, 11 January 1922, p. 11.

CHAPTER FORTY-FOUR, McNeil Island, Washington, Late December 1921

"Sonny's Actors Find Water Cold." *The Tacoma News Tribune* (Tacoma, Washington), 28 December 1921, p. 9.

CHAPTER FORTY-FIVE, Long Beach, California, January 9, 1922

"City Powerless to Prevent Mrs. Roy Gardner's Stage Appearance." *The Long Beach Press*, 9 January 1922, p.1.

"Gardner's Wife Hopes To See Him Freed." *The Long Beach Press*, 9 January 1922, p. 10.

CHAPTER FORTY-SIX, Bay Area, California, and Spokane, Washington, Late January 1922

Pantages Ad. *San Francisco Chronicle*, 22 January 1922, p. 5.

"Mrs Roy Gardner In Person Star At Pantages." *San Francisco Chronicle*, 16 January 1922, p. 14.

"City May Bar Bandit's Wife From Spokane Theater Stage." *Spokane Chronicle* (Spokane, Washington), 25 January 1922, p. 3.

"City Dads To Pass On Mrs. Roy Gardner." *Spokane Chronicle* (Spokane, Washington), 26 January 1922, p. 3.

"Lindsley Bans Bandit Picture." *The Spokane Review* (Spokane, Washington), 31 January 1922, p. 6.

Pantages Ad. *The Spokesman-Review* (Spokane, Washington), 25 January 1922, p. 5.

"Seattle Censors Place Ban on Act of Noted Bandit's Wife." *Santa Ana Register* (Santa Ana, California), 4 February 1922, p. 1.

CHAPTER FORTY-SEVEN, Vancouver, British Columbia, February 14, 1922

"Tells Story of a Bandit Husband." *The Vancouver Sun* (Vancouver, British Columbia), 14 February 1922, p. 14.

"Wife Tries to Help." *Vancouver Daily World* (Vancouver, British Columbia), 16 February 1922, p. 10.

"Pantages-Vaudeville." *The Tacoma Daily Ledger* (Tacoma, Washington), 24 February 1922, p. 5.

CHAPTER FORTY-EIGHT, Los Angeles, California, March 1922

"Roy Gardner, World Famous Bandit, at La Petite Theatre." *Evening Vanguard* (Venice, California), 8 March 1922, p. 6.

"Roy Gardner Motion Pictures Create Sensation." *Evening Vanguard* (Venice, California), 9 March 1922, p. 6.

"Roy Gardner's Spouse Treads Burbank Stage." *Los Angeles Evening Express*, 20 March 1922, p. 21.

"Roy Gardner's Wife at Burbank." *Los Angeles Evening Post-Record*, 20 March 1922, p. 10.

Neptune Theatre Ad. *Evening Vanguard* (Venice, California), 27 March 1922, p. 6.

Harley Davidson Ad. *The Oregon Daily Journal* (Portland, Oregon), 8 January 1922, p. 28.

Schaefers Bros. Skin Care Ad. *The Eugene Guard* (Eugene, Oregon), 15 March 1922, p. 2.

"Notorious Mail Bandit's Wife in Fight Over Film." *Los Angeles Evening Express*, 29 March 1922, p.1.

"Pasadena's Trustees Ban 'Shimmy,' Also 'Toddling' and Flirting Must Stop." *Los Angeles Evening Express*, 29 March 1922, p. 1.

CHAPTER FORTY-NINE, USP Leavenworth, June 1922

"Gardner Seeks 'Crime Cure.'" *The Kansas City Times* (Kansas City, Missouri), 23 September 1922, p. 3.

"Mrs. Roy Gardner, Wife of Notorious Outlaw, In Person at American." *The Bulletin* (Pomona, California), 7 April 1922, p. 4.

"Brain Pressure Makes Me Bad, Avers Gardner." *Arizona Republican* (Phoenix, Arizona), 16 June 1922, p. 2.

"Our Russian Policy." *The Los Angeles Daily Times*, 26 June 1922, p. 20.

CHAPTER FIFTY, Maricopa, Arizona, July 1922

"Mail Sacks Rifled by Roy Gardner Found by Boy." *The Coconino Sun* (Flagstaff, Arizona), 14 July 1922, p. 11.

By "Del." "Cheerful Chirps." *The Coconino Sun* (Flagstaff, Arizona), 4 August 1922, p. 2.

"Post Office Dept." *The Holbrook News* (Holbrook, Arizona), 4 August 1922, p. 1.

"Letters Stolen by 'Smiling Roy' Will be Be Re-Mailed Soon." *The Bisbee Daily Review* (Bisbee, Arizona), 12 July 1922, p. 6.

"The Famous Bandit Roy Gardner Did It." *The Holbrook News* (Holbrook, Arizona), 29 September 1922, p. 1.

CHAPTER FIFTY-ONE, Fresno, California, August 1922

"Roy Gardner and His Captor Now Go 50–50 in 'Freedom' Venture." *The Fresno Morning Republican*, 14 August 1922, p. 2.

"Roy Gardner, Bandit, To Undergo Operation." *The Bellingham Herald* (Bellingham, Washington), 21 September 1922, p. 2.

"Gardner Faces Jail Operation." *The San Francisco Examiner*, 21 September 1922, p. 3.

CHAPTER FIFTY-TWO, Washington, DC, October 1922

"No Operation For Bandit." *The Kansas City Times* (Kansas City, Missouri), 18 October 1922, p. 1.

CHAPTER FIFTY-THREE, USP Leavenworth, November 1922

Perry, Ray Sumner. "Roy Gardner As I Knew Him." *Oakland Tribune Magazine*, 17 December 1922, p. 5+.

"'Houdini of the Bandits' Offers Brain to Science." *Lima Republican-Gazette* (Lima, Ohio), 12 November 1922, p. 7.

"'California Smile Bandit' Is Appearing at Queen." *Fort Worth Record-Telegram*, 11 November 1922, p. 4.

Grand Central Theatre Ad. *The Dallas Express*, 11 November 1922, p. 7.

Grand Theatre Ad. *Corsicana Daily Sun* (Corsicana, Texas), 18 December 1922, p. 13.

CHAPTER FIFTY-FOUR, USP Leavenworth, 1923

"Roy Gardner is Segregated When He Makes Threats." *The Pittsburg Sun* (Pittsburg, Kansas), 15 March 1923, p. 1.

United Press Leased Wire. "Roy Gardner Put in Solitary Cell." *Hollywood Daily Citizen* (Hollywood, California), 15 March 1923, p. 1.

Clegg, Ben, "Caged! Chapter III." *Los Angeles Record*, 3 October 1928, p. 1.

"Captor Now Fights for Smiling Bandit." *The Courier* (Waterloo, Iowa), 14 March 1923, p. 2.

"New Attempt Being Made to Obtain the Release of Gardner." *Monrovia Daily News* (Monrovia, California), 20 August 1923, p. 6.

"Torn Mail Pouch Recalls Activities of Roy Gardner." *The Sacramento Star*, 25 July 1923, p. 10.

The Editors of Encyclopaedia Britannica. "Teapot Dome Scandal." britannica.com.

"Roy Gardner is Placed In Solitary Confinement for Assault on Prison Warden." *The Arizona Republican* (Phoenix, Arizona), 8 May 1923, p. 6.

"Behavior in Prison." *St. Louis Post-Dispatch* (St. Louis, Missouri), 10 June 1923, p. 11.

"Roy Gardner Plots Against Life of Prison Guard." *The Tacoma Daily Ledger* (Tacoma, Washington), 3 October 1923, p. 7.

CHAPTER FIFTY-FIVE, Dixon, California, Winter 1924

"Sagebrush, Climate, Water." *The Press-Telegram* (Long Beach, California), 18 May 1924, p. 28.

"Brother-In-Law of Roy Gardner Fined for Bootlegging." *The Sacramento Bee*, 21 February 1924, p. 8.

"Asks Court to Confiscate Wine." *Napa Valley Register*, 26 March 1930, p. 1.

CHAPTER FIFTY-SIX, Phoenix, Arizona, September 1924

"Mrs. Roy Gardner Returns to Phoenix on Mission to Aid Notorious Mail Bandit." *Arizona Republican* (Phoenix, Arizona), 6 September 1924, p. 3.

"Mrs. Roy Gardner Departs After Securing Affidavits from Jurors Urging Operation for Mail Bandit." *Arizona Republican* (Phoenix, Arizona), 10 September 1924, p. 8.

CHAPTER FIFTY-SEVEN, The West Coast, Spring 1925

"Buick Figures in Long Journey." *Arizona Republican* (Phoenix, Arizona), 16 November 1924, p. 28.

"Captor of Bandit Thief is 'Nicked' on Traffic Charge." *Santa Ana Register* (Santa Ana, California), 11 February 1924, p. 11.

"Roy Gardner's Captor Loses Cuffs to Yegg." *The Los Angeles Times*, 17 February 1925, p. 30.

"Bandits Return Stolen Machine." *The Daily Tulare Register* (Tulare, California), 5 September 1923, p. 5.

"Criminals Can Be Restored by Skull Operations Says Man Who Captured Bandit, Roy Gardner." *Daily Review* (Hayward, California), 25 April 1925, p. 1.

"Bandit Capturer Will Appear at California." *The Petaluma Argus* (Petaluma, California), 27 May 1925, p. 1.

Editorials. *The Selma Enterprise* (Selma, California), 29 August 1924, p. 4.

International News. "Wife Starves to Pay for Operation on Roy Gardner." *The San Francisco Examiner*, 3 October 1924, p. 1.

"Gardner Not Going Blind Warden Says." *The Press Democrat* (Santa Rosa, California), 27 November 1924, p. 1.

International News Service. "Gardner's Hunger Strike a Farce, Asserts Warden." *The San Francisco Examiner*, 26 February 1925, p. 20.

CHAPTER FIFTY-EIGHT, USP Atlanta, October 1925

"A Prison Train to Nevada." *The Kansas City Times* (Kansas City, Missouri), 1 August 1925, p. 21.

Associated Press. "Halts Hunger Strike Today." *The Iola Register* (Iola, Kansas), 16 October 1925, p. 1.

Bolger, Jim. "Here's A 'Kick.'" *Los Angeles Record*, 9 January 1926, p. 1.

Sun Bureau. "Rum and Drug Probes Halted, Burns Asserts." *The Baltimore Sun*, 5 April 1924, p. 1+.

"Federal Prison Officials to Face Court Today." *The Atlanta Constitution*, 19 December 1924, p. 1+.

"Former Prison Chiefs Attack Probe Methods." *The Atlanta Constitution*, 20 December 1924, p. 1+.

"Sartain and Riehl Declared Guilty; Seek New Trials." *The Atlanta Constitution*, 21 February 1925, p. 1+.

"Sartain, Fletcher Will Take Stand in Bribery Case." *The Atlanta Constitution*, 16 February 1925, p. 1+.

"Snook Is Named Warden Atlanta Federal Prison." *The Columbia Record* (Columbia, South Carolina), 8 January 1925, p. 3.

"Legend of Soapy Smith." *Clark County Courier* (Kahoka, Missouri), 6 October 1933, p. 6.

Cooper, Ben. "Few Breaks for Liberty Have Been Successfully Carried Out by Inmates of U.S. Penitentiary Here." *The Atlanta Constitution*, 4 December 1927, p.6.

"Oil Just Poured from this Negro Ponzi's Mouth." *Chicago Tribune*, 20 June 1921, p. 21.

"Chicago's Negro Ponzi Found Guilty by Jury." *Pittsburgh Post-Gazette*, 3 December 1920, p. 8.

CHAPTER FIFTY-NINE, Napa, California, Summer 1926

"Bandit's Wife Becomes Nurse." *Oakland Tribune*, 13 July 1926, p. 1.

CHAPTER SIXTY, USP Atlanta, July 1928

"Deputy Who Arrested Roy Gardner, Notorious Mail Car Bandit, Thinks Federal Convict is Curably Insane." *Arizona Republican* (Phoenix, Arizona), 22 October 1926, p. 4.

"Roy Gardner Glad Holohan Is Warden." *The San Francisco Examiner*, 11 September 1927, p. 18.

Cooper, Ben. "Escape Plans Foiled." *The Atlanta Constitution*, 4 December 1927, p. 6.

Cooper, Ben. "Trades Are Taught." *The Atlanta Constitution*, 4 December 1927, p. 6.

"Mail Bandits Battle Guards at Federal Pen." *The Atlanta Constitution*, 19 July 1928, p. 1+.

"Snook's Collapse Halts Riot Probe." *The Atlanta Constitution*, 20 July 1928, p. 1+.

"'Undercover' Man Reported in Pen To Get Evidence." *The Atlanta Constitution*, 26 September 1928, p. 1+.

"U.S. Pen Chiefs Planning to Segregate Drug Addicts, Says Washington Dispatches." *The Atlanta Constitution,* 5 August 1926, p. 3.

Burke, Jefferson. "Aids Sneak to Mabel with Snook Jail Yarn." *Daily News* (New York, New York), 22 November 1928, p. 3+.

"Snook Resigns As Warden of Federal Penitentiary; To Leave Position on April 1." *The Atlanta Constitution,* 18 March 1929, p. 1+.

CHAPTER SIXTY-ONE, Napa, Summer 1929

"Wife of Daring Train Bandit Ill." *The Modesto Bee* (Modesto, California), 28 May 1929, p. 11.

McGee, Agnes. "Good Husband." *Stockton Independent* (Stockton, California), 4 July 1929, p. 8.

CHAPTER SIXTY-TWO, USP Atlanta, September 1929

"Roy Gardner In Hunger Strike." *Oakland Tribune,* 27 September 1929, p. 3.

CHAPTER SIXTY-THREE, St. Elizabeth's Hospital, Washington, DC, Autumn 1929

"Physicians Declare Roy Gardner Sane." *The San Francisco Examiner,* 29 December 1929, p. 18.

CHAPTER SIXTY-FOUR, USP Leavenworth, Winter 1930

United Press Leased Wire. "Roy Gardner on Way to Leavenworth for Balance of Big Term." *The Pomona Progress-Bulletin* (Pomona, California), January 17, 1930, p. 2.

"Horse Abandoned in Cold After it Falls Exhausted." *St. Louis Post-Dispatch* (St. Louis, Missouri), 18 January 1930, p. 8.

CHAPTER SIXTY-FIVE, The West Coast, The Great Depression

Roy Gardner, Mechanic Ad. *The Lebanon Express* (Lebanon, Oregon), 16 July 1930, p. 10.

"Officer Sonney Has Wax Figure Exhibition Here." *Tulare Advance-Register* (Tulare, California), 6 September 1930, p. 3.

"Wax Figures Cause Plenty of Trouble." *The Los Angeles Record,* 29 August 1930, p. 1.

Sonney Historical Museum Ad. *Tulare Advance-Register* (Tulare, California), 6 September 1930, p. 2.

"Surprise Party Honors Mr., Mrs. John Bacci." *The Napa Valley Register* (Napa, California), 14 October 1932, p. 2.

"Mrs. J. Gardner Honored at Dinner Party." *Napa Journal* (Napa, California), 12 September 1931, p. 3.

CHAPTER SIXTY-SIX, Washington, DC, 1933
"Kelly, Gardner in New Cargo of 125 Bound for Alcatraz." *The San Francisco Examiner* 3 September 1934, p. 3.

CHAPTER SIXTY-SEVEN, Alcatraz, September 1934
Associated Press. "Prisoners Off for New 'Home.'" *The Morning Chronicle* (Manhattan, Kansas), 4 September 1934, p. 5.

"Nearly Inch of Rain Falls Within Few Minutes." *The Wichita Eagle* (Wichita, Kansas), 3 September 1934, p. 1.

Larry, Henry. "Mere Sight of Alcatraz Makes 'Big Shots' Meek." *San Francisco Examiner*, 22 September 1936, p. 1.

CHAPTER SIXTY-EIGHT, Alcatraz, November 1934
"Gardner Asks Roosevelt for Commutation." *The San Francisco Examiner*, 26 November 1934, p. 5.

"Roy Gardner in Plea." *The San Francisco Examiner*, 26 November 1934, p. 1.

"Wife and McPike Differ Over Gardner." *The San Francisco Examiner*, 27 November 1934, p. 9.

CHAPTER SIXTY-NINE, Alcatraz, December 4, 1934
Associated Press. "Paris and Berlin Sign Saar Peace; Equality for Jews." *The San Francisco Examiner*, 4 December 1934, p. 1.

Shippy, Sam. "Roy Gardner's Wife Allows Interview by Journal Scribe." *Napa Journal* (Napa, California), 27 November 1934, p. 1.

"Wife Sees Roy Gardner; Shocked, May End Visits." *Oakland Tribune*, 18 February 1935, p. 7.

"U.S. Attorney Recommends Serving Entire Term." *Napa Journal* (Napa, California), 16 December 1934, p. 1.

"Mrs. Gardner Seeks Release of Husband." *Oakland Tribune*, 6 February 1935, p. 3.

"The Prison on Alcatraz." *Oakland Tribune*, 9 September 1934, p. 20.

CHAPTER SEVENTY, Napa, California, June 1935
"Roy Gardner's Wife Ill on Her Birthday." *Oakland Tribune*, 22 June 1935, p. 5.

Oliver, Myrna. "William Parkes, 106; WWI Member of Welch Fusiliers." *The Los Angeles Times*, 22 October 2002, p. B11.

"Court's Decree Annuls Marriage." *Napa Journal* (Napa, California), 3 October 1933, p. 1.

"Mrs. Dolly Gardner Makes Statement." *The Napa Valley Register* (Napa, California), 18 October 1933, p. 1.

CHAPTER SEVENTY-ONE, Alcatraz, Winter and Spring 1936
"Prison Head to Probe Revolt." *Oakland Tribune*, 22 January 1936, p. 1+.

"Racketeer is Wounded by Fellow Convicts." *Santa Rosa Republican* (Santa Rosa, California), 22 February 1936, p. 1+.

Reed, P. F. "Al Capone Blocks Murder Attempt." *The San Francisco Examiner*, 29 October 1938, p. 7.

United Press. "Annulment Asked by Wife of Roy Gardner." *The Sacramento Bee*, 21 1936, p. 7.

CHAPTER SEVENTY-TWO, USP Leavenworth, August 1936

United Press. "Gardner Ex-Wife Weds." *The Press Democrat* (Santa Rosa, California), 10 July 1936, p. 1.

Reed, P. F. "Murder on Alcatraz-How Celluloid Blocked Escape." *The San Francisco Examiner*, 25 October 1938, p. 10.

"Gardner 'Promoted,' Robber Moved from Alcatraz." *The San Francisco Examiner*, 14 August 1936, p. 6.

PART FOUR Opening Quote

United Press. "Last of Western Train Robbers is 'Tired of Living.'" *The Chico Record* (Chico, California), 11 January 1940, p. 1.

CHAPTER SEVENTY-THREE, USP Leavenworth, June 1938

Associated Press. "Gardner, Notorious Bandit, To Be Freed." *The Wichita Eagle* (Wichita, Kansas), 4 June 1938, p. 11.

"Roy Gardner, Bandit, Free in Two Months." *The San Francisco Examiner*, 4 June 1938, p. 1.

Associated Press. "Gardner Free, Tells 'Rock' Experiences." *The San Francisco Examiner*, 18 June 1938, p. 11.

Movie Ad for "Narcotic." *The Napa Valley Register* (Napa, California), 19 February 1935, p. 8.

"Noted Officer Will Be Seen in Person At Neptune." *Venice Evening Vanguard* (Venice, California), 22 May 1926, p. 3.

"Al Capone Described As Man Whose Mind is Fully 'Gone.'" *The Amarillo Globe* (Amarillo, Texas), 27 June 1938, p. 4.

"Starts Life Anew." *The Press Democrat* (Santa Rosa, California), 2 July 1928, p. 7.

"Roy Gardner Meets Daughter, Husband." *Oakland Tribune*, 2 July 1938, p. 2.

CHAPTER SEVENTY-FOUR, California, Summer 1938

"Smart People Don't Break the Laws, Roy Gardner Tells Lions." *The Press-Tribune* (Roseville, California), 30 September 1938, p. 8.

Radio Ad for "Calling All Cars." *Richmond Daily Independent* (Richmond, California), 11 August 1938, p. 14.

Radio Ad for "Calling All Cars." *The Long Beach Sun*, 11 August 1938, p. 14.

"Roy Gardner, On Crime Crusade, Visits in Visalia." *Visalia Times-Delta* (Visalia, California), 19 August 1938, p. 2.

"Master Criminal and Nemesis to Meet in Yreka." *Siskiyou Daily News* (Yreka, California), 6 October 1938, p. 1.

"Last Train Robbery." *Santa Ana Register* (Santa Ana, California), 2 September 1938, p. 19.

"Roy Gardner Says Al Capone Crazy." *Santa Ana Register* (Santa Ana, California), 2 September 1938, p. 1+.

CHAPTER SEVENTY-FIVE, Nevada City, California, Christmas, 1938

"Roy Gardner Purchases Ranch at Nevada City." *The Press-Tribune* (Roseville, California), 2 December 1938, p. 7.

United Press. "Roy Gardner Learns Ranch Home Burned." *The San Bernardino County Sun*, 28 December 1938, p. 12.

"Officer's Widow Falls to Death." *Oakland Tribune*, 2 March 1939, p. 17.

CHAPTER SEVENTY-SIX, The West Coast, Winter and Spring 1939

"George Murphy Assigned." *Hollywood Citizen News* (Hollywood, California), 13 January 1939, p. 6.

Chesnutt, James G. "New Fortune Lost." *The San Francisco Call Bulletin*, 11 January 1940, p. 1+.

Gould, Jay. "Race Track & Gossip." *The California Eagle* (Los Angeles, California), 5 January 1939, p. 4.

Associated Press. "Roy Gardner Again Faces U.S. Charge." *Roseburg News Review* (Roseburg, Oregon), 8 March 1939, p. 1.

"Roy Gardner Faces Prison for Wrongful Use of Mails." *Oakland Tribune*, 9 March 1939, p. 22.

The Editors of Encyclopedia Britannica. "Nanjing Massacre." britannica.com, https://www.britannica.com/event/Nanjing-Massacre

"Roy Gardner Opens Crime Show at Fair." *The Press Democrat* (Santa Rosa, California), 6 April 1939, p. 1.

"Roy Gardner to Talk In Portland Theater." *Corvallis Gazette Times* (Corvallis, Oregon), 24 March 1939, p. 1.

"Roy Gardner's Show Draws Crowds." *The San Francisco Examiner*, 5 April 1939, p. 10.

"Fair Half Over; Visitor No. 5 Million Awaited Today." *The San Francisco Examiner*, 12 July 1939, p. 9.

"Fair Will Become 'Biggest Playground.'" *The San Francisco Examiner*, 24 June 1939, p. 14.

International News Service. "Roy Gardner, Bay Man Hurt When Auto Hits Truck." *The Fresno Bee*, 15 April 1939, p. 2.

Associated Press. "Gardner, Policeman Friend Clash in Court." *The Fresno Bee*, 20 October 1939, p.14.

CHAPTER SEVENTY-SEVEN, San Francisco, Summer and Autumn 1939
Associated Press. "Roy Gardner is Freed of Charge." *Statesman Journal* (Salem, Oregon), 11 July 1939, p. 1.
"Exposition News." *The San Francisco Examiner*, 9 July 9 1939, p. 16.
"4 Events Hold Fair Spotlight." *Oakland Tribune*, 9 July 1939, p.6.
"Daily Program of Exposition Given in Full Detail." *Oakland Tribune*, 6 August 1939, p. 7.
"5,000 See Horse Show." *The San Francisco Examiner*, 1 July 1939, p. 7.
"Roy Gardner Hired As Launch Lecturer." *Oakland Tribune*, 30 June 1939, p. 14.
"'Alcatraz' By Roy Gardner, Famous Train Robber. To Begin Next Thursday in The News Messenger." *Lincoln News Messenger* (Lincoln, California), 13 July 1939, p. 3.
Gardner, Roy. "Alcatraz." *Lincoln News Messenger* (Lincoln, California), 20 July 1939, p. 3.
Gardner, Roy. "Alcatraz." *Indian Valley Record* (Greenville, California), 3 August 1939, p. 1.
Gardner, Roy. "Alcatraz." *Lincoln News Messenger* (Lincoln, California), 17 August 1939, p. 3.
Associated Press. "German Air Bombers Raid Warsaw, Other Polish Cities," *The Sacramento Bee,* 1 September 1939, p. 1+.
"Exposition Lifted from Summer Slump by Free Entertainment, Early Closing." *Oakland Tribune*, 27 October 1939, p. 25.
"'Taps' To Sound At Fair Tonight." *Oakland Tribune*, 29 October 1939, p. 1.
"Gardner Suicide Laid to Sight." *The Los Angeles Times*, 12 January 1940, p. 12.

CHAPTER SEVENTY-EIGHT, San Francisco, Thanksgiving 1939
"At the Liberty." *Honolulu Star-Bulletin*, 18 December 1939, p. 12.
"Roy Gardner, Ex-Mail Bandit. Kills Self Here." *The San Francisco Call Bulletin*, January 11, 1940, p. 1+.

CHAPTER SEVENTY-NINE, Hotel Governor, January 10, 1940
Associated Press. "Roy Gardner Ends Life By Poison Fumes." *Santa Cruz Sentinel* (Santa Cruz, California), 11 January 1940, p. 1+.
"The Self Execution of Roy Gardner Is Striking Proof That 'Crime Does NOT Pay.'" *Santa Rosa Republican* (Santa Rosa, California), 11 January 1940, p. 1+.

CHAPTER EIGHTY, Phoenix, Arizona, January 11, 1940
International News Service. "Two Claim Dead Train Robber Was Seen Today." *Santa Rosa Republican* (Santa Rosa, California), 11 January 1940, p. 1+.

EPILOGUE
Associated Press. "Former Policeman, Louis Sonney, Dies." *Spokane Chronicle*, 27 June 1949, p. 42.

"Dollie Parkes." *The Napa Valley Register* (Napa, California), 8 December 1979, p. 2.

"Gardner's Kin Sue Over Film." *Santa Rosa Republican* (Santa Rosa, California), 14 February 1940, p. 9.

"Jean Janofsky." *The Napa Valley Register* (Napa, California), 10 September 1995, p. 19.

Hartzell, Frank. "World War I Veterans Still Proud, Busy." *The Napa Valley Register* (Napa, California), 14 August 2002, p. 1+.

"William Parkes." *The Napa Valley Register* (Napa, California), 11 October 2002, p. 5.